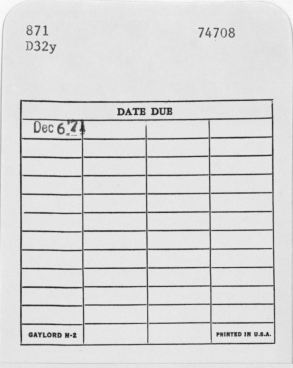

# YALE CLASSICAL STUDIES

# YALE CLASSICAL STUDIES

EDITED FOR THE DEPARTMENT OF CLASSICS

*by*

CHRISTOPHER M. DAWSON

*and*

THOMAS COLE

*VOLUME XXI*
*STUDIES IN*
*LATIN POETRY*

CAMBRIDGE
AT THE UNIVERSITY PRESS
1969

Published by the Syndics of the Cambridge University Press
Bentley House, 200 Euston Road, London N.W.1
American Branch: 32 East 57th Street, New York, N.Y.10022

Library of Congress Catalogue Card Number 69–14392
Standard Book Number: 521 07395 2

Printed in Great Britain
at the University Printing House, Cambridge
(Brooke Crutchley, University Printer)

# Contents

| Thomas Cole | The Saturnian Verse | 1 |
| Erich Segal | The *Menaechmi*: Roman Comedy of Errors | 75 |
| H. D. Jocelyn | *Imperator histricus* | 95 |
| David O. Ross, Jr. | Nine Epigrams from Pompeii (*CIL* 4.4966–73) | 125 |
| Anne Amory | *Obscura de re lucida carmina*: Science and Poetry in *De Rerum Natura* | 143 |
| Leo C. Curran | Catullus 64 and the Heroic Age | 169 |
| Edmund T. Silk | Bacchus and the Horatian *Recusatio* | 193 |
| Ross S. Kilpatrick | Two Horatian Proems: *Carm.* 1.26 and 1.32 | 213 |
| E. J. Kenney | Ovid and the Law | 241 |

# The Saturnian Verse

THOMAS COLE

# The Saturnian Verse

THE PRESENT ESSAY does not seek to advance any new set of
theories with regard to the Saturnian. Its purpose is rather to
criticize some of those already current and to restate others in
such a way as to make them more convincing to the skeptics.
There is no dearth of correct observations in the scholarly
literature devoted to the Saturnian, and there is even one general
discussion, that of Leo,[1] which seems to me to be right in many
of its essential conclusions. What is most needed at present is
some attempt to disengage valid observations from the fanciful
contexts in which they are often embedded and, more important,
some attempt to point the way, by example if possible, out of a
methodological difficulty that has never been handled in a
completely satisfactory fashion and is too often ignored altogether.
The character of the difficulty is best stated in the words of
A. W. De Groot, the scholar who has faced it most openly and
coped with it most successfully:

> La méthode usuelle d'investigation consiste à vérifier
> l'hypothèse, adoptée dès le début, que tel ou tel principe de
> versification est primaire...sans qu'on s'occupe sérieuse-
> ment de la question de savoir si le principe reconnu comme
> primaire peut être secondaire, ou s'il peut y avoir deux
> principes primaires en même temps. Ainsi, par manque de
> contre-épreuve, on ne réussit ni à écarter tous les doutes sur
> ces points ni à déterminer le caractère et la mesure d'inter-
> dépendance de toutes les tendances observées.[2]

In practice, the *hypothèse* to which De Groot refers is often only an
*a priori* assumption as to what the basic or normal scheme of the
Saturnian must have been, and *vérification* a simple catalogue of

1. "Der Saturnische Vers," *AbhGöttingen*, N.F. 8, Nr. 5 (1905).
2. "Le vers saturnien littéraire," *REL* 12 (1934), 285.

the lines which do and do not conform to this scheme, together with some effort to minimize as much as possible the number and significance of the latter. Readers who accept an author's starting assumption may find his demonstrations persuasive; others, as De Groot notes, are likely to remain unconvinced, and with good reason. For skeptics are certainly right in pointing out that neither Leo nor anyone else has been able to start with a single metrical scheme that is prevalent enough throughout the whole corpus of extant Saturnians to inspire confidence;[3] and they are also right in pointing out that there is no valid evidence outside this corpus to justify beginning with one scheme rather than another—as will be shown by a glance at some of the facts that are time and again adduced as if constituting such evidence.

One such fact is provided by the testimony of ancient metricians. These men had at least the opportunity of knowing much more about the Saturnian than we can ever know; hence, some would argue, they ought to be heeded when they confidently explain it as a quantitative verse identical with a Greek type used by Archilochus, Callimachus and the dramatists.[4] But on closer examination this confidence turns out to be based on assumptions which modern scholars cannot share—that the laws of Greek quantitative verse are valid for all poetry, and that one may posit as the regular or normal form of a metre a sequence of syllables rarely found in the poems supposedly composed in that metre.[5]

3. For a sample of such criticism see the views cited by W. Beare, *Latin Verse and European Song* (London 1957), p. 122.

4. Cf. Marius Victorinus (*GL* 6.139.1–3) and Terentianus Maurus 2498–510 (*GL* 6.399–400). Both passages derive from a common source, probably the anonymous discussion that is printed in *GL* 2.265.8–21 and generally attributed to Caesius Bassus.

5. The most revealing commentary on this aspect of the ancient metricians' method is, of course, *GL* 6.265.10–14: *nostri...antiqui...usi sunt eo* [the Saturnian] *non observata lege nec uno genere custodito ut inter se consentiant versus, sed praeterquam quod durissimos fecerunt, etiam alios breviores, alios longiores inseruerunt, ut vix invenerim apud Naevium quos pro exemplo ponerem.*

Equally unsatisfactory is the brief statement of another ancient commentator (Servius *ad Georg.* 2.385) about the "rhythmic" (i.e. non-metrical) character of the Saturnian, a statement that has often been cited[6] in an effort to show that the Romans themselves believed the verse to be constructed on principles different from those operative in Greek theory and practice—hence in accordance with some non-quantitative scheme. But Servius' observation falls into line with several others in the Roman metricians (*GL* 6.41.25 – 42.3, 96.15–19, 282.16–20, 374.1632–3, 585.17 – 586.4, 588.23–5) that draw a purely quantitative contrast between *metra* and *rhythmi*. In the former there must be a regular succession of feet; in the latter a great variety of metrical feet may be used so long as the time ratio between thesis and arsis remains the same. So far from being non-quantitative, rhythmical verse is the quantitative form *par excellence*, whereas the composer of *metra* pays attention to qualitative differences (e.g. that between dactyl and anapest) which the composer of *rhythmi* ignores (cf. Quintilian 9.4.46; Diomedes, *GL* 1.474.5–8).[7]

Also adduced as evidence for the way a Saturnian should be scanned is the undeniably quantitative character of the metres

6. See, most recently, O. J. Todd, "Servius on the Saturnian Metre," *CQ* 34 (1940), 145; and L. Herrmann, "Vers vulgaires et vers Saturniens," *Hommages à Albert Grenier* (Brussels 1962), pp. 792–93.

7. Servius classes the Saturnian with the poems of certain *vulgares* (cf. *GL* 6.206.9–10) as an example of non-metrical verse. It is conceivable that the latter were works of Servius' contemporaries in which the syllabic and accentual verse of the Middle Ages was already anticipated—as it is in Augustine's *Psalmus contra partem Donati*; cf. H. J. Rose, "Unmetrical Triumph Songs," *CP* 39 (1944), 258, who compares Servius' statement with Augustine's own remark (*Retrac.* 1.20) on the disregard of *metrica necessitas* in the *Psalmus*. But there is no reason to believe that Servius himself realized that the verse to which he referred might be non-quantitative as well as non-metrical. The first writer who explicitly associates *rhythmi* with syllabic and accentual versification is Bede (*GL* 7.258.24–7). On the re-definition of the term *rhythmus* which this association involved, see R. L. Crocker, "*Musica Rhythmica* and *Musica Metrica* in Antique and Medieval Theory," *Journal of Music Theory* 2 (1958), 9–10.

used in the dramas of Livius and Naevius—it being unlikely, so the argument goes, that the same man should have composed epic in a metrical idiom totally unrelated to that which he used for drama. Yet "rhythmic" versification, based on syllable counting, word accent, and rhyme, is to be found throughout the Middle Ages alongside the "metrical" forms inherited from antiquity, often in the work of the same author,[8] at times within the confines of a single poem.[9] If Hildebert of Lavardin could celebrate the past glories of Rome and the future glories of the new Jerusalem in lines as different as:

> par tibi Roma nihil cum sis prope tota ruina;
>> quam magni fueris integra fracta doces. (Migne clxxi, col. 1409)

and:

> urbs caelestis, urbs beata,
> súper pétram collocata,
> urbs in portu sátis tuto
> de longinquo te saluto    (Migne clxxi, col. 1414)

there is no reason to deny the possibility of a comparable versatility in Livius and Naevius. On the other hand, the fact that Saturnians must have been written at Rome before Livius introduced direct imitation of Greek literary models does not prove, as some have assumed, either that the metre was basically

8. First and most regularly in the Latin poetry of Anglo-Saxon writers. Both Bede and Aldhelm are known to have composed *rhythmi* as well as *metra*—cf., in the catalogue of the former's works (*MGH, Auct. Ant.* 15.235.8–11), the title *Liber hymnorum diverso metro sive rhythmo* and Lull's request (*MGH, Epist. Mer. et Karol. Aevi* 1.338.24–5) for *Adhelmi episcopi aliqua opuscula sive prosarum seu metrorum aut rhythmicorum.* Samples of St Boniface's poems in both genres survive: cf. *MGH, Poet. Aevi Karol.* 1.18 (*rhythmi*) and 1.3–17 and 19–23 (*metra*).

9. Cf. *Carmina Burana* 39, 44, and 46, pp. 127–8 and 134–5 Schmeller (cited by W. Meyer, "*Ludus de Antichristo*," *SBMunich* 1882, Nr. 1, 183 = *Gesammelte Abhandlungen zur Mittellateinischen Rhythmik* [Berlin 1905], 1, 333).

different in character from the quantitative verse of the Greeks, or even that it was not a Greek import from a much earlier period.[10]

It is undeniable that there is one later Latin verse which seems to resemble the Saturnian more than any other: the dramatic senarius. Hence it is tempting to use the known in explaining the unknown and appeal to dramatic practice for criteria in dealing with the many disputed points of Saturnian prosody (elision, hiatus, synizesis, syncope, metrical lengthening).[11] But the temptation should be resisted. Among the hundred or so surviving Saturnians there are seven which begin with a pair of iambic words:

(1) malum dabunt Metelli Naevio poetae.   (*GL* 6.266.7)

(2) virum mihi Camena insece versutum.   (Livius 1 Morel)

(3) ibi manens sedeto donicum videbis   (Livius 18.1)

(4) novem Iovis concordes filiae sorores   (Naevius 1 Morel)

(5) ubi foras cum auro illinc exibant   (Naevius 5.3)

(6) patrem suum supremum optumum appellat

(Naevius 14)

(7) parens timens heic vovit, voto hoc soluto

(*CEL* 4.2 Buecheler)

One would have to search through several thousand senarii to find seven which open in the same way.[12] So striking a difference in metrical technique naturally makes one wonder whether there is any rule or tendency of dramatic versifica-

10. See G. Pasquali, *Preistoria della poesia Latina* (Florence 1936), pp. 59–75.

11. Cf. Leo (above, n. 1), pp. 20–1, where the scansion *insecē versutum* is justified by an appeal to senarius and septenarius endings of the type *fingerē fallaciam*.

12. I count only sixteen certain examples in Plautus and Terence (over 11,000 senarii). Cf. R. Klotz, *Grundzüge altrömischer Metrik* (Leipzig 1890), p. 237, and P. W. Harsh, *Iambic Words and Regard for Accent in Plautus* (Stanford 1949), pp. 94–5.

tion that can be accepted without question as valid for the Saturnian.[13]

The above is fairly typical of the sort of guidance one can expect to receive from examination of the ancient metricians, application to the Saturnian of principles which govern later verse forms, or considerations based on what is known of early Roman literary history. All such arguments are either so vague as to be of little value, or else cancelled out by arguments of opposite tendency that can be derived with equal plausibility from the same sources. It is not external evidence of this kind, but the internal evidence provided by the Saturnian itself that must be the point of departure for any sound inquiry into the character of the metre.

It is such an inquiry that De Groot undertakes to conduct in the article already cited (above, p. 3). His method is to examine the surviving epic fragments of Livius and Naevius with a view to discovering "régularités de toute sorte", on the assumption that the type of *régularité* which is most pronounced and most consistently present is likely to be the one which the poets were consciously striving for. Such an investigation is subject, of course, to difficulties of its own. The task it sets itself is complex, inasmuch as the regularities involved include recurrent patterns, not only of longs and shorts, but also of accented and unaccented syllables, isosyllabic words and phrases, and words and phrases linked by assonance and alliteration. Moreover, the findings of a statistical method such as this are far less significant in a study of

13. The divergence is noted by E. Fraenkel, *Iktus und Akzent* (Berlin 1928), pp. 12–13, and explained by him as part of the contrast between the sung verse of the Saturnian and spoken verse of comic *diverbium* (*ibid.* pp. 355, n. 1). But the word pattern in question is just as alien to the *Langzeile* of the comic *cantica* as it is to the senarius (roughly one example for every 800 septenarii and every 450 octonarii, as against one example for every 700 senarii). With the shorter iambic cola found in the *mutatis modis cantica* the proportion is higher (I count two certain examples in approximately 260 lines). But the total number of lines is so much smaller here that statistics are less indicative—and the frequency of occurrence is still strikingly different from that encountered in the Saturnian.

the Saturnian than they would be were a larger body of material involved. We can never be sure that what is common to all our fragments is an essential feature of the verse rather than merely a preferred one, nor can we be sure that what is not found among them at all is an excluded form rather than merely an uncommon one. And, if the metre happens to be one which, like English blank verse or the Aeolic rhythms of Greek poetry, allows a great deal of variation within a fairly simple overall scheme, the recurrent patterns which such a method reveals may be so numerous or so rudimentary as to make us wonder whether we are not dealing with a kind of rhythmical prose or with a verse based on a type of recurrence not taken into account during the investigation. Finally, the method, precisely because of its complexity, is an easy one to misuse. De Groot himself is too selective and arbitrary in his conception of what a regularity is. He devotes insufficient attention, for example, to the possibility that syllable counting might be the *principe primaire* of the Saturnian; and in weighing the claims of quantitative and accentual hypotheses he insists that only a strict sequence of long and short syllables can give quantitative pattern to a line, while allowing a much freer succession of stressed and unstressed syllables to establish what he regards as a significant accentual pattern. He pronounces too quickly, by the application of this double standard, in favor of an accentual Saturnian; and, once this conclusion has been reached, he is just as prone as other scholars to gratuitous assumptions in support of a preconceived opinion.[14] Finally, he never offers any detailed documentation for his assumption that the inscriptional Saturnian is essentially different in metrical character from the literary, and so can legitimately be ignored in an investigation of the latter.

The present essay begins, therefore, with an effort to realize

14. Tetrasyllabic words, for example, are allowed a secondary initial accent, and ∪∪≥ at the end of a line or half-line is assumed to be equivalent to ∠≥, an equivalence which, if it in fact existed, would suggest quantitative rather than accentual verse.

the advantages of De Groot's method by applying it more thoroughly and rigorously than it was applied by De Groot himself, and with greater regard for its possible pitfalls and limitations. The result may still fall short of being a methodologically satisfactory study of the Saturnian; but it will represent, I hope, a further step in the right direction, and provide a firmer starting point than exists elsewhere for the speculation about the metre's origin and history with which the essay concludes.

## I

An investigation such as De Groot's is confronted at the outset by a difficulty which may be partially circumvented, though never completely removed. One must begin with a body of material, and to obtain this body of material one must have criteria for deciding whether a given poem or fragment is in fact composed in Saturnians. Ancient authorities are not very helpful here, for the only works they specifically identify as composed in Saturnians are the *Bellum Poenicum* of Naevius, the Metelli verse, and a pair of lines from *tabulae triumphales*. It is thus impossible to lay down criteria for recognizing a Saturnian without some preconception about the metrical character of the verse. The best one can do is base one's criteria on preconceptions that all students of the metre are likely to share, and so define the Saturnian as, very roughly, any archaic Latin verse that is used stichically and divided by a caesura into two parts, the first of which contains five to nine syllables, the second (usually one to three syllables shorter than the first) five to eight syllables.[15]

15. To define the Saturnian by reference to the number of syllables it may contain involves some risk of committing the investigation at the outset to a syllabic analysis of the metre. But less risk is involved here than would be with any other type of definition. In quantitative and accentual verse there is usually some metrical rule determining the number of syllables per foot, or the number of unstressed syllables that may intervene between two stressed ones. As a result there is also a metrical relationship between the

Probably no one would wish to maintain that any line satisfying these conditions is a Saturnian;[16] but certainly no line which does *not* satisfy them can be considered one. The body of verse so delimited may eventually be shown to contain divergences of metrical technique sufficiently striking that it can no longer be regarded as a meaningful unit. But our definition does provide a convenient point of departure; and it is, in fact, far less inclusive than might at first seem. For one is certainly justified in excluding from consideration any passage so short or fragmentary that its conformity to the definition may be fortuitous,[17] as well as any excerpt—even if from a work which other evidence shows to have been composed in Saturnians— where the line division is not certain or where textual difficulties are sufficient to make the metrical structure doubtful. We need

number of accents or feet per line and the total number of syllables. On the other hand, the number of accents or quantitative *morae* which appear in a syllabic verse is likely to be limited solely by the nature of the poet's vocabulary. A definition of a non-syllabic verse in terms of the maximum and minimum number of syllables it may contain is thus likely to include a far lower percentage of non-verses than a quantitative or accentual definition that is not applicable. If we were to define the Latin hexameter, for example, as any verse of twelve to seventeen syllables, the definition would include most senarii and many septenarii and octonarii; on the other hand, an accentual definition, one which called any line with three to eight stresses a hexameter, would include almost all senarii, septenarii, and octonarii as well as many lyric metres; and the task of isolating within this much larger body of material the true hexameters and the metrical principle on which they were actually constructed would be correspondingly more difficult.

16. With the possible exception of Beare (above, n. 3), whose investigations lead him to the conclusion (p. 130) that the Saturnian is "...simply one short group of words followed by another short group of words of about equal (or slightly less) weight."

17. Into this category fall most citations and fragments from ancient *carmina* (e.g., the lines assigned to the *Carmen Priami*, the *Carmen Saliorum*, and the *praecepta* of Marcus vates in Morel, pp. 1, 6, and 29) as well as the Saturnians which have been manufactured by excerpting bits and pieces from the religious and legal formulae quoted by authors such as Cato and Livy (for representative samples, see L. Havet, *De Saturnio Latinorum versu* [Paris 1880], pp. 415–16).

not consider any of the model Saturnians that are cited without indication of source by the imperial metricians, for they are under suspicion of having been invented expressly for the purpose of illustrating a particular metrical theory; nor need we consider any fragments of classical or post-classical poetry which satisfy our definition, for the "Saturnians" they contain may represent a post-archaic stage in the development of the metre.[18] Finally, any lines metrically identical with senarii, septenarii, octonarii, or hexameters must be excluded—on the probable assumption that these lines were either intended to be scanned as such by their authors, or else have been altered in transmission to make them conform to metrical patterns with which later antiquity was more familiar.[19]

If with these restrictions in mind we apply our definition to the surviving remnants of archaic Latin poetry we obtain a corpus of 125 Saturnians. Of these, twenty-seven are from Livius Andronicus' translation of the *Odyssey*:

Livius 1 Morel:[20]

|  |  |
|---|---|
| virum mihi Camena | insece versutum |
| 3: mea puera quid verbi | ex tuo ore supra (codd., |
| *supera* Morel) fugit |  |
| 4: argenteo polubro | aureo eclutro |
| 5: tuque mihi narrato | omnia disertim |
| 8: in Pylum devenies | ⟨h⟩aut ibi ommentans |
| 9: tumque remos iussit | religare struppis |
| 10: ibidemque vir summus | adprimus Patroclus |

18. On the question of Varronian Saturnians, see below, pp. 64–5.

19. Into this category go three verses of Livius (see below, n. 20) as well as, in all probability, the *versus ex antiquo carmine* cited by Nigidius Figulus (*ap.* Aulus Gellius 2.9.1 = fr. 4 Funaioli): *religentem esse oportet religiosus ne fuas* (i.e. *rélligentem ⟨te⟩ ésse*... or *réligentem ⟨ted⟩ ésse*...: a trochaic septenarius).

20. Literary Saturnians are cited throughout with the numbering and (except in four instances) text of Morel. Emendations and variant readings not accepted by Morel, even if they seem possible or likely, are not mentioned unless their acceptance might alter the metrical pattern of a

line. Excluded from the enumeration altogether are the following fragments
in Morel's edition:

Livius 6: quae haec daps est, qui festus dies
    12: atque escas habemus mentionem
    24: quoniam audivi     paucis gavisi
    25: inferus an superus tibi fert deus funera Ulixes
    28: parcentes praemodum
    29: sic quoque fitum est
    31: dusmo in loco
    32: cum socios nostros mandisset impius Cyclops
    35: at celer hasta volans perrumpit pectora ferro
    40: celsosque ocris arvaque putria et mare magnum
    41: affatim edi bibi lusi
    42: iam in altum expulsa lintre
    44: erant et equorum inaurata tapeta
    45: auratae vaginae, aurata baltea illis erant
Naevius 24: manusque susum ad caelum sustulit suas rex
        Amulius divis⟨que⟩ gratulabatur
    32: ...Manius Valerius
        consul partem exerciti    in expeditionem
        ducit...
    33: fames acer augescit hostibus
    34: apud emporium in campo    hostium pro moene
    39: ...transit Melitam
        Romanus exercitus; insulam integram urit
        populatur, vastat, rem    hostium concinnat.
    40: eam carnem victoribus danunt
    41: vicissatim volvi victoriam
    62: quianam Saturnium    populum pepulisti?

Livius 6, 12, 28, 29, 31, 41 and 42 and Naevius 33, 40 and 41 are all too
short to be full lines and cannot be located with any certainty as part of a
single line or two consecutive lines; Livius 24 is corrupt; the provenance of
Livius 40, 41, 42, 44, and 45 and of Naevius 34 and 62 is uncertain; and
Livius 25, 32 and 35 can be scanned as hexameters and are probably from a
later *retractatio* (cf. Leo [above, n. 1], pp. 60–1, n. 4). The line division in
Naevius 32 is uncertain (see below, p. 18, with n. 28) as is the text of
Naevius 24 (*isque* codd., *manusque* Merula; *res* codd., *rex* Stephanus; *gratulabatur divis* codd., *divisque gratulabatur* Luc. Müller); and both text and line
division are doubtful in Naevius 39 (*exercitus* codd., del. Vahlen; *populatur
vastat* codd., transpos. Thulin, *populat* Havet, *vastam* Palmer—cf. O. Skutsch,
*CR* 72 [1959], 59, n. 2).

11: quando dies adveniet     quem profata Morta est
13: partim errant nequinont     Graeciam redire
14: sancta puer Saturni     filia regina
15: apud nympham Atlantis     filiam Calypsonem
16: igitur demum Ulixi     cor frixit prae pavore
17: utrum genua amploctens     virginem oraret
18.1–2: ibi manens sedeto     donicum videbis
    me carpento vehentem     domum venisse
19: simul ac dacrimas de ore     noegeo detersit
20.1–3: namque nullum peius     macerat humanum
    quamde mare saevom:     vires cui sunt magnae
    topper confringent     importunae undae[21]
21: Mercurius cumque eo     filius Latonas
22: nexebant multa inter se     flexu nodorum dubio
23: nam diva Monetas     filia docuit
26.1–3: topper citi ad aedis     venimus Circae.
    simul duona eorum     portant ad navis.
    multa alia in isdem     inserinuntur.
27: topper facit homines     ut prius fuerunt
38: neque tamen te oblitus sum     Laertie noster.

Forty-three come from Naevius:

Naevius 1 Morel:

    novem Iovis concordes     filiae sorores
3.1–3: postquam avem aspexit     in templo Anchisa,
    sacra in mensa Penatium     ordine ponuntur;
    immolabat auream     victimam pulchram.
4.2–3: noctu Troiad exibant     capitibus opertis,
    flentes ambae abeuntes     lacrimis cum multis

---

21. The line is often emended (e.g. ⟨eum⟩ *topper*..., *topper* ⟨vel hunc⟩..., ⟨tamen⟩ *topper*...) in an effort to give concessive force and some sort of antecedent to the *cui* clause. But the antecedent is unnecessary, and the concessive idea is more naturally supplied by rejecting Augustinus' *vires cui* (*viret cui* codd.) in favor of *vis et cui* (Lindsay), *vires et cui* (Havet), or—since this use of *et* is not attested elsewhere in archaic Latin—*vi⟨re⟩s etsi*; cf., in the Homeric original, εἰ καὶ μάλα καρτερὸς εἴη (8.139).

5.1–3: eorum sectam sequuntur    multi mortales.
    multi alii e Troia    strenui viri.
    ubi foras cum auro    illinc exibant.

7: ferunt pulchras creterras    aureas lepistas

12.1–2: senex fretus pietati    deum adlocutus,
    summi deum regis    fratrem Neptunum.

14: patrem suum supremum    optumum appellat

19.1–3: inerant signa expressa    quomodo Titani
    bicorpores Gigantes    magnique Atlantes
    Runcus ac Purpureus    filii Terras

20: ei venit in mentem    hominum fortunas

21: silvicolae homines    bellique inertes

22: iamque eius mentem fortuna    fecerat quietem

23.1: blande et docte percontat    Aenea quo pacto

28: res divas edicit    praedicit castus

29: prima incedit Cereris    Proserpina puer

30.1–2: dein pollens sagittis    inclutus arquitenens,
    sanctus Iove prognatus    Pythius Apollo.

31: scopas atque verbenas    sagmina sumpserunt

35: simul atrocįa[22] proicerent    exta ministratores

36: virum praetor advenit    auspicat auspicium

42.1–2: seseque ei perire    mavolunt ibidem
    quam cum stupro redire    ad suos popularis

43.1–2: sin illos deserant    fortissimos viros
    magnum stuprum populo    fieri per gentes

44: censet eo venturum    obviam Poenum

45: superbiter contemptim    conterit legiones

46: onerariae onustae    stabant in flustris

47: convenit regnum simul    atque locos ut haberent

48: septimum decimum annum    ilico sedent

49: Sicilienses paciscit    obsides ut reddant

51: magnam domum decoremque    ditem vexarant[23]

22. Trisyllabic scansion of *atrocįa* is necessary; otherwise the first colon will have ten syllables.

23. *Vexarant* is the reading of most manuscripts, as against the rarer *vexerant* favored by Morel.

52: simul alius aliunde        rumitant inter se
53: magnae metus tumultus       pectora possidit
54: plerique omnes subiguntur    sub suum iudicium[24]
55: quod bruti nec satis        sardare queunt
63: atque prius pariet          lucusta lucam bovem.

Three are from the epigrams attributed to Appius Claudius Caecus:

amicum cum vides        obliscere miserias;
inimicus si es commentus     nec libens aeque
ne quid fraudis stuprique    ferocia pariat   (p. 5 Morel),

two from an imperial metrician's citation of the *tabulae trium-phales* of Acilius Glabrio and L. Aemilius Regillus:

fundit fugat prosternit      maximas legiones (*GL* 6.265.29)
duello magno dirimendo       regibus subigendis
                (*GL* 6.265.25; cf. Livy 40.52.4),

two from the epitaph of Atilius Calatinus as quoted by Cicero (*Sen.* 61; *Fin.* 2.116):

hunc unum plurimum       consentiunt gentes
populi primarium      fuisse virum,

one from the reply of the Metelli to Naevius:

malum dabunt Metelli      Naevio poetae   (*GL* 6.266.7)

and four from the funeral epitaph ascribed to Naevius (64 Morel). The remaining forty-three are found on archaic inscriptions (28 in the epitaphs of the Scipios and Marcus Caecilius; 15 in the dedications of Mummius, the Vertuleii, and the *coqui Falisci*—cf. nrs. 2–4, 6–9, and 11 in Buecheler's *CEL*).

There are in addition fifteen incomplete or corrupt lines from each of which half of a Saturnian can be recovered:

Livius 2 Morel:
            pater noster Saturni      filie...

---

24. The manuscripts are divided between *suum* and *unum* (the reading in Morel); in defense of the former, see S. Mariotti, *Il Bellum Poenicum e l'arte di Nevio* (Rome 1955), pp. 79–80, n. 53.

7: ...matrem procitum     plurimi venerunt.[25]
30: vestis pulla purpurea     ampla...
34: inque manum suremit     hastam...
36: vinumque quod libabant     anclabatur...
37: deque manibus dextrabus...
39: ...⟨topper⟩ capesset     flammam Volcani

Naevius 4.1:

    ...amborum uxores
10: pulchraque...ex auro     vestemque citrosam
12.3: regnatorem marum...
15: summe deum regnator     quianam †genusisti
23.2: Troiam urbem liquerit...
50.1–2: id quoque pasciscunt     †moenia sint quae
      Lutatium†
      reconciliant captivos     plurimos...[26]

Naevius 58 Strzelecki:
     cum tu arquitenens sagittis     pollens dea...[27]

25. The line is a complete Saturnian by our definition, but the Greek original (1.248: τόσσοι μητέρ' ἐμὴν μνῶνται) gives some support to Havet's *matrem ⟨meam⟩*....

26. The line division follows Leo (above, n. 1), p. 35, on the reasonable assumption that, given the paratactic character of early Latin style and the rarity of enjambment in the Saturnian, the two indicative verbs are likely to be the beginnings both of verses and of sense units. E. Norden's interpretation, reported by C. Cichorius (*Römische Studien* [Bonn 1922], p. 50, n. 51) and accepted in the editions of Morel, Marmorale, and Mariotti, tries to make sense of the fragment with minimal emendation: *id quoque pasciscunt, moenia sint quae | Lutatium reconcilient, captivos plurimos.* ("Auch dies bedingen sie [the Carthaginians] aus, Abgaben sollten sein, die den Lutatius wieder aussöhnten, (ferner) die sehr vielen Gefangenen.") But this rendering involves construing *captivos* in a very awkward way, and I doubt that the verb *reconciliant* could be used to describe coming to terms with an enemy commander.

27. On the provenance of the fragment, see L. Strzelecki, "Miscellanea Naeviana," *Eos* 47.1 (1957–8), 65–8. The line may be complete as it stands (*cum tu arquitenens   sagittis pollens dea*), but the version given in the text is more likely in view of the parallel position of *sagittis* in Naevius 30.1: *dein pollens sagittis inclutus Arquitenens.*

        

and the final two words of the Mummius inscription:

> imperator dedicat.   (*CEL* 3.5)

should probably be regarded as composing another half-line.

It is worth noting that in only one instance does a poem composed in Saturnians contain a sequence of words which one would be tempted to regard as a line but for the fact that it lacks a central break. The line division which the sense of Naevius 32 demands is certainly the following:

> ...Manlius      Valerius consul
> partem exerciti in expeditionem ducit;

but the nine syllables of *in expeditionem ducit* would be unparalleled as the second half of a Saturnian. One must either locate the verse end differently, or posit a missing or irregular caesura (*partem exerciti in expe-      ditionem ducit*). The latter alternative seems to me preferable,[28] but our definition of the Saturnian is not seriously affected by this single exception to the caesura requirement.

The bipartite character of the verse is shown not only by the absence, or near absence, of lines that fail to show a caesura at one of the permitted places, but also by the frequency with which there is a pause or partial pause in sense at one of these places (cf., for example, Naevius 19:

> inerant signa expressa, quomodo Titani,
> bicorpores Gigantes, magnique Atlantes,
> Runcus ac Purpureus, filii Terras),

---

28. The usual division: *Manlius Valerius | consul partem exerciti   in expeditionem | ducit...* is improbable, for the enjambment which leaves *ducit* (followed, presumably, by a full stop) at the beginning of a line is just as unparalleled as a caesuraless verse of the form suggested in the text. *Manlius Valerius consul      partem exerciti | in expeditionem   ducit* is, for similar reasons, almost as objectionable.

as well as by the poets' fondness for linking the component parts of the line by parallels both of sound and of sense:

Livius 4: ARgent*eo* poLUbRO, AUR*eo* ecLUtRO
*CEL* 9.1–3: *m*agna sapientia, *m*ultasque virtutes
            aetate quom *p*arva *p*ossidet hoc saxum.
            quoiei vita defecit, non honos, honore.

Only slightly less striking in its regularity, though less universally taken into account in analyses of the metre, is the break that is sometimes called, after its discoverer,[29] the *caesura Korschiana*. Korsch, who viewed the Saturnian as a quantitative verse, pointed out that in lines which can be scanned as hypercatalectic iambic senarii there is usually a break not simply in the middle of the verse but in the middle of the first half of the verse as well, and that the latter break comes after the second arsis:

$$\overset{1}{\cup} - \overset{2}{\cup} - \Big| \overset{3}{\cup} - \cup \quad \overset{4}{-} \cup - \overset{5}{\cup} - \overset{6}{\cup}$$

The phenomenon to which he called attention is, however, of much wider applicability; and the law which describes it is independent of Korsch's own quantitative formulation. I would propose that it be restated as follows: in any half-line that contains seven or more syllables the last three or (more rarely) the last four must be preceded by word end. This rule is violated only when absolutely necessary—to allow for the inclusion within a half-line of a word of five or more syllables:

Naevius 35: ...exta ministratores
     *CEL* 2.5: ...imperatoribus summis
     *CEL* 3.1: ductu auspicio imperioque...
     *CEL* 6.5: ...Aleriaque urbe[30]
     *CEL* 6.6: dedet Tempestatebus...
     *CEL* 9.1: magna sapientia...

29. T. Korsch, *De versu Saturnio* (Moscow 1868), p. 40.

30. Hexasyllabic scansion (*Aleriaqu(e) urbe*) is, of course, possible; see below, n. 52.

The only other possible exceptions are

    Livius 19: simul ac dacrimas d(e) ore...

    Naevius 48: septimum decimŭm annum...

        *CEL* 3.1: ...ēĭus Achaia capta

        *CEL* 8.4: ...tibē utier vita

But if the third and fourth of these cola are read with elision (*tib(e) utier vita*) and synizesis (*ei͡us*) they become hexasyllabic and cease to be covered by our rule; and the first and second are regular if we allow hiatus between *de* and *ore* and elision between *decim(um)* and *annum*. The scansions *tib(e) utier* and *decim(um) annum* would be, of course, the normal ones in Latin poetry; and *dĕ ore* and *ei͡us* can be paralleled in comedy.[31] But, even if these scansions were less unexceptionable in the general context of Latin usage, they should probably be allowed here. There is no evidence to indicate how closely Saturnian practice with regard to synizesis, elision, and hiatus approximated that of later poetry (cf. above, pp. 7–8). Hence, if the only exceptions to a rule that otherwise holds good for all surviving Saturnians are in lines where alternative scansions are possible, and if accepting one alternative rather than the other removes the exception, this scansion is probably to be preferred—even if there are only sporadic parallels in later literature. For, if the rule involved were in fact one to which exceptions were permitted, we should expect at least one or two of the surviving exceptions to be in lines where the possibility of removing the irregularity by an alternate scansion did not exist. This principle is important and will be used on several occasions in the analysis that follows.

    Like the bipartite structure produced by the central break, the quadripartite structure which the *caesura Korschiana* gives to the Saturnian is often underlined by alliteration, assonance, and syntactic parallelism:

    31. Cf., for the former, *Amphitruo* 736 and 829. *Ei͡us* is the regular scansion in Plautus.

Naevius 63: ATque *prius*     *p*ArieT     *luc*usta     *luc*am
bovem

Naevius 45: superb*ITER*     CONTEMp*TIM*     CON*TERIT*
legiones

*GL* 6.265.25: *D*uell*o* magno     *d*irimen*d*o     re*G*IBUS
suBIGen*d*is;

and the care which the archaic poets must have taken to achieve this structure is evident if we contrast their verses with the model Saturnians of the imperial metricians, three of which (over a quarter of the total) contain violations of Korsch's law:

*GL* 6.265.17: turdis edacibus dolos     comparas amice
*GL* 6.265.21: consulto producit eum     quo sit impudentior
*GL* 4.466.7: Isis pererrat orbem     crinibus profusis.[32]

Korsch's law is the most striking of the regularities which can be observed in the structure of the cola that make up the Saturnian line. Nothing comparable by way of quantitative, accentual, or alliterative pattern has been discovered.[33] It is, therefore, a logical starting point for further investigations.

32. The remaining eight are:
(1) cum victor Lemno classem     Doricam appulisset   *GL* 6.139.15
(2) iam nunc vocat Camenas     ⟨quis⟩ novem sorores   *GL* 6.139.29
(3) quem non rationis egentem     vicit Archimedes   *GL* 6.265.19
(4) quid invides amicis     invides amicis   *GL* 6.266.14
(5) summas opes qui regum     regias refregit   *GL* 6.294.1
(6) trahuntque siccas multas     machinae carinas   *GL* 6.531.19
(7) merulae quod os vetustae     mane dulce cantat   *GL* 6.594.6
(8) magnum numerum triumphat     hostibus devictis   *GL* 6.615.8
(5) and (8) may come from archaic dedications, in which case the incidence of violation of the *lex Korschiana* in verses for which the imperial metricians are themselves responsible is even higher. Moreover, (1), (3) and (6) can be made to conform to the *lex Korschiana* only by allowing other violations of normal archaic practice ($-- \cup \cup - \cup$ before the caesura in (3)—cf. below, pp. 22–25; $---- $ after the caesura in (1) and (6)—cf. below, pp. 28–9).

33. The nearest approach is the regularity with which the second colon of the verse shows a quantitative cadence of the form $\cup\cup \; \underset{\smile}{}$. But to this rule there are at least five exceptions (Naevius 5.2: *strenui viri*, 43.1: *fortissimos*

Four is the maximum number of syllables that the second part of any colon may contain. The first part may contain as many as five or (much more rarely) six. A consideration of the metrical structure which these five- and six-syllable word groups display reveals another regularity of the greatest significance. In pentasyllabic word groups there is almost always at least one pair of consecutive short syllables; in hexasyllabic groups there are always two such pairs:

> Livius 3: mea puera,      quid verbi...
> 19: simul ac dacrimas      de ore...
> 37: deque manibus      dextrabus...
> Naevius 35: simul atrociạ      proicerent...
> 49: Sicilienses      paciscit...
> 50.2: reconciliant      captivos...
> 52: simul alius      aliunde...
> Naevius epitaph 4: ...loquier lingua      Latina
> CEL 3.2: ...Romam redieit      triumphans
> CEL 4.3: decuma facta      poloucta...
> CEL 7.6: subigit omne      Loucanam...
> CEL 8.5: facile facteis      superases...
> CEL 11.3: bene rem geras      et valeas...

The following lines adhere to the rule if we allow elision at the places indicated and, in the third example, a final -*s* which does not make position:

*viros*, 48: *ilico sedent*, 63: *lucusta lucam bovem*; *CEL* 3.3: *quod in bello voverat*). During the period when all Latin words were stressed on the first syllable, the pattern created by adherence to the *lex Korschiana* would have tended, of course, to be accompanied and reinforced by a regular accent falling on the first syllable of each colon and on the third or fourth syllable from the end (*súperbiter cóntemptim cónterit légiones*, etc.). Initial word accent may, therefore, have played a role alongside syllable grouping in giving metrical structure to the verse. But that the role was an essentially subordinate one, at least in the Saturnians of the third and second centuries B.C., is indicated by the number of instances in which the main stress in a group would fall on some syllable other than the first (e.g. *CEL* 4.5: *semol te orant se vóti*...; Livius 18: *me cárpento vehentem*....

Naevius 58 Strzelecki: cum t(u) arquitenens     sagittis...
         *CEL* 8.1: qu(ei) apic(e) insigne     Dialis...
         *CEL* 8.4: quibus s(ei) in longa     licuisset...
Appius Claudius: inimicus s(i) es     commentus...;

and elision and/or synizesis removes the opening five- or six-syllable group altogether in the following:

Livius 3: ...ex tu(o) ore     supra fugit
     22: nexebant     mult(a) inter se...
Naevius 3.2: sacr(a) in mensa     Penatium...
     5.1: eorum sectam     sequuntur...
     22: iamqu(e) eius mentem     fortuna...
     23.1: bland(e) et docte     percontat...
     29: prim(a) incedit     Cereris...
     42.1: sesequ(e) ei     perire...
   *CEL* 4.5: semol t(e) orant     se voti...
   *CEL* 8.2: mors perfecit     tu(a) ut essent...[34]
   *CEL* 8.6: qua re lubens     t(e) in gremiu...
  *CEL* 11.2: hospes grat(um) est     qu(om) apud meas...
   *CEL* 2.1: ...acipt(um) aetat(ei)     agedai

It is probably significant that of the above cola only the last requires elision at the *caesura Korschiana*,[35] and that the colon in question is from the dedication of the Faliscan cooks. This poem, as will be seen, diverges from the metrical practice of all other Saturnians often enough to suggest that its author, while obviously trying to reproduce the metre of Livius, Naevius, and the Scipio epitaphs, had a very imperfect idea of what the metre was. One is accordingly tempted to suppose that in standard Saturnians elision was prohibited or at any

34. In this and the two following examples failure to elide would necessitate placing the *caesura Korschiana* after rather than before the elided word—hence the illegitimate five- or six-syllable opening.

35. *Nexebant mult(a) inter se* may be another example; but it is possible to take it as an example of the rare type × × × | × × × × (e.g. *lucusta lucam bovem* [Naevius 63]).

rate avoided at this point in the line. If so, two additional cola:

Livius 17: utrum genua     amploctens...
Naevius 46: onerariae     onustae...

and possibly three more:

Livius 16: igitur demum     Ulixi...
Naevius 19.1: inerant signa     expressa...
Naevius epitaph 3: itaque postquam     est Orchi...

should be added to the list of those which show a regular penta-syllabic opening.[36] This can only be a suggestion at the present point in our investigation, but it will be supported by further evidence adduced later.

Besides an anomalously placed elision the dedication of the Faliscan cooks contains one of the two Saturnian half-lines that show an irregular five- or six-syllable opening:

*CEL* 2.2: opipar(um) ad veitam     quolundam...

Because of its provenance this colon does not constitute a significant exception to the rule. More problematic is Livius 22:

...flexu nodorum dubio.

The half-line is suspect, however, because of its length. Octo-syllabic second cola are found nowhere else in Livius or Naevius. They appear only four times in the entire Saturnian corpus:

Naevius epitaph 4: ...loquier lingua Latina
Appius Claudius: ...obliscere miserias
*CEL* 3.2: ...Romam redieit triumphans
*CEL* 2.5: ...imperatoribus summis;

36. The last three examples are more dubious, inasmuch as all of them would allow for placing the caesura after the first word: *igitur | dem(um) Ulixi*, etc.; see, however, below, p. 29. Also more dubious, because not certainly from the *Bellum Punicum* (cf. above, n. 20), is Naevius 34 (*apud emporium in campo     hostium pro moene*). If the line is a Saturnian, admission of hiatus after *emporium* is necessary and will create another hexasyllabic opening of the type $\cup \cup - \cup \cup \underset{\smile}{} |$ (*simul ac dacrimas dĕ ore*...).

and one of these appearances is in the dedication of the Faliscan cooks. It is tempting, therefore, to follow Buecheler and read *nodum* for *nodorum*.

It can hardly be coincidental that, of the thirty-two possible patterns which a sequence of five long and/or short syllables may display, there are fully twelve (represented by the schemata $- \cup - - \cup$, $\underset{\smile}{-} - \underset{\smile}{-} - \underset{\smile}{-}$, $- \underset{\smile}{-} - \underset{\smile}{-} -$ and $\cup - - \cup -$) which, with one possible exception, are never found in the portion of a half-line which precedes the *caesura Korschiana*. Since there is no comparable restriction on the order of longs and shorts in tetra-syllabic openings,[37] the only plausible explanation for the phenomenon is that the composers of the Saturnian regarded a succession of two short syllables as equivalent, at certain points in the verse at any rate, to a single syllable, whether long or short, so that pentasyllabic units could substitute for tetra-syllabic ones only when they contained one such pair and hexasyllabic units only when they contained two. And this means that the verse must, to some extent at any rate, have obeyed a combination of metrical principles similar to that which is operative in the comic senarius, septenarius, and octonarius. There, in addition to the syllabic equivalence of $\cup$ and $-$ which is regular in the thesis of each foot, we find (also confined to theses) the equivalence of $\cup$ and $\cup \cup$, and (throughout the verse) the quantitative equivalence of $-$ and $\cup \cup$. This hybrid metrical system, by which under certain conditions $\underset{\smile}{-} = \cup \cup$ (i.e. $\cup = - = \cup \cup$), will explain, as no set of accentual principles can, why a sequence like *\*spléndide facteis superases* should not be just as acceptable an opening as *fácile facteis superases* (*CEL* 8.5); and it will also explain, as no purely syllabic system can, why a sequence like *\*subegit omne Loucanam* is less metrical than *subigit omne Loucanam* (*CEL* 7.6).

The $\underset{\smile}{-} = \cup \cup$ equivalence that has been detected in the opening portion of certain Saturnian cola seems to have been operative elsewhere in the verse as well. Turning our attention

37. For a partial tabulation of tetrasyllabic verse openings in Livius and Naevius see De Groot (above, n. 2), p. 303.

from the first to the second part of the colon we find the
following metrical patterns (lines where alternate scansions are
possible are enclosed in parentheses):[38]

∪ ∪ − ∪

| Naevius | 4.3: | flentes ambae | abeuntes... |
| | 12.1: | senex fretus | pietati... |
| | 42.2: | ...ad suos | popularis |
| | 45: | ...conterit | legiones |
| | 47: | ...atque locos | ut haberent |
| | 48: | septimum | decimum annum... |
| | 51: | magnam domum | decoremque... |
| | 52: | simul alius | aliunde... |
| | 54: | plerique omnes | subiguntur... |
| *GL* 6.265.29: | | ...maximas | legiones |
| *GL* 6.265.25: | | duello magno | dirimendo... |
| *Ibid.*: | | ...regibus | subigendis |
| *CEL* 3.3: | | ob hasce res | bene gestas... |
| *CEL* 7.2: | | ...fortis vir | sapiensque |
| *CEL* 8.2: | | mors perfecit | tua ut essent... |
| *CEL* 8.4: | | quibus sei in longa | licuiset... |
| *CEL* 8.5: | | facile facteis | superases... |
| *CEL* 11.1: | | hoc est factum | monumentum... |
| *CEL* 11.3: | | ...dormias | sine qura |

− ∪ ∪ ∪

| Livius | 8: | in Pylum | devenies... |
| | 11: | quando dies | adveniet... |
| | 30: | vestis pulla | purpurea... |
| Naevius | 19.3: | Runcus ac | Purpureus... |
| | 30.1: | ...inclutus | arquitenens |

38. In view of our uncertainty as to the quantity of final syllables in early
Latin (see J. Vendryes, *Recherches sur l'histoire et les effets de l'intensité initiale
en Latin* [Paris 1902], pp. 82–7) and our complete ignorance as to what, if
any, special rules applied to the quantity of the syllables before the central
break and at the end of the line, all final syllables are regarded as anceps for
the purposes of the tabulation.

36: ...auspicat auspicium
54: ...sub suum iudicium
*CEL* 8.3: ...gloria atque ingenium
*CEL* 8.6: qua re lubens te in gremiu...
*CEL* 11.3: bene rem geras et valeas...

∪ ∪ ∪ ⌣

Appius Claudius: ...obliscere miserias

– – ∪ ⌣

Livius 38: (neque tamen te oblitus sum...)
Naevius 47: convenit regnum simul...
63: ...lucusta lucam bovem.
Calatinus epitaph: populi primarium...
*CEL* 2.3: quei soveis a⟨rg⟩utieis...
*CEL* 2.4: gondecorant sai⟨pi⟩sume...

∪ – ∪ ⌣

Livius 3: (...ex tuo ore supra fugit)
Naevius 3.2: sacra in mensa Penatium...
*CEL* 11.2: (hospes gratum est quom apud meas...)

– – – ⌣

Livius 22: (nexebant multa inter se...)
38: (neque tamen te oblitus sum...)
Naevius 19.1: (inerant signa expressa...)
Naevius epitaph 3: (itaque postquam est Orchi...)

∪ – – ⌣

Livius 3: (...ex tuo ore supra fugit)
15: ...filiam Calypsonem[39]

– ∪ – ⌣

Livius 16: (igitur demum Ulixi...)
16: ...cor frixit prae pavore
*CEL* 6.3: Luciom Scipione...

39. Usually scanned *filiam Calypsŏnem*, but such an example of iambic shortening would be unique in early Saturnians; cf. G. Jachmann, "Zu altlateinischer Prosodie," *Glotta* 7 (1916), 61–3.

– ‿ ⌣

   Livius 21: Mercurius     cumque eo...
Naevius 3.3: immolabat     auream...
    *CEL* 3.3: ...quod in bello     voverat
    *CEL* 3.5: imperator    dedicat
    *CEL* 4.4: donu danunt    Hercolei...
    *CEL* 7.1: Cornelius    Lucius...

⌣ ⌣ ⌣

      Livius 22: ...flexu nod[or]um     dubio
          27: topper facit     homines...
    Naevius 21: silvicolae     homines...
          29: prima incedit     Cereris...
          43: magnum stuprum     populo...
          63: atque prius     pariet...
Appius Claudius: ...ferocia     pariat

The remaining cola (over sixty in number) all show the ending
⌣ – ⌣ with no significant preference for initial long or short. The
overall predominance of this form is partially paralleled by the
evident preference, among tetrasyllabic sequences, for those
which show a pair of short syllables: ‿ ‿ – ⌣ and ⌣ ‿ ‿ ⌣. It is
tempting to explain this preference in terms of the same
⌣ = ‿ ‿ equivalence that was seen to be operative in the first
half of the colon, for both ‿ ‿ – ⌣ (= ‿̑‿ – ⌣) and ⌣ ‿ ‿ ⌣
(= ⌣ ‿̑‿ ⌣) thereby become permissible substitutes for the
predominant ⌣ – ⌣. It is hard to see any other reason why word
groups of the form – ‿ ⊥ ⌣ should be so much less frequent than
those of the form ‿ ‿ ⊥ ⌣; or why, outside the kitchen Saturnians
of *CEL* 2, ⌣ ⊥ ‿ ⌣ word groups are found much less frequently
than ⌣ ‿ ‿ ⌣ groups. On the analogy of ‿̑‿ – ⌣ and ⌣ ‿̑‿ ⌣,
one might expect that ⌣ – ‿ ‿ (= ⌣ – ‿̑‿) would be a third
possible variant on ⌣ – ⌣. But the rarity of this form as an
ending (four possible instances: Naevius 3.2, 47, and 63;
Livius 3) is explicable on the plausible assumption that substitution of ‿ ‿ for ⌣ was not allowed at the end of the colon, just
as it is not allowed at the end of the senarius or Greek trimeter.

⌣ – ⌣ ⌣ therefore belongs with – ⌣ – ⌣ and ⌣ – ⌣ – as a tetra-syllabic cadence that cannot be analyzed as a variant on the trisyllabic ⌣ – ⌣.

These cadences are rare enough to make alternate scansions preferable whenever possible. In three lines, therefore,

> Livius 16: igitur demum     Ulixi...
> Naevius 19.1: inerant signa     expressa...
> Naevius epitaph 3: itaque postquam     est Orchi...

the *caesura Korschiana* should come after the second word rather than, as indicated in the above lists, the first. (Hiatus in each instance rather than elision should accompany the caesura— cf. above, pp. 23–4).[40] The remaining examples of the cadence in question are remarkable not only for their rarity, but also for a restriction in their use to which forms containing a pair of consecutive short syllables are not subject. There is no certain example of – ⌣ – ⌣ or ⌣ – ⌣ ⌣ following a tetrasyllabic opening. In the line which most editors give as *neque tamen te oblitus sum...* (Livius 38) *neque enim* is an alternate reading and *nec tamen* a possible emendation; *hospes gratum est quom apud meas...* (*CEL* 11.2) may be scanned with synizesis of *meās*; elision plus synizesis gives *ex tu(o) ore supra fugit* in Livius 3; and in *sacra in mensa Penatium* (Naevius 3.2) it is possible to read *Penatum* (Buecheler)[41] or scan *Penatịum* (Baehrens). *Gondecorant sae⟨pi⟩-sume* does not admit of heptasyllabic scansion, but like *aciptum aetatei agedai* and *opiparum ad veitam quolundam* (cf. above, pp. 23–4), it belongs to the metrically aberrant *CEL* 2.

The contrast both of frequency and use between those tetra-syllabic endings which contain a pair of short syllables and those which do not suggests, when taken in conjunction with the facts about pentasyllabic and hexasyllabic openings presented

---

40. One is left with Livius 22 (*nexebant multa inter se...*) as a solitary example of the type × × × | – – – ×; but the alternate scansion, with elision at the *caesura Korschiana* (*nexebant mult(a) inter se...*), is just as anomalous.

41. Cf. Pasquali (above, no. 10), p. 27, n. 1, who compares, from Ennius, *caelestum* and *partum*.

earlier, that one should posit as a tentative scheme for the
longer Saturnian cola the following:

x x x x | x x x;   or   x x x | x x x x;   or   ⏑⏑⏑⏑⏑⏑⏑⏑ | ⏑⏑⏑⏑ x

where (x) represents a syllable that may be either long or short,
and (|) indicates word end. The normal colon has seven syllables
with word end after the fourth. Variant forms arise through
placement of word end after the third syllable, or through the
substitution of ⏑ ⏑ for x at one or two of the places indicated.
Both types of variation are never found in the same colon, and
consecutive syllables are never replaced by consecutive pairs of
shorts. These two restrictions account for Korsch's law and the
prohibition of tetrasyllabic openings in cola which end in
– ⏑ – ⏒ or ⏒ – ⏒ ⏒. Korsch's law would be violated were it
possible to substitute ⏑ ⏑ for x in the second half of a colon of
the type x x x | x x x x; and a tetrasyllabic opening followed by
– ⏑ – x or ⏒ – ⏒ ⏒ would be a colon of the type ⏑⏑⏑⏑⏑⏑ | x x x x
or x x x x | x x x x. The six cola (see above, p. 19) which, because
they contain a pentasyllabic word, necessarily violate the rules
about caesura placement, adhere to the rule that x may be
replaced only by ⏑ ⏑. The one octosyllable among them:

*CEL* 2.5: . . . imperatoribus summis

may be scanned as x x x x ⏑⏑⏑ x x; and the one enneasyllable:

*CEL* 3.1: duct(u) auspici(o) imperioque. . .

scans as x x ⏑⏑⏑ x ⏑⏑⏑ x x.
   One other fact about the placement of pairs of short syllables
is worth noting. No colon begins with the sequences ⏒ – – ⏑ ⏑ |,
– ⏑ ⏑ – ⏒ |, or – ⏑ ⏑ – ⏑ ⏑ |. This may indicate that ⏑ ⏑ could
only be substituted for the first and third syllables in the line.
On the other hand, since the sequences in question represent
only a small percentage of the total number possible, their
absence may be owing to chance. In deciding between the
alternate explanations here one is tempted to be guided by the
parallel usage in the second part of the colon, where ⏑ ⏑ – ⏒ is

preferred, though not to the exclusion of ⌣̲ ⌣ ⌣ ⌣̲. The relationship between the sequences ⌣ ⌣ – ⌣̲ and – ⌣ ⌣ – at the beginning of the line may have been similar. On the other hand, ⌣ ⌣ seems unlikely ever to have been substituted for the final syllable in the colon (above, pp. 28–9). The same may have held for the syllable immediately before the *caesura Korschiana*.

The metrical structure of tetrasyllabic openings is much freer (cf. above, p. 25 with n. 37). The preference for word arrangements of the form × × | × × or, less frequently, × × × × (as against × | × × × and × × × | ×) has often been noted. That syllabic considerations rather than a desire for an accented first and third syllable are at work here is indicated by the absence of any striking preference for tetrasyllables of the form × × ⌣̲ × over those of the form × ⌣̰̲ ⌣ ×. The one absolute rule is quantitative: the sequence ⌣ ⌣ – × appears only in the following lines:

Livius 16: igitur demum      Ulixi...
Naevius 19.1: inerant signa      expressa...
Naevius 46: onerariae      onustae...

and in every instance the opening becomes pentasyllabic if hiatus is allowed at the *caesura Korschiana*. The scansion with hiatus is therefore, according to the principle already enunciated, the preferred one (above, p. 20). Similarly the absence of any certain example of an initial colon with the opening sequence ⌣ ⌣ ⌣ × | favors scansion with hiatus in

Naevius epitaph 3: itaque postquam      est Orchi...

Both these conclusions, it should be noted, are in accord with the argument advanced earlier (above, pp. 23–4) against admitting elision at the *caesura Korschiana* and provide an important support for that argument.

There are two occurrences of the opening sequence ⌣ ⌣ ⌣ × | where the possibility of an alternate scansion does not exist, both of them in the second half of the line:

Naevius 4.2: ...capitibus      opertis
*CEL* 2.6: ...bene iovent      optantis

The sequence should be considered a legitimate, though rare, form of the initial tetrasyllable, as is – ∪ – × |, of which there are three certain and five possible occurrences:

| | | |
|---|---|---|
| Naevius 3.3: | immolabat | auream... |
| *CEL* 3.5: | imperator | dedicat |
| *CEL* 8.7: | terra Publi | prognatum... |
| Livius 30: | vestĭs pulla | purpurea... |
| *CEL* 7.3: | quoiŭs forma | virtutei... |
| *CEL* 7.6: | obsidesqu(ĕ) | abdoucit... |
| *CEL* 8.3: | ...gloria atqu(ĕ) | ingenium |
| *CEL* 9.6: | ...quei minŭs sit | mandatus |

More common is – ∪ ∪ × | (at least six examples),[42] all other tetrasyllabic openings being covered by the formula × – × × |.

Taking these rules or preferences into account we may write the scheme for the Saturnian half-line of seven or more syllables as follows:

$$\underset{×}{∪∪}\ (\underset{–}{∪∪})\ \underset{×}{∪∪}\ × \mid \underset{×}{∪∪}\ \underset{×}{∪∪}\ ×\quad \text{or}\quad × × × \mid × × × ×$$
$$(– ∪ × ×)$$
$$(∪ ∪ ∪ ×)$$

Sequences and substitutions of only sporadic occurrence are enclosed in parentheses.

The general rarity of tetrasyllabic openings that show the sequence ∪ ∪ is worth noting, and naturally raises the questions of whether these openings are not variants on shorter ones—just as pentasyllabic openings, all of which contain at least one such sequence, seem to be variants on tetrasyllabic ones. We cannot, however, attempt an answer to the question until we have considered the shorter Saturnian cola in themselves.

These cola all contain either five or six syllables. Aside from

42. See the inventory and discussion in Leo (above, n. 1), pp. 46–7.

the exceedingly common $- \cup - \mid \times - \times,$[43] the following hexasyllabic forms are attested (cola in which there is the possibility
of an alternate scansion are enclosed in parentheses):

(1)   $- \cup \cup \mid \times - \times$

        Livius 5: ...omnia      disertim
            14: ...filia       regina
            17: (...virginem      oraret)
            21: (...filius     Latonas)
            27: (...ut prius     fuerunt)
    Naevius 3.1: (postquam avem    aspexit...)
           3.2: ...ordine    ponuntur
            14: (...optumum    appellat)
         23.1: (...Aenea[44]    quo pacto)
         30.2: ...Pythius    Apollo
            31: ...sagmina   sumpserunt
         50.1: id quoque    paciscunt...
            53: ...pectora    possidit
  Naevius epitaph 3: (...traditus   thesauro)
        *CEL* 3.4: (...Herculis   victoris)
        *CEL* 6.3: (...filios   Barbati)
        *CEL* 8.1: (...flaminis   gesistei)

(2)   $- \cup - \mid \cup \cup \times$

        *CEL* 4.4: ...maxime    meretod
        *CEL* 8.6: ...Scipio    recipit

(3)   $- \cup \cup \mid \cup \cup \times$

      Livius 23: ...filia    docuit
        *CEL* 8.2: ...omnia    brevia

43. See the inventory in Leo (above, n. 1), pp. 17–19. Here and in what
follows, forms with the cadence $- - \times$ are assumed to be metrically equivalent to those with the cadence $\cup - \times$, on the analogy of heptasyllables,
where $\times - \times$, with no significant preference for initial long or short (above,
p. 28) is the most common closing sequence.

44. For the scansion *Aené̆a* see Leo (above, n. 1), pp. 34–5, n. 5.

(4)    $- - - \mid \times - \times$

       Livius 10: (...adprimus     Patroclus)[45]
             13: partim errant     nequinont...
          20.2: (...vires cui     sunt magnae)
    Naevius 3.1: (...in templo     Anchisa)
            28: res divas     edicit...
          30.1: dein pollens     sagittis...

(5)    $- - \cup \mid \times - \times$

       Livius 10: (...adprimus     Patroclus)
    Naevius 4.1: (...amborum     uxores)
            10: ...vestemque     citrosam
          19.2: (...magnique     Atlantes)
            21: (...bellique     inertes)
          23.1: (...Aenea[44]     quo pacto)
      *CEL* 3.4: (hanc aedem     et signu)...
      *CEL* 9.1: ...multasque     virtutes
      *CEL* 9.2: aetate     quom parva...

(6)    $\cup - - \mid \times - \times$

       Livius 15: (apud nympham     Atlantis...)
      *CEL* 3.2: Corinto     deleto...

(7)    $\cup - \cup \mid \times - \times$

     Livius 26.2: (simul duona     eorum...)

(8)    $- - - \mid - \cup \times$

    Naevius 23.2: Troiam urbem     liquerit...
          43.1: sin illos     deserant...
            55: quod bruti     nec satis...
Calatinus epitaph: hunc unum     plurimum...
      *CEL* 6.5: hec cepit     Corsica...

---

45. *Patroclus*, the usual scansion in classical Latin, seems preferable to the *Patroclus* which would be regular in archaic drama. The name is so scanned in the Homeric verse from which Livius 10 is translated (3.110: ἔνθα δὲ Πάτροκλος...); and, so scanned, it produces a more normal colon (*Patroclus* would give the otherwise unattested hexasyllable $- - \times \mid \cup \cup \times$).

(9)  ∪ − − | − ∪ ×

Appius Claudius: amicum     cum vides...

(10)  ∪ − ∪ | − ∪ ×

        *CEL* 6.2: (duonorum     optumo...)

(11)  ∪ ∪ − | × − ×

     Naevius 4.3: ...lacrimis     cum multis
           20: ...hominum     fortunas

(12)  × × × × | × ×

        Livius 9: tumque remos     iussit...
          9: ...religare     struppis
        11: ...quem profata     Morta est
      20.1: namque nullum     peius...
      20.2: quamde mare     saevom...
      20.2: (...vires cui sunt     magnae)
      20.3: (...importunae     undae)
        38: ...Laertie     noster
   Naevius 5.3: (ubi foras     cum auro...)
     12.2: summi deum     regis...
     12.3: regnatorem     marum...
       29: ...Proserpina     puer
     43.1: ...fortissimos     viros
Naevius epitaph 4: (obliti sunt     Romae...)
Calatinus epitaph: ...consentiunt     gentes
     *CEL* 2.1: conlegium     quod est...
     *CEL* 3.1: ...eius Achaia     capta
     *CEL* 6.1: (...cosentiont     R[omae])
     *CEL* 6.5: (...Aleriaque     urbe)
     *CEL* 7.3: ...parisuma     fuit
     *CEL* 8.4: ...tibe utier     vita
     *CEL* 11.2: ...restitistei     seedes

(13)  − − | − ∪ ∪ ×

     *CEL* 11.1: ...Maarco     Caecilio

The sequence – ∪ ∪ | is used as an opening for hexasyllables in exactly the same way as the more common – ∪ – |: before × – × (category 1 above); before ∪ ∪ × (cf. categories 2 and 3), never before – ∪ × (cf. 8–10 above); and rarely in a colon that forms the first half of a line. It can plausibly be analyzed, therefore, as a metrical equivalent for – ∪ – |. The cola listed in categories 1–3 above will thus be examples of the two types – ∪ × | × – × and – ∪ × | ∪ ∪ ×.

It would be possible to analyze the opening sequences – – – | and – – ∪ | as further variants on – ∪ × |, on the assumption that the second as well as the third syllable of the sequence could be either long or short. But though – – – | and – – ∪ |, like – ∪ × |, appear most often before × – × (cf. 4 and 5 above) their use in other respects is rather different. Unlike – ∪ × |, they appear just as often in the first as in the second half of the line, and they are never found before ∪ ∪ × (cf. 2 and 3 above). Moreover, one of them, – – – |, differs further from – ∪ × | in that it appears before – ∪ × (cf. 8 above). Rather than link – – – | and – – ∪ | with – ∪ × |, it is preferable to associate them with the two rarer sequences, ∪ – – | and ∪ – ∪ |, whose use parallels theirs more closely. There are certain examples of ∪ – – | and possible examples of ∪ – ∪ | before both × – × and – ∪ × (6–9); and neither form ever precedes ∪ ∪ ×. This identification would make all the cola listed in categories 4–10 examples of the two types × – × | × – × and × – × | – ∪ ×.

Further support for the separation of – ∪ × | × – × and – – × | × – × which this classification involves comes from a series of heptasyllabic sequences which show the form × × × | ×̆ ∪̆ ∪̆ ×̆ :

| | | |
|---|---|---|
| Livius 8: in Pylum | devenies... |
| Naevius 19.3: Runcus ac | Purpureus... |
| 30.1: ...inclutus | arquitenens |
| 36: ...auspicat | auspicium |
| 42: ...ad suos | popularis |
| 45: ...conterit | legiones |

48: septimum      decimum annum...
54: ...sub suum     iudicium
*GL* 6.265.25: ...regibus    subigendis
*GL* 6.265.29: ...maximas    legiones
*CEL* 7.2: ...fortis vir    sapiensque
*CEL* 11.3: ...dormias    sine qura

It has already been suggested (above, p. 28) that cadences of the form $\overset{\times}{\cup}\overset{\cup}{\cup}\overset{\times}{\underset{-}{}}$ are variants on x – x, and the suggestion is borne out by the sequences just enumerated. The latter occupy a peculiar position among cola of the form x x x | x x x x. They make up over half the total (twelve out of twenty-one; cf. above, pp. 26–7; and, unlike the other varieties, they always open with the sequence – ∪ x |.[46] Rather than posit x x x | $\overset{\times}{\cup}\overset{\cup}{\cup}\overset{\times}{}$ as an unaccountably popular subspecies of the otherwise rare x x x | x x x x, it is natural to assume that these cola are alternate forms of the common – ∪ x | x – x (i.e. – ∪ x | x ∪∪ x and – ∪ x | $\overset{\cup\cup}{\times}$ – x). To the characteristics already mentioned which distinguish – ∪ x | from – – x | as an opening for hexasyllables

---

46. The only possible exceptions are Naevius 4.3: *flentes amb(ae) abeuntes*... $\overset{-\ -\ -}{}\ \overset{\cup\cup-\ \times}{}$
and *CEL* 7.2: ...*fortis vir sapiensque*. But our analysis of heptasyllables (above, pp. 23–4) gives us reason to prefer scansion with hiatus (– – – x | ∪ ∪ – x) in the former example; and *CEL* 8.4: *quibus s(ei) in longa licuiset*... (cf. above, p. 23) favors the scansion *fortis vir* in which -*s* does not make position. The percentage of cola of the type x x x | x x x x which show the sequence – ∪ x | $\overset{\times}{\cup}\overset{\cup}{\cup}\overset{\times}{}$ is even higher if one accepts monosyllabic scansion of *atque* in Naevius 45 (...*atque locos ut haberent*) and *CEL* 8.3 (...*gloria atque ingenium*); and there are several reasons for preferring this scansion. The sequence – ∪ ∪ – ∪ ∪ – x (*atque locos ut haberent*) is not paralleled elsewhere in the Saturnian corpus, nor is – ∪ – x | – ∪ ∪ x (*gloria atque ingenium*). Even the form – ∪ – x | x – x, on which – ∪ – x | – ∪ ∪ x is, presumably, a variant (– ∪ ∪ x being substituted for x – x), has only one certain occurrence—cf. above, p. 32. Moreover, general archaic usage, which favors the form *atque* before vowels and *ac* before consonants (cf. F. Skutsch, *Plautinisches und Romanisches* [Leipzig 1892], p. 53) indicates that the word was regularly monosyllabic.

one may therefore add the fact that the colon $-\cup\times \mid \times - \times$, unlike $--\times \mid \times - \times$, shows the same substitution of $\cup\cup$ for $\underset{\smile}{\phantom{.}}$ that was observed in certain heptasyllables.

Besides supporting our classification of hexasyllables, cola of the form $-\cup\times \mid \times - \times$ provide some guide for the analysis of the heptasyllables $\cup\cup\cup\times \mid \times\times\times$ and $-\cup\cup\times \mid \times\times\times$. Since $\cup\cup$ seems capable of replacing $\underset{\smile}{\phantom{.}}$ in both halves of the heptasyllables in which this substitution occurs, it is reasonable to expect the same to hold true for hexasyllables, and so to analyze ...*capiti-bus opertis* and ...*bene iovent optantis* (Naevius 4.2 and *CEL* 2.6; cf. above, p. 31) as $\underset{\smile\smile}{\phantom{.}}\cup\times \mid \times - \times$. On the other hand, the absence of evidence for cola of the form $\times - \times \mid \times - \times$ in which $\cup\cup$ substitutes for $\underset{\smile}{\phantom{.}}$ in the cadence provides some reason for not importing this substitution into the first part of the colon by analyzing heptasyllables of the form $-\cup\cup\times \mid \times - \times$ as $\times\underset{\smile\smile}{\phantom{.}}\times \mid \times - \times$. This consideration is strengthened by the general rules governing the use of $-\cup\cup\times \mid$ as a colon opener. The sequence is found regularly in the first half of the line,[47] unlike $\times - \times \mid \times - \times$, which is roughly as frequent there as in the second half; moreover, unlike $\times - \times \mid$, $-\cup\cup\times \mid$ precedes final $\cup\cup\times$ as well as $-\cup\times$ and $\times - \times$. The restriction of $-\cup\cup\times \mid$ to the first of the line also makes it unlikely that $-\cup\cup\times \mid \times - \times$ is a variant on $-\cup\times \mid \times - \times$ (i.e. $-\overset{\smile\smile}{\cup}\times \mid \times - \times$), as does the existence of the form $-\cup\cup\times \mid -\cup\times$ (Livius 21: *Mercurius cumque eo*...). The corresponding hexasyllabic sequence, $*-\cup\times \mid -\cup\times$, is unattested. For these reasons, $-\cup\cup\times \mid \times\times\times$ is best analyzed as an isosyllabic variant on the more common $\times - \times\times \mid \times\times\times$. If the general formula for the heptasyllable is now restated so as to exclude the types ($\cup\cup\cup\times \mid \times\times\times$ and $\times\times\times \mid \overset{\times}{\cup}\overset{\cup}{\cup}\overset{\smile}{\phantom{.}}\overset{\times}{\phantom{.}}$) that seem to be variants on hexasyllables, it will go as follows:

$$\overset{\cup\cup}{\underset{\circ}{\phantom{.}}}\overset{(\cup\cup)}{\underset{\circ}{\phantom{.}}}\overset{\cup\cup}{\times}\times \mid \overset{\cup\cup}{\times}\overset{\cup\cup}{\times}\times \quad \text{or} \quad \times\times\times \mid \overset{-\cup-}{\underset{\times-\times}{\phantom{.}}}\overset{\times}{\times}$$

$(\circ\circ = \overset{\cup\,-}{\underset{\cup\,-}{\phantom{.}}}; \quad (\cup\cup) = \text{rare substitution}).$

---

47. The only possible exception is *CEL* 9.6: ...*quei minus sit mandātus* (*sit mactus* Lachmann, Weil and Benloew).

All hexasyllabic cola show a preference for central caesura or, failing that, for caesura after the fourth syllable. The preference is so marked that one is probably justified in scanning $\bar{M}\bar{a}arco$ | $\bar{C}\bar{a}ecil\underset{\cdot}{i}o$ (category 13 above) to remove the solitary exception.[48] Among forms with the central caesura there is a striking preference for $- \cup \times$ | as an opening and an even more striking preference for $\times - \times$ as a cadence. The arrangement of syllabic quantities in cola of the form $\times \times \times \times$ | $\times \times$ is freer, though there is only one possible example of $\cup \cup \cup \times$ | $\times \times$ (*CEL* 6.5: ...*Aleriaque urbe*) and one of $\cup \cup - \times$ | $\times \times$ (Livius 9: ...*religare struppis*).[49] The situation here recalls that which exists in heptasyllables of the type $\times \times \times \times$|$\times \times \times$(above, pp. 31–2), of which $\times \times \times \times$ | $\times \times$ may, therefore, be a shortened or catalectic version: $\circ \circ \times \times$ | $\times \times$ $(\times)$. The one fact which goes against this analysis is the frequency of $- \cup - \times$ | as an opening in the hexasyllable: five examples in sixteen certain occurrences of the colon. In the much larger body of heptasyllables there are only three certain examples of such an opening (above, p. 32). It is possible, therefore, that our single category $\times \times \times \times$ | $\times \times$ is a conflation of two separate types: the shortened heptasyllable $\circ \circ \times \times$ | $\times \times$ and $- \cup - \times$ | $- \times$: a variant (with irregular caesura) of the most common hexasyllable, $- \cup -$ | $\times - \times$.

The invariability with which the caesura appears after the third or fourth syllable of each hexasyllable, the predominance of the form $- \cup \times$ | $\times - \times$, and the relationship between this form and $- \cup \times$ | $\overset{\times}{\cup}\overset{\cup}{\cup}\overset{\cup}{-}\overset{\times}{\times}$ are all such as to suggest the same hybrid system of versification that was observed in heptasyllables. Analysis is more difficult with pentasyllables, of which the following are certain examples (cadences which show the

48. Cf. S. Mariotti (above, n. 24), p. 75, n. 39, and S. Timpanaro, 'Per una nuova edizione critica di Ennio," *SIFC* 21 (1946), 67–8, with the parallels cited there: Ennius 251 (*Serviljo*), 94, 104, 436, 473 Vahlen; and Naevius, Fr. com. 17 Ribbeck.

49. The quantity of the first syllable in *Aleria* is not known; and the first syllable of *religare* may, of course, be long, as often in *religio* and *religiosus*.

sequences $--\times$ and $\cup-\times$ are assumed to be equivalent—cf.
above, n. 43):

(1)   $-\cup-\mid-\times$
     Livius 26.1: (...venimus    Circae)
    Naevius 3.3: ...victimam    pulchram
        19.3: ...filii    Terras
         44: ...obviam    Poenum
  Appius Claudius: ...nec libens    aeque

(2)   $-\cup\cup\mid-\times$
     Livius 26.1: (...venimus    Circae)

(3)   $-\cup-\mid\cup\times$
    Naevius 5.2: ...strenui    viri
        48: ...ilico    sedent

(4)   $-\cup--\times$
     Livius 26.3: ...inserinuntur

(5)   $--\mid\times-\times$
     Livius 20.3: topper    confringent...
        26.2: ...portant    ad navis
         39: ...flammam    Volcani
    Naevius 5.1: ...multi    mortales
        5.3: ...illinc    exibant
       12.2: ...fratrem    Neptunum
        46: ...stabant    in flustris
     *CEL* 4.2: ...voto hoc    soluto
     *CEL* 4.5: ...crebro    condemnes

(6)   $\cup-\mid\times-\times$
     Livius 18.2: ...domum    venisse
     *CEL* 2.5: ququei huc    dederunt...

(7)   $\cup-\cup-\times$
    Naevius 12.1: ...deum adlocutus

(8)  $-\,-\,\cup\mid\cup\,\times$

      Naevius 55: ...sardare     queunt
          *CEL* 2.2: ...festosque     dies

(9)  $\cup\,-\,\cup\mid\cup\,\times$

    *CEL* 6.2 and
Calatinus epitaph: ...fuisse     virom

(10)  $-\,-\,-\mid-\,\times$

      Naevius 28: ...praedicit     castus

(11)  $-\,-\mid\cup\,\cup\,\times$

        *CEL* 6.6: ...aide     meretod

Two types of sequence—those beginning with $-\,\cup\,-$ (categories 1, 3 and 4) and those with the second and fourth syllable long (categories 5–7 and 10) seem to be preferred, as is caesura after the third syllable in the one type and after the second syllable in the other. With one exception (*praedicit castus*) violations of the latter rule occur only when a four- or five-syllable word must be accommodated within the colon (*inserinuntur, deum adlocutus*).

Sequences opening in $-\,\cup\mid$ or ending in $\mid-\,\cup\,\times$ seem to be avoided altogether, so that in seven cola:

    Livius 4: ...aureo     eclutro
        8: ...haut ibi     ommentans
      17: ...virginem     oraret
Naevius 3.1: postqu(am) avem     aspexit...
      14: ...optumum     appellat
    *CEL* 4.1: ...asper⟨e⟩[50]     afleicta
    *CEL* 6.2: duonorum     optumo...

we are justified in scanning with hiatus to replace the anomalous pentasyllable with a regular hexasyllable of the form $-\,\cup\,\times\mid\times\,-\,\times$

50. There is no trace of an "*e*" in the inscription, but the supplement is demanded by the sense of the line and can be supported by the parallel of *capt*⟨*a*⟩ and *duct*⟨*u*⟩ in *CEL* 3.1.

or $x - x \mid - \cup x$.[51] It follows that hiatus rather than elision was regular at the central caesura in hexasyllables, a rule which favors scansion with hiatus in five additional metrically ambiguous cola:

Livius 15: apud nympham     Atlantis...
      26.2: simul duona      eorum...
      26.3: multa alia        in isdem...
Naevius 5.2: multi alii        e Troia...
      21: silvicolae       homines...[52]

In pentasyllables, however, there are three pieces of evidence to suggest that the reverse was true: (1) the second syllable of cola which show a 2|3 division of syllables into words is always long, not indifferently long or short, as is the syllable which precedes central hiatus in hexasyllables and heptasyllables; (2) among the twenty-five certain pentasyllables there is no *multi exibant* or *obviam ire*, in which hiatus would be necessary to avoid an otherwise unexampled tetrasyllabic half-line; (3) if one excludes elision from the pentasyllable there will be five cola:

Naevius 3.1: ...in templo     Anchisa
     4.1: ...amborum      uxores

51. Cf. S. Mariotti, *Livio Andronico e la traduzione artistica* (Milan 1952), p. 89; J. Soubiran, *L'élision dans la poésie latine* (Paris 1966), p. 29.

52. The only hexasyllable which one might be tempted to scan with elision at the central caesura is *CEL* 7.6: *obsidesque abdoucit*, inasmuch as the sequence $- \cup x \mid x - x$ is very common, particularly in the second half of the line, whereas $- \cup - x \mid x - x$ has only one sure parallel (*CEL* 8.7: *terra Publi prognatum*...). But, since early Latin shows apocope of final -*e* in *perque, quodque, quomque* and a number of other words (see Skutsch [above, n. 46], pp. 151–3), it is possible that the scansion *obsidesqu(e) abdoucit* would not involve ordinary elision; compare ...*gloria atque ingenium* (*CEL* 8.3), a colon which with the scansion *atqu(e)* suggested above (n. 46) differs from *obsidesque abdoucit* only in that it does not involve the cadence $x - x$ but rather its metrical equivalent $x \cup \cup x$. (Whether elision or hiatus was preferred at the caesura in hexasyllables of the form $x x x x \mid x x$ is uncertain. Hiatus is possible in *importunae undae* [Livius 20.3] and elision in *Aleriaque urbem* [*CEL* 6.5]; but there is no reason for preferring either scansion over its possible alternate.)

> 19.2: ...magnique     Atlantes
> 21: ...bellique     inertes
> *CEL* 3.4: hanc aedem     et signu...

of the type × – × | × – × which show hiatus. Since there are only fifteen possible examples all-told of the colon,[53] this incidence of hiatus seems unusually high. It is reasonable to assume that at least one or two of the cola cited are to be scanned with elision, as pentasyllables.

There is no simple quantitative or accentual explanation for the syllabic sequences which are favored in pentasyllabic cola. From a quantitative point of view the solitary – – – | – × (*praedicit castus*) would be just as acceptable as the common – – | × – ×; and accentual scansion would not distinguish ⊥ – | × ⊥ × from the unexampled ⊥ ∪ | × ⊥ ×. Perhaps the best explanation of these cola is one based on attention to the placement of caesura and to hexasyllabic analogies. In pentasyllables, as in hexasyllables, forms with caesura after the third syllable open most often with the sequence – ∪ ⊻ | (categories 1–4 above), and the pentasyllabic forms which show this sequence can plausibly be analyzed as shortened versions of the hexasyllabic ones: – ∪ × | × × = – ∪ × | × – (×).[54] If we posit a similar shortening of the relatively infrequent hexasyllable × – ×|× – × we can account for the other pentasyllabic forms (– – ∪ | ∪ ×, ∪ – ∪ | ∪ ×, – – – | – ×; cf. categories 8–10) with caesura after the third syllable (× – × | × × = × – × | × – (×)), as well as for the relative infrequency of these forms. Pentasyllables in categories 5 and 6 (∪ – | × – ×, – – | × – ×) can also be explained as shortened versions of this hexasyllable, on the assumption that initial × – × | was subject even more strongly than final × – × to the loss of its last syllable (× – | × – × = × – (×) | × – ×). Finally, opening – ∪ × | will not have been subject to this

<hr>

53. See the list given in the text (p. 34), from which one should subtract the probably heptasyllabic *apud nympham Atlantis* and *simul duona eorum*.

54. The catalectic form of final × – × must be written × × ×, given our ignorance (above, n. 38) as to the rules concerning the quantity of the final syllable in line or colon.

shortening at all—hence the absence of $- \cup \mid x - x \ (= - \cup (x) \mid x - x)$.

This leaves one pentasyllabic form (*aide meretod*) $\overset{- \ - \ \cup\cup\times}{}$ without an analysis. The colon must be considered in conjunction with others that display a word of the form $\cup \cup \times$:

$\cup \cup - \mid x - \cup \times$

    Calatinus epitaph: populi    primarium...
          Livius 38: (neque enim    te oblitus sum...)[55]

$x \, x \, x \, x \mid \cup \cup \times$

        Livius 27: topper facit    homines...
      Naevius 21: silvicolae    homines...
           29: prima incedit    Cereris...
         43.2: magnum stuprum    populo...
           63: (atque prius    pariet...)[56]
  Appius Claudius: ...ferocia    pariat

$\cup \cup - \mid - - -$

      Naevius 4.3: ...lacrimis    cum multis
          20: ...hominum    fortunas

$- \cup \times \mid \cup \cup \times$

      Livius 23: ...filia    docuit
    Naevius 63: (atqu' prius    pariet...)[56]
     *CEL* 4.4: ...maxsume    meretod
     *CEL* 8.2: ...omnia    brevia
     *CEL* 8.6: ...Scipio    recipit

Our investigation has indicated that at several places in the Saturnian a pair of short syllables alternates with a single syllable, whether long or short; hence one might suppose that the same holds true here and so analyze the above cola as:

$\overset{\cup\cup}{\times} - \mid x - \cup -; \quad x \, x \, x \, x \mid \overset{\cup\cup}{\times} \, x; \quad \overset{\cup\cup}{\times} - \mid - - - \quad$ and $\quad - \cup \times \mid \overset{\cup\cup}{\times} \, x.$

---

55. The alternative is to read *nec tamen*; cf. above, p. 29.
56. On the scansion of *atque* in early Latin see above, n. 46.

On the other hand, the equivalence × = ∪ ∪ has been accepted hitherto only at positions in the verse where a pair of short syllables was not interchangeable with any other sequence of two syllables, or where single syllables and pairs of short syllables were noticeably more frequent than other disyllabic sequences. In all of the examples with which we are now dealing, ∪ ∪ *is* interchangeable with other pairs. Alongside ∪ ∪ × | × − −, for example, we find × − × | × − −; alongside ∪ ∪ − | × − ∪ ×, × − × | × − ∪ ×; alongside × × × × | ∪ ∪ ×, × × × × | × − ×; and, alongside − ∪ × | ∪ ∪ ×, − ∪ × | × − ×. Moreover, there is no correlation between the frequency and use of those cola which, on the assumption that ∪ ∪ × substitutes for × ×, ought to be metrically equivalent to each other. The form × × × × | × × is fairly common in the second half of the line (ten out of sixteen certain occurrences), whereas its counterpart with a disyllable in the penultimate position (× × × × | ∪ ∪ ×) appears there only once. ∪ ∪ − | × − ∪ − and − − | ∪ ∪ × would correspond, if the ∪ ∪ × = × × equation is accepted, to cola (× × | × − ∪ − and − − | × ×) that are not attested at all. One might expect that if × − | × − × corresponds to ∪ ∪ × | × − × there would be a similar correspondence between × − × | × − × and ∪ ∪ − × | × − ×; but the last form is not certainly attested. Finally, though the pair − ∪ × | × ×: − ∪ × | ∪ ∪ × is exactly paralleled by the pair − ∪ × | × − ×: − ∪ × | ∪ ∪ − ×, cola showing the form − ∪ × | ∪ ∪ × are almost half as frequent as those with the form − ∪ × | × × whereas − ∪ × | ∪ ∪ − × occurs less than a fourth as often as − ∪ × | × − ×. For these reasons it seems likely that, whenever it appears, ∪ ∪ × is an isosyllabic variant for − ∪ × or × − × (a relatively rare variant, except possibly in half-lines of the type × × × | × × × ×, where the type itself is too rare to allow us to determine whether ∪ ∪ × was a favored opening).

Since the equation × = ∪ ∪ is operative only in certain types of colon these are best isolated from the rest in a full inventory of attested forms. The general scheme of the Saturnian half-line, not taking this equation into account, is as follows:

o o x x | x x (x)   or   x x x | $\overset{x}{-}\overset{-}{\cup}\overset{x}{-}\overset{x}{x}$

$\begin{array}{c} - \cup x \\ x - (x) \\ (\cup \cup x) \end{array}$ $\begin{array}{c} x - (x) \\ (\cup \cup x) \end{array}$   or   x - x | - ∪ x

The deletions or substitutions denoted by parentheses are allowed in any colon, but (except in very unusual cases—e.g. *aide meretod*) no one colon contains more than one of them.

Substitution of ∪ ∪ for x is allowed in the following cola, at the places indicated:

$\overset{\cup\cup}{o} \overset{[\cup\cup]}{o} \overset{\cup\cup}{x} x$  |  $\overset{\cup\cup}{x} \overset{\cup\cup}{-} x$
$\overset{\cup\cup}{-} \cup x$

subject to the restriction that no colon contains more than two such substitutions and that these substitutions never occur at adjacent positions.

The basic units of the Saturnian are thus six- and seven-syllable cola that display certain preferred groupings of long and short syllables, and certain propensities toward catalexis and toward the resolution of a single syllable into two short syllables. The preferred syllable groupings are 4|3 and 3|3, with x – x the preferred cadence and o o x x or – ∪ x the preferred opening. Resolution occurs in cola which show a preferred opening followed by a preferred cadence; catalexis in the sequence x – x when it forms the cadence of a colon or when it opens a colon for which it also serves as a cadence.

There is, I believe, an historical explanation for the restriction on the type of colon in which resolution is allowed, but the explanation must be delayed until the whole question of the origin and history of the Saturnian has been considered.

## II

As has been pointed out (above, p. 25) the x = ∪ ∪ equation characteristic of the Saturnian is found in the Latin senarius, septenarius, and octonarius. It is also found in certain Greek metres, notably in the comic trimeter (where ∪ ∪ = ∪ or × in the thesis of any foot but the last), in the choriambic or poly-schematist dimeters of Euripides and Corinna (∪∪∪ ∘ ∘ − ∪ ∪ − or ∪∪ ∪∪ ∪∪ ∪∪ − ∪ ∪ −), and in many of the Aeolic metres of both tragedy and comedy (where ∪ −, − ∪, − − and ∪ ∪ ∪ are inter-changeable openings). It is natural, therefore, to ask whether the Saturnian was not derived from Greek models. As long as it was assumed that Roman imitation of Greek literature began with Livius' translation of the *Odyssey* this question tended to be answered in the negative. The choice of so alien and un-Homeric a metre for a translation of one of the two master-pieces of Greek epic poetry is hardly explicable except as a concession to native taste, which must have been used to verse composed in this metre, and hence more receptive to a Saturnian *Odyssey* than it would have been to one composed in prose or hexameters. The whole problem of Saturnian origins was, therefore, reopened when, in his *Preistoria della poesia latina*, Pasquali argued that native taste was itself nurtured on Greek models. According to this theory, the Saturnian used by Livius was ultimately derived from Greek metres introduced to Rome at a much earlier date, during that period of extensive contact with and borrowing from the Hellenic East and South which ancient tradition associated with the reigns of the Tarquins and which can be dated, on archaeological evidence, to the sixth or fifth century B.C.[57]

Pasquali's theory fits with the facts of Roman cultural and literary history in so far as they are known. It is plausible enough that the period which witnessed the introduction of an alphabet based on the Greek, the dedication of temples to Greek gods (cf. Dion. Hal. 6.17.2 and 94.3), the summoning of Greek artists to superintend their construction (Pliny, *NH*

57. The exact dating is a matter of dispute (see, for a recent discussion, A. Momigliano, "An Interim Report on the Origins of Rome," *JRS* 53 [1963], 101–7), but as to the general character of the period and the lessened contact with the Hellenic world during the century that immediately followed it there is general agreement.

35.154), and the use of Ionian models for their decoration,[58] should also see the importation of an Hellenic poetic genre. The oldest surviving specimen of Latin poetry, the *Carmen Arvale*, can plausibly be dated to this Hellenizing period in the early history of Rome,[59] and the poem is composed almost entirely of cola which reappear later in the Saturnian. It lacks only the regular pairing of longer and shorter units that creates the characteristic Saturnian line:

> enos Lases      iuvate.
> neue lue rue      Marmar sins      incurrere in      pleoris.
> satur fu      fere Mars.      limen sali      sta berber.
> semunis      alternei      advocapit      conctos.
> enos Marmor      iuvato.
> triumpe triumpe triumpe triumpe triumpe.

The hymn contains four heptasyllables of the form $\circ \circ \times \times \mid \times - \times$ (*enos Lases iuvate, incurrere in pleoris, limen sali sta berber, enos Marmor iuvato*); one hexasyllable of the type $\times - \times \mid \times - \times$ (*semunis alternei*), another of the type $\times \times \times \times \mid \times \times$ (*advocapit conctos*), and a third of the form $\times - \times \mid \cup \cup \times$ (*satur fu fere Mars*). The last is not found in any Saturnian, but is one of the variants whose sporadic appearance our analysis of the verse would lead us to expect (cf. above, p. 46). The final *triumpe* is a refrain and may be regarded as *extra metrum*, which leaves *neue lue rue Marmar sins* ($- (\cup) \cup - \cup - \mid - - -$) as the only colon that would be anomalous in a Saturnian context.[60] The affinity between the

58. See Pasquali (above, n. 10), pp. 59–70.

59. The form *lases* establishes *c.* 350 B.C. as a *terminus ante quem* for the *Carmen*, though the general feeling that it is much older is probably correct. On the other hand, the probable etymology of *triumpe* (< Gk. θρίαμβε via Etruscan) shows that the poem does not antedate the era of close contact with Etruria.

60. The line can be made regular by scanning $\overset{- \ \cup\cup\ \cup-}{neu'\ lue\ rue}$ (see Pasquali [above, n. 10], pp. 29–30); and there are several possible parallels to the apocope of final *-e* that this scansion requires (see above, n. 52). But the iambic shortening $\overset{\cup\cup}{lue}$ cannot be supported by anything that is found elsewhere in early Saturnians (cf. above, n. 39).

metre of the Arval hymn and that of Livius, Naevius and the Scipio epitaphs is clear; and the poem also has structural affinities (threefold repetition of cola, division into five lines followed by refrain) with certain Greek hymns of a popular character.[61] It can therefore be plausibly viewed as one of the first products of such a Latinization of Greek lyric forms as Pasquali posits. Subsequent developments could easily have made the pairing of cola which appears in three of the five lines of the Arval hymn obligatory and introduced the preference for the sequence heptasyllable plus hexasyllable that is characteristic of the Saturnians of the third and second centuries. And it is understandable how the resulting form might seem barbarous and alien to one poet brought up on Greek literary traditions (Ennius), and yet to another (Livius) enough like the sort of verse with which he was familiar that he could seek to adapt it to Greek themes and Greek literary techniques.

For all of these reasons, Pasquali's hypothesis has, from the Latinist's point of view, much to recommend it. From the Hellenist's point of view, on the other hand, it has serious shortcomings, shortcomings which, to my mind, make it unacceptable. It is Pasquali's contention that all the regular Saturnian cola have Greek analogues, and that these analogues are sufficiently close to make the theory of the Greek origin of the metre highly likely. The parallels adduced by Pasquali are fairly numerous and require an extended examination; but examination will show, I believe, that some of them are nonexistent and that the rest are not striking enough, either individually or as a body, to be significant.

It is undeniable that all, or almost all, Saturnian cola can be paralleled in Greek verse, and that occasionally not merely separate cola but whole Saturnian lines have exact Greek counterparts. This is only to be expected. It would be hard to devise a sequence of five to nine long and short syllables, or even one of eleven to sixteen long and short syllables, which

61. See E. Norden, *Aus altrömischen Priesterbüchern = Skrifter Utgivn. av kungl. Humanistiska Vetenskapssamfundet i Lund* 29 (1939), 236–44.

could not be found somewhere in the corpus of Greek lyric
verse. Greek parallels, if they are to be significant, must involve,
not simply isolated lines, but entire metrical contexts which
show a configuration recalling that created by a series of
Saturnians.[62] And the contexts adduced by Pasquali, principally
those in which regular or syncopated iambic dimeters appear in
conjunction with each other and with aeolic clausulae, differ
in several important ways from anything which one would find
in a stanza of Saturnians.

The Greek iambic dimeter shows full $(\times - \cup -)$ or singly
$(\cup - \wedge -, \wedge - \cup -)$ and doubly $(\wedge - \wedge -)$ syncopated iambic metra
in a variety of combinations. This being so, and given the fact
that an iambic metron is occasionally replaced by a choriamb,
the number of forms which may appear alongside each other in
a single passage is large (e.g. $\cup - - \mid \cup - \cup -$, $\cup - - \mid - \cup -$,
$- \cup \cup - \mid - -$, $\cup - \cup - \mid - -$, $- \cup \cup - \mid - \cup -$, $- \cup \cup - \mid \cup - \cup -$);
and anyone coming across one of these cola in an iambic
context would have no hesitation—as Pasquali rightly points
out[63]—in calling it a dimeter. Yet the possible combinations,
numerous as they are, do not account for all those which appear
in the Saturnian, or even for all the most common ones. The
sequence $\cup \cup - \times$ is, as we have seen (above, p. 28), a fairly
common variant of $\times - \times$ in the second half of the Saturnian
heptasyllable; but, unlike the choriamb, $\cup \cup - \times$ may not be
substituted for an iambic metron in either regular or syncopated
dimeters. Nor are cola of the form $\cup \cup - \times \times \mid \times - \times$ or $- - - \times \mid$
$- - -$ capable of scansion as iambic dimeters.

Latin iambic verse is, of course, much freer with irrational
longs than Greek; hence one might argue that, just as the

62. Cf. W. J. W. Koster, "Versus Saturnius," *Mnemosyne* 57 (1929), 286:
"Concedo in infinita fere copia poeseos graecae cola erui posse, quorum
singula singulis Saturnii partibus respondeant. Aliud tamen est in cantico
semel vel bis schema quoddam metricum occurrere, aliud in versu recitato
κατὰ στίχον iterari..." A similar point is made by Pasquali himself at the
outset of his discussion (above, n. 10), pp. 2–3, but not sufficiently borne in
mind in the sequel.

63. (Above, n. 10), p. 8.

senarius begins with certain sequences (e.g. $--\mid--\mid--\mid-$) never found in the Greek trimeters on which it is modeled, so the presence of these same sequences in the Saturnian is no telling argument against its derivation from the lyric iambic dimeter. One might also argue that in the process of being Latinized this same lyric dimeter acquired the ability to substitute $\cup\cup$ for $\cup$ in the thesis that was characteristic of another kind of Greek iambic verse, the spoken or recitative trimeter of comedy; and thereby one would establish the iambic provenance of lines like

$$\overset{\cup\ \cup\ -\ \ \cup\ \cup\ -\ \ \ \ \ \cup\ -\ \times}{\text{Livius 19: simul ac dacrimas \quad de ore...}}$$

Finally, one might import iambic scansion into lines of the type

$$\overset{-\ \ -\ \ \cup\ \cup\ \ -\ -\ \times}{\text{Naevius 30.2: sanctus Iove prognatus...}}$$

by saying that the fourth syllable is *brevis in longo*. The extension of this license from period or verse end, where it regularly appears in Greek, to metron end, as here, can be defended by calling attention to the regularity of caesura, occasionally combined with hiatus, at this point in the line and the greater phonetic autonomy of the Latin as compared with the Greek word.[64]

Yet, even when this much has been granted,[65] there remain

---

64. On which see De Groot (above, n. 2), pp. 309–10 and "Le mot phonétique et les formes littéraires du latin," *REL* 12 (1934), 117–39; M. Barchiesi, *Nevio epico* (Padua 1962), pp. 321–2; and Vendryes (above, n. 38), p. 130.

65. This is, of course, more than some of Pasquali's critics would grant. See, in particular, E. Kapp, who in reviewing Pasquali's work rightly points out that the equivalence of Greek forms like $\times-\cup-\mid\times-\cup-$ and $\times-\cup-\mid--$ is only possible because certain longs were allowed three *morae* in delivery rather than two (e.g. $\times-\cup-\mid--$ became in delivery $\times-\cup-\mid\underline{\quad}\ \underline{\quad}$) and that it is difficult to see how such a system of delivery could establish the iambic character of sequences like $----\mid---$ or $\cup\cup-\cup\cup-\mid---$ (*GGA* 198 [1936], 481–2). This, along with certain other objections, while damaging to Pasquali's thesis, does not seem to me to be fatal. A kind of answer can be found for it. I have preferred, therefore, to confine my criticism of Pasquali to points which seem to me unanswerable.

further divergences to be accounted for. The most common Saturnian hexasyllable ($- \cup \times \mid \times - \times$) resembles the Greek ithyphallic ($- \cup - \cup - \times$), a form which can be analyzed as a syncopated iambic dimeter (i.e. $\wedge - \cup - \mid \cup - \wedge -$) and is used frequently, both κατὰ στίχον and in association with other dimeters. Cola of the type

$$\text{Livius 1: ...insecĕ} \quad \text{versutū͞m}$$

and

$$\textit{CEL 7.2: ...fortĭs vir} \quad \text{sapiĕnsque}$$

can be scanned as ithyphallics by the expedients just discussed (admission of *brevis in longo* at the central caesura of the colon, and admission of theses in which $\overline{\cup\cup} = \cup$). Use of the same expedients will also allow us to equate most examples of the normal heptasyllable ($\circ \circ \times \times \mid \times - \times$) with forms common in syncopated iambics. But with these exceptions the varieties of "iambic dimeter" preferred by the Saturnian are not those preferred in Greek poetry, and *vice versa*. After $- \cup \times \mid \times - \times$, the most common Saturnian hexasyllables are $\circ \circ \times \times \mid \times \times$, $\times - \times \mid$ $\times - \times$ and $\times - \times \mid - \cup \times$ (sixteen, ten and seven certain occurrences respectively). All could be Latin adaptations of permitted forms of iambic syncopation. But these forms, though attested in Greek, are all rarer than $- \cup - \mid - \cup \times$, which does not appear in the Saturnian at all; and rarer still in Greek is the reasonably common Saturnian colon $- \cup \times \mid - \times$ (eight occurrences).[66] On the other hand, two of the most common forms of syncopated dimeter in Greek are $\times - \cup - \mid - \cup \times$ and $- \cup - \times - \cup \times$, of which the Saturnian corpus contains, respectively, three and two examples.

66. *Heraclidae* 898 = 907 and *Lysistrata* 1309–11 offer the only certain examples, from an iambic context, in all of lyric and drama. In the *amoebaion* of *Troades* 235–91 $- \cup - - -$ appears in the vicinity of iambs (287 and, possibly, 282), but its immediate neighbors are dochmiacs and anapests. Elsewhere $- \cup - - -$ is regularly associated with trochaic or cretic sequences.

As has been pointed out, the heptasyllable o o x x | x – x, like the ithyphallic, is common in both Greek and Latin. On the other hand, this heptasyllable is not merely common in the Saturnian but obviously the "regular" or "normal" form of the longer cola. Hexasyllables of the type x x x x | x x (above, p. 39) as well as octosyllables and enneasyllables seem to be based on it. In Greek, however, the heptasyllable is itself a shortened or catalectic version of the normal octosyllable x – ◡ – | x – ◡ –. It appears often as part of larger iambic units—usually trimeters— but is rarely predominant through an entire poem. As a rule it introduces or terminates a series of octosyllables, or alternates with the latter—not, as in the Saturnian, with cola shorter than itself—to form a kind of distich. Sequences in which the hepta-syllable predominates are not unknown,[67] but it is hard to see why Latin poets should have taken the exceptional as their principal model rather than the usual. There is certainly no corresponding tendency among dramatic poets to use a cata-lectic senarius.

The only Greek genre which exhibits anything like such a tendency towards catalexis is the anapest. The catalectic anapestic dimeter, or paroemiac, is in fact identical with Saturnian cola of the form ◡◡ ◡◡ ◡◡ – | ◡◡ – –; and this di-meter bears at least an external resemblance to another metre,

67. *Heracles* 1065–8 and *Trachiniae* 893–5 are, to my knowledge, the only passages which show as many as three catalectic dimeters in succession; the *Anacreontea* contain whole poems composed in these dimeters, but it is not at all certain that this is a metrical heritage from Anacreon himself. The pair cited by Hephaestion (5.3 = Fr. 84 Page) are identical with *Ana-creontea* 47.8–9 Rose, which may have been Hephaestion's source. The alternation of x – ◡ – | ◡ – x and ◡◡ – ◡ – ◡ – x is better attested in pre-Hellenistic Greek (cf. Aristophanes, *Thesm.* 352–6 and Sappho, Fr. 102 Page: γλύκηα μᾶτερ οὔτοι...), and such an alternation could easily have been misunderstood by a Latin poet as a stichic use of the colon x̰ – ◡ – ◡ – x. But there is no evidence to suggest that this type of composition was ever associated with iambic dimeters. There is more evidence for stichic use of heptasyllables of the form – x – ◡ ◡ – x, x – ◡ ◡ – ◡ –, and x – ◡ – ◡ ◡ –, occasionally in iambic contexts. But these all show sequences of longs and shorts that are rare or unexampled in the Saturnian.

also called a paroemiac, which shows the form $\underset{\smile}{=} - \smile\smile - \smile\smile - \underset{\smile}{=}$.
In some ways these paroemiac metres provide a better analogue
to the Saturnian than does the iambic dimeter. They have
anapestic affinities, and anapestic dimeters, unlike their iambic
counterparts, display a tendency towards central caesura that
recalls the *lex Korschiana*. Moreover, unlike anapestic dimeters
and like the Saturnian, paroemiacs may open with either ͜ ͜
or ͜. Elsewhere in the colon there is, of course, no parallel to
the $\underset{\smile}{=} \mid \smile\smile$ alternation that is characteristic of the Saturnian.
It was suggested by Bergk, however,[68] and the suggestion was
often taken up by German metricians during the succeeding
century, that the classical Greek paroemiac is a regularized
version of a much freer verse form which exhibited this alternation in all of its theses. The *Urvers* thus posited:

$$\overset{\smile\smile}{\smile} - \overset{\smile\smile}{\smile} - \overset{\smile\smile}{\smile} - \sigma$$

bears a certain resemblance to the general formula for Saturnian
cola of seven or more syllables as given above (p. 38); and it
would provide a Greek parallel for most of the Saturnian heptasyllables and octosyllables which cannot be scanned as iambic
dimeters by the regular laws of Greek versification, as well as
for the Saturnian preference for catalexis. Yet Bergk's primitive
paroemiac is largely hypothetical.[69] Its very existence is nothing
more than an inference from the fact that certain lines of a
proverbial, and so "paroemiac", character display the scansion
$\overset{\smile\smile}{\smile} - \overline{\smile\smile} - \smile - \sigma$ or $\overset{\smile\smile}{\smile} - \smile - \overline{\smile\smile} - \sigma$ rather than the usual
$\overset{\smile\smile}{\smile} - \overline{\smile\smile} - \overline{\smile\smile} - \sigma$; and that one or another of these forms
appears occasionally beside $\overset{\smile\smile}{\smile} - \overline{\smile\smile} - \overline{\smile\smile} - \sigma$ in several
archaic inscriptions whose "metrical" character may be
purely fortuitous. Equally gratuitous is the assumption, often
made by followers of Bergk, that the comic parody Ἐρασμονίδη

68. *Über das älteste Versmass der Griechen* (Progr. Freiburg 1854), pp. 3–18
= *Kleine Philologische Schriften* (Halle 1886), 2.394–404.

69. See W. J. W. Koster, *Traité de métrique grecque²* (Leiden 1953),
p. 158; "De studiis recentibus ad rem metricam pertinentibus," *Mnemosyne*
Ser. 4, 3 (1950), 47–8 and 152–3; and A. M. Dale, *The Lyric Metres of Greek
Drama²* (Cambridge 1968), pp. 159–60.

βάθιππε of Archilochus' Ἐρασμονίδη Χαρίλαε was intended to be metrically equivalent to the latter and so evidence for the existence of a colon of the form ᴗ – ∪ ∪ – ᴗ̆ᴗ̆ – ᴗ.[70] And, even if Bergk's theory were acceptable, the difficulties in the way of assuming a Greek origin for the Saturnian would not be substantially lightened. Any Greek pedigree for the Saturnian half-line is forced to make it an elaborate hybrid; and the hybrid is scarcely less elaborate if we assume that it combined only two strains (the iambic dimeter with its capacity for suppressing theses at will and the hypothetical paroemiac with its preference for catalexis and its admission of the equivalence ᴗ̆ᴗ̆ = ∪) than it would be if we assume the last-named trait to be a heritage from a third parent, the comic trimeter or choriambic dimeter. It would of course be rash to say that either pedigree is impossible, but it would be even more rash to accept one or the other. And even this complex reconstruction of *preistoria* would not create a formula sufficiently inclusive to provide a place for forms like

| | | |
|---|---|---|
| – – ∪ – \| ∪ – | Naevius 43.1: ...fortissimos | viros |
| – ∪ ∪ – \| ∪ ∪ – | Naevius 21: silvicolae | homines... |
| × – × – × | Naevius 12.1: ...deum adlocutus | |
| | Naevius 5.3: ...illinc exibant | |

The first of these, an iambic tripody,[71] is never found with iambic dimeters in Greek; the second, a hemiepes, appears only sporadically, by way of metrical contrast.[72] Yet the Saturnian

---

70. See Dale (above, n. 69), p. 160, n. 1.

71. It would be possible to scan *fortis|simos viros* (i.e. – – ∪ – ᴗ– | ∪ – ∪ –, a permitted form of syncopated iambic dimeter), but word end between rather than within metra is the rule in the Saturnian cola for which analogues in Greek iambic verse can be adduced.

72. E.g. in *Eumenides* 956–67, where – ∪ ∪ – ∪ ∪ – along with longer dactylic sequences alternates with syncopated iambs in an *ababa* pattern. A similar alternation between dactylo-anapestic and iambic elements can be found in the Elean cult hymn to Dionysus adduced by Leo (above, n. 1), pp. 71–2, as a Greek analogue to the Saturnian.

was used by Livius to translate the stichic verse of the *Odyssey* and by Naevius for the imitation in Latin of a Greek genre which was always stichic in form. It is reasonable to assume, therefore, that these poets themselves regarded their verse as a fairly homogeneous series of lines composed of units which were metrically interchangeable, if not identical. And this is something quite different from the epodic or stanzaic structure created in Greek by the alternation of iamb and hemiepes.

The third of the forms quoted is an iambic penthemimeres. Like the tripody, it does not appear with dimeters in Greek.[73] It is analyzed by Pasquali, however, as a reizianum ($\overset{\smile\smile}{\times} - \overset{\smile\smile}{\times} - \times$) and so identified both with a sequence ($\times - \smile\smile - \times$) found often in conjunction with iambs and with the colon $\smile\smile - \smile\smile - \times$ that is used κατὰ στίχον in the famous Rhodian swallow song (848 Page). But this identification relies on the assumption that the Greek reizianum admitted the equivalence of $\smile\smile$ and $\smile$, an assumption for which there is just as little evidence as there is for Bergk's paroemiac.[74] Hence the commonness of $\times - \smile\smile - \times$ in Greek iambic contexts says nothing at all about the probable provenance of $\times - \times - \times$, a colon which is very rare in Greek except in alternation with dactylo-anapestic sequences.[75]

$\times - \times - \times$ and $\times - \smile\smile - \times$ are, of course, used as interchangeable cola in the reiziana and *versus reiziani* of Latin comedy; but even were it certain that these forms are entirely based on Greek models—which in the absence of extensive parallels must

---

73. The few Greek cola which might be adduced as parallels all show the forms $- - \smile - -$ (*Helen* 194 = 213; *Philoctetes* 1211), $\smile - - - -$ (*Eumenides* 961 = 981; the Seikelos song—see K. von Jan, *Musici Scriptores Graeci*, pp. 452-3) or $- - - - -$ (*Septem* 770; Sophocles, *Electra* 510). The Seikelos song is accompanied by metrical notation which shows that the scansion of the line in question was $\smile - \overset{}{\_} \overset{}{\_} \overset{}{\_}$, and presumably the other cola cited would have been given the time value of full dimeters in similar fashion: $\overset{}{\_} \overset{}{\_} \smile - \overset{}{\_}$ and $\overset{}{\_} \overset{}{\_} - - -$. But a line like *deum adlocutus* cannot be equated with a full dimeter by any of the laws of syncopated iambics.

74. See Koster, *Traité* (above, n. 69), p. 227, n. 2 and Dale (above, n. 69), p. 138, n. 1.

75. The sequence is, for example, common in dactylo-epitritic verse.

remain dubious[76]—there is good reason to believe that the
$\times - \times - \times$ of comedy was very different metrically from its
supposed Saturnian counterpart. The comic reizianum allows
any word arrangement that exhibits the metrical pattern
$\overset{\cup}{\times} \underset{\smile}{\cup} \overset{\cup}{\times} \underset{\smile}{\cup} \times$. In the Saturnian, on the other hand, the colon
$\times - \times - \times$ regularly shows word end after the second syllable.
This sets it apart, not only from the reiziana of comedy, but
also from those Saturnian half-lines which might be analyzed
as reiziana of the type $\times \underset{\smile}{\cup} \cup \cup \underset{\smile}{\cup} \times$:

> Livius 23: nam diva Monetas...
> 27: topper facit homines...
> 38: ...Laertie noster
> Naevius 4.2: ...capitibus opertis
> 10: ...vestemque citrosam
> Appius Claudius: ...ferocia pariat
>
> *CEL* 7.3: (...parisuma fūit)

The latter are in turn linked by their syllabic structure to a
number of cola that cannot possibly be reiziana: *capitibus
opertis* falls together with *bene iovent optantis* (*CEL* 2.6) as a
resolved version of the regular hexasyllable ($\underset{\smile}{\cup} \cup \times \mid \times - \times$);
*nam diva Monetas* and *vestemque citrosam* parallel *multasque virtutes*
(*CEL* 9.1) and *res divas edicit* (Naevius 28)—i.e. $\times - \times \mid \times - \times$,
a less common hexasyllabic type; *parisuma fūit* and *Laertie noster*
are probably, like *fortissimos viros* (Naevius 43.1) or *consentiunt
gentes* (Calatinus epitaph), shortened versions of the ordinary
heptasyllable $\circ \circ \times \times \mid \times - \times$; and *ferocia pariat* and *topper facit
homines* take their place alongside *magnum stuprum populo*
(Naevius 43.2) as rare variants on this heptasyllable. The
reizianum is thus, on the most plausible reading of our evidence,
a colon totally alien to the Saturnian,[77] into which it can be

76. Lines which may be scanned as *versus reiziani* do appear in Greek—
see the examples cited by Pasquali (above, n. 10), p. 34—but there is no
trace in Greek of the stichic use of it that is characteristic of Latin comedy.

77. As is, one may note, another very common Greek colarion, the
Adonic ($- \cup \cup - \times$).

imported only by artificial conflation of several distinct though superficially similar types. The occurrence of reiziana along with iambs in Greek is therefore irrelevant, not only to the analysis of $\times - \times - \times$, but also to the whole question of Saturnian origins.

The only Greek colon, in fact, which in frequency and function as well as external form has a close parallel in the Saturnian is the ithyphallic. That the Romans should have developed this form independently of Greek models is more likely than that they should have in one instance remained faithful to a system of versification toward which they displayed the greatest independence elsewhere. And this conclusion is not altered by the fact that the Greek ithyphallic is occasionally made to follow longer cola in somewhat the same way that it often follows longer cola in the Saturnian, or by the fact that one of these bipartite verses, the "Archilocheum" ($\underset{\smile}{-} - \smile \smile - \smile \smile$ $- \underset{\smile}{} \mid - \smile - \smile - \times$), happens to be identical with one of our 125 Saturnians:

CEL 3.1: ductu auspicio imperioque      eius Achaia capta.[78]

Such a similarity is even more likely to be fortuitous than the general resemblance between the ithyphallic and the most common Saturnian hexasyllable. Moreover, as Pasquali himself has shown, there is reason to believe that the regular alternation of longer and shorter cola is subsequent to the composition of the Arval hymn, and so an indigenous Roman development, whatever we assume the ultimate origin of the cola themselves to be (cf. above, pp. 48–9).

Should we by some chance recover a poem of Alcman or Corinna written in what are obviously Saturnians the problem

78. Cf. Archilochus, Frs. 107–9 Diehl (= 153, 155–6 Lasserre). The Archilocheum is used κατὰ στίχον and so offers a somewhat closer parallel to the Saturnian line than the two examples of iambic colon plus ithyphallic, cited by E. Fraenkel, "The Pedigree of the Saturnian Metre," *Eranos* 49 (1951), 170–1: *Troades* 529–30 = 549–50 and the first line of the Cretan hymn to Zeus (Diehl, *Anthol. Lyr.*², *Suppl.* pp. 131–3 = Powell, *Coll. Alex.* p. 160). The first of these serves as a clausula to a series of iambic dimeters, the second introduces a poem in trochaics and major ionics.

of the origin of the Roman metre would, of course, be solved, and along the lines Pasquali has suggested. But the discovery would raise another problem, hardly less formidable, of the origin of the model the Romans used, so anomalous would it be in the general context of Greek lyric versification. Until such a discovery actually forces us to confront this problem, there is no reason why we should manufacture it for ourselves.

## III

Pasquali, whose analysis of the Saturnian follows Leo's quite closely in other respects, differs sharply from his predecessor in his view of the metre's origin. The point at issue is the proper interpretation of the $-$ $=$ $\cup\cup$ and $\cup\cup$ $=$ $\cup$ equivalences that are allowed at certain places in the verse. For Leo the latter of these is a vestige of the *Urfreiheit* which characterized the common Indo-European ancestor of both Greek and Latin verse (cf. above, p. 54). Since there are only isolated survivals of this freedom in classical Greek verse its presence in the Saturnian would indicate direct derivation—independent of Greek influence—from some Indo-European model.[79]

Pasquali, on the other hand, accepts A. Meillet's theory, propounded eighteen years after the publication of Leo's monograph,[80] of an Indo-European verse partially indifferent to patterns of longs and shorts but insisting on a fixed number of syllables. He therefore regards the $-$ $=$ $\cup\cup$ equivalence as an innovation peculiar to Greek and, in particular, Ionian verse. And so the presence of this equivalence in the Saturnian is a telling argument in favor of its Greek origin.[81]

Pasquali is certainly right in preferring Meillet's view of the Indo-European *Urvers* to Leo's, but the use he makes of Meillet's hypothesis is more questionable. Vedic poetry is entirely

79. (Above, n. 1), pp. 75–8, and *Geschichte der römischen Literatur* (Berlin 1913), p. 16.

80. *Les origines indo-européennes des mètres grecques* (Paris 1923).

81. (Above, n. 10), pp. 21–4.

syllabic, but classical Sanskrit knows of metres based on the equivalence of a single long with two shorts.[82] What could occur in one language independently of Greek influence could certainly occur in any other, particularly in one such as Latin, where the coexistence of contracted forms with a single long vowel and non-contracted forms with two short vowels (e.g. $\overline{cogo}:\overset{\cup\cup}{coago}$; $nihil:\overline{nil}$) would make the innovation a natural one.[83] And, even if the innovation itself is Greek in origin, it need not follow that the metre is. Greek metres which had been purely syllabic in the hands of the Lesbian poets came, once they had been taken over by the Attic dramatists, to show the $\cup = \cup\cup$ and $- = \cup\cup$ equivalences characteristic of certain types of Ionian and Dorian verse.[84] It is perfectly possible that the influence of the Greek hexameter and comic trimeter led to an identical development in a Latin metre that had been more nearly syllabic to begin with.

This hypothesis of a predominantly syllabic Indo-European metre partially though never wholly transformed by the application of principles borrowed from Greek versification has in fact been propounded in several studies of the Saturnian, though never developed in any detail.[85] It is, I believe, the

---

82. See H. Jacobi, "Über die Entwicklung der indischen Metrik in nachvedischer Zeit," *ZDMG* 37 (1883), 595–602, and "Zur Kenntniss der Āryā," *ZDMG* 40 (1886), 336–42.

83. Cf. E. Bignone, *Storia della letteratura latina* I (Florence 1942), pp. 158–9, n. 1.

84. The most striking case in point is the so-called Aeolic base, which takes the form x x in Sappho and Alcaeus but in Greek drama becomes $-$ x, x $-$ or $\cup\cup\cup$ (i.e. $--$, $\cup\overset{\cup\cup}{}$ or $\overset{\cup\cup}{}\cup$). A more complex example of the same phenomenon is offered by a comparison of the choriambic dimeters of Corinna ($\overset{\cup\cup}{\circ}\overset{\cup}{\circ} \circ \circ - \cup\cup$ x) with those of Euripides ($\overset{\cup\cup}{\circ}\overset{\cup\cup}{\circ}\overset{\cup\cup}{\circ}\overset{\cup\cup}{\circ} - \cup\cup$ x).

85. Cf. E. A. Sonnenschein, *What is Rhythm?* (Oxford 1925), pp. 66–8; L. Nougaret, *Traité de métrique latine classique*³ (Paris 1963), pp. 22–3. Barchiesi (above, n. 64), p. 325, posits a somewhat similar evolution, though the point of departure is, in his view, a verse characterized by "ritmo verbale" (cf. G. B. Pighi, "Il verso saturnio," *RFIC* [1957], 54–9) rather than isosyllabism.

hypothesis which fits best with the evidence, both Latin and non-Latin, at our disposal; and in the remaining portion of this essay I wish to call attention to two sets of facts which seem to me to make it at once more probable and more precise.

As was pointed out at the end of section I, the substitution of ◡ ◡ for ◡ and – is confined to cola of the types o o x x | x – x and – ◡ x | x – x. Pentasyllables show no certain examples of this substitution, nor do hexasyllables of the types x – x | x – x, x – x – ◡ x and o o x x | x x.[86] There is also one further restriction on its use that has not yet been noted. Substitution of ◡ ◡ for ◡̱ is not certainly attested in cola which show the forms – ◡ ◡ – | x – x and – ◡ – x | x – x.[87] The only two cola in which ◡ ◡ replaces ◡̱ are therefore x – x x | x – x and – ◡ x | x – x. It follows that, if *brevis in longo* before the central caesura is assumed to have been permitted, all the cola in which the substitution takes place are identical with either the first or the second half of a hypercatalectic iambic senarius divided by hephthemimeral caesura and constructed in strict accordance with the rules of quantitative verse. When, as often happens, a heptasyllable of the type x – x x | x – x is followed by the hexasyllable – ◡ x | x – x, the result is, of course, an entire hypercatalectic senarius.

The most natural explanation for this restriction on the use of the equation ◡ ◡ = ◡̱ is that the starting point for its introduction into the Saturnian was lines of the type:

$$x - x - \mid x - x \quad - ◡ - \mid x - x,$$

and that such lines struck the Romans as similar to Greek iambic trimeters lengthened by a syllable, and so capable of showing the same alternation between ◡, ◡ ◡ and – that was

86. On the possible exceptions see above, n. 46 (Naevius 4.3: *flentes ambae abeuntes*... and *CEL* 7.2: *fortis vir sapiensque*...), p. 38 (cola of the form – ◡ ◡ x | x x x), p. 39 (*CEL* 11.1: ...*Maarco Caecilio*) and pp. 44–5 (cola which begin or end with the sequence ◡ ◡ x).

87. In *CEL* 8.3 (...*gloria atque ingenium*) and Naevius 47 (...*atque locos ut haberent*) monosyllabic scansion of *atque* is, for the reasons given above (n. 46) preferable to disyllabic scansion.

allowed at certain points in these trimeters. Extension of the license would have naturally followed, so that even in isolation from each other the component parts of this Roman "trimeter" could alternate ∪∪ with ⊻, and cola with a short syllable before the central caesura could be considered as metrically equivalent to those with a long syllable, and so capable of showing the same alternation.[88] It is worth noting that the earliest appearance of the ⊻ = ∪∪ equation in the Saturnian is in Appius Claudius Caecus:

amicum cum vides     obliscere mi$\overset{\smile\smile}{\text{se}}$rias;

$\overset{\smile\smile}{\text{in}}$imicus si es commentus     nec libens aeque

and that the first of these lines may have been translated from a couplet of Philemon[89] in which ∪∪ is twice substituted for –:

οὕτως ἐπάν τις τυγχάνῃ λυπούμενος
ἧττον ὀδυνᾶται φίλον ἐὰν παρόντ᾽ ἴδῃ          (Fr. 108 Kock).[90]

If this explanation of the presence of the equivalence ⊻ = ∪∪ in the Saturnian is correct, one would expect the frequency, both of the verses in which this equivalence is allowed and of verses identical with hypercatalectic senarii, to increase with the passage of time and the progressive Hellenization of Roman poetry. As the tabulation on p. 64 shows, the expectation is

88. Presumably a short syllable before the central caesura came to be regarded by Saturnian poets as *brevis in longo*. In allowing this license, as well as in admitting hiatus and excluding the substitution of ∪∪ for × (above, pp. 28–9) they would have been treating the position in the colon immediately before the caesura exactly like the final position in a Greek verse or period (cf. above, p. 51).

89. See F. Marx, "Appius Claudius und Philemon," *Zeitschr. f. österr. Gymn.* (1897), 218.

90. Equally reminiscent of the Greek trimeter is the Saturnian's aversion to the substitution of ∪∪ for ∪ or – in two adjacent positions; see above, p. 46, and, for Greek practice, J. W. White, *The Verse of Greek Comedy* (London 1910), pp. 49–50 and 62.

amply confirmed by the evidence.[91] Both types of verse are more abundant in Naevius than in Livius, and more abundant in the post-Naevian Naevius epitaph than in either. And a similar progression is evident if one compares the earliest inscriptional Saturnians with later ones. Equally in accordance with our hypothesis of the "Hellenic" origin of these verse types is the fact that in any given period they seem to have been more frequent in literary than in epigraphical texts.[92]

91. In the tabulation lines of the forms $\times - \times \mid - \cup \times \quad \times - \times \times \mid \times - \times$ and $\times - \times \times \mid \times - \times \quad - \cup - \times \mid - \times$, as well as the more common $\times - \times \times \mid$ $\times - \times \ - \cup \times \mid \times - \times$, are counted as hypercatalectic senarii. Omitted from the tabulation are the irregular Saturnians of *CEL* 2 as well as the following four lines:

| | | |
|---|---|---|
| Naevius 1: | novem Iovis concordes | filiae sorores |
| 7: | ferunt pulchras creterras | aureas lepistas |
| GL 6.265.25: | duello magno dirimendo | regibus subigendis |
| GL 6.265.29: | fundit fugat prosternit | maximas legiones. |

All four are preserved in the citations of imperial metricians, obviously because of their conformity to the hypercatalectic senarius pattern, and so do not represent a metrically random sampling.

92. The statistics for the *sententiae* of Appius Claudius (2 out of 3 verses showing substitution of $\cup \cup$ for $\times$; 1 out of 3 verses identical with a hypercatalectic senarius) are out of line with the rest. But this may be owing either to the smallness of the sampling, or to the fact that Appius is reproducing the content as well as the form of specific Greek trimeters. On the other hand, our statistics are borne out by what remains of the dedicatory inscription (*CEL* 1859) of C. Sempronius Tuditanus (consul 129 B.C.):

| | |
|---|---|
| ...re et Tauriscos c... | |
| ...us coactos m... | |
| ...r quineis qua... | ...avit |
| ....signeis consi... | ...os Tudita[nus] |
| ...e egit triumpu[m]... | ....dedit Tim[avo] |
| ...ria ei restitu[it]... | ...reis tradit |

If, as seems likely, the inscription is in Saturnians, we have the ends of four lines and of five initial cola. Of these, five or (scanning *Tudĭtā́nus*) six show the colon cadence found in $\times - \times \times \mid \times - \times \ - \cup \times \mid \times - \times$; a seventh example (...*avit*) may be a portion of this cadence, and the remaining two sequences can be paralleled in the rarer types of Saturnian that are identical with hypercatalectic senarii (with *quineis* in the third verse compare Naevius epitaph, 4: *obliti sunt Romae*...; and with ...*reis tradit* in the last compare

| Source | Nr. of lines preserved | Nr. of lines showing $\cup = \cup\cup$ or $- = \cup\cup$ equivalence | (%) | Nr. of lines identical with hyper-catalectic senarii | (%) |
|---|---|---|---|---|---|
| Livius (3rd cent. B.C.) | 27+7/2 | 7 | 23 | 6 | 22 |
| Naevius (*c.* 200 B.C.) | 41+8/2 | 19 | 42 | 13 (15)[93] | 32 (37) |
| Naevius epitaph (late 2nd cent.?) | 4 | 2 | 50 | 3 (4)[94] | 75 (100) |
| Calatinus epitaph and *CEL* 6 (3rd cent. B.C.) | 8 | 0 | 0 | 1 | 12½ |
| *CEL* 7 (*c.* 200 B.C.) | 6 | 2 | 33 | 2 | 33 |
| *CEL* 3–4, 8–9, 11 (after 170 B.C.) | 25+1/2 | 12 | 47 | 12 | 48 |

Were the evidence at our disposal less fragmentary the development of the Saturnian might be seen to take the form of a gradual approximation to the perfectly regular hypercatalectic senarius that appears in Varro's Menippeans:

| | | |
|---|---|---|
| quia plus inquit merere | debet in quost virtus | |
| | | (157 Buecheler) |
| primum iste qui meret | sestertios vicenos | (158) |
| | novos maritus | |
| tacitulus taxim uxoris | solvebat cingillum | (187) |
| procella frigida ante | obruat celocem | (214) |

*CEL* 11.2: . . . *restitistei seedes*). It is possible, therefore, that every line in the dedication showed a regular iambic pattern; and a fairly high incidence of the equivalence $\cup\cup = \times$ is indicated by the fact that there may be as many as three examples (*restituit, Tudĭtānus* and *consiliis*, which is restored by Buecheler in the fourth line) in the half of the inscription that survives.

93. The number will be 13, 14 or 15, depending on the scansion of *atque* in 31: *scopas atque verbenas | sagmina sumpserunt*, and of *Aenea* in 23.1: *blande et docte percontat Aenea quo pacto*. Monosyllabic scansion of *atque* seems preferable in general (above, n. 46) but disyllabic scansion gives a commoner opening colon ($\circ \circ \times \times \mid \times - \times$ as against $\times - \times \mid \times - \times$). On *Aenea* see above, n. 44.

94. The number will be 3 or 4 depending on the scansion of *obliti sunt Romae*—see below, n. 97.

aliae mitram ricinam     aut mitram Melitensem   (433)

ubĭ tum comitia habebant    ibĭ nunc fit mercatus (497)

tunc nuptiae videbant     ostream lucrinam     (501)[95]

The development would have been completed once the succession of syllables that had come more and more to be preferred became the required one, and once the restrictions as to placing of word end observed by the early Saturnian had been dropped (cf., in the Varronian examples, 187 and 497, which have elision at the *caesura Korschiana*, and 214, which shows the exceedingly rare word division $\times - \times \mid - \cup - \times$).[96] The Naevius epitaph, whose lines can be scanned either as Saturnians or (with one possible exception)[97] as hypercatalectic senarii, would belong, on this assumption, to a penultimate stage in the development; and this would accord well with the date of composition (last half of the second century) which scholars are inclined, on other grounds, to posit for it.[98]

95. 157–8 were first identified as Saturnians by G. Hermann, *Elementa Doctrinae Metricae* (Leipzig 1816), p. 640. L. Müller, *Der Saturnische Vers und seine Denkmäler* (Leipzig 1885), pp. 151–2, rejected the identification, while accepting 497 and 501 (first proposed by A. Meineke, "De Saturniis Varronianis," *Zeitschrift für die Alterthumswissenschaft* 93 [1845], 740). C. Zander, "Versus Saturnii," *Lunds Universitets Årsskrift* N.F. 1. Avd., Bd. 14.2, Nr. 23 (1918), 17–18, made further additions, two of which, 187 and 214, are accepted by Koster (above, n. 62), 340–1. The list in the text is Koster's, plus 433 (from Zander) and minus 499 Buecheler (...*avidus* | *iudex reum ducebat esse* κοινὸν Ἑρμῆν by Koster's scansion, but more likely to be an iambic septenarius). Zander's extensive collection, in so far as it is not duplicated by those of other scholars, consists of lines which it is difficult to scan either as Saturnians or hypercatalectic senarii.

96. The solitary example is Livius 16: ...*cor frixit* | *prae pavore*.

97. In *obliti sunt Romae loquier lingua Latina, Romae* is conceivably trisyllabic.

98. See E. V. Marmorale, *Naevius poeta* (Florence 1953), p. 141, with the earlier discussions cited there. Roughly contemporary would be the Saturnians of *CEL* 1839 (above, n. 92) and those which, according to the scholiast on Cicero, *Arch.* 11.27, were composed by the poet Accius. Cf. Müller (above, n. 95), pp. 8–9, who suggests that Accius may have been the first theoretician of the Saturnian as well.

The statistics relating to the occurrence of ᴗ ᴗ alternating
with ᴗ̱ in Saturnian cola and of lines of the type x – x x | x – x
– ᴗ x | x – x thus point to the same conclusion as do the theories
of comparative metrics. Even without the latter evidence one
would be tempted to suppose that in the earliest stage of its
development the Saturnian was more nearly syllabic in
character than it was during the second century B.C. Against
assuming that this isosyllabism was an inheritance from some
Indo-European prototype there exists, however, an objection
similar to one of those raised in discussing Pasquali's theory of a
Greek pedigree for the Saturnian. The Greek and Vedic lines
on whose similarity to each other the theory of a common Indo-
European prototype is based are for the most part sequences of
twelve, eleven or eight syllables. A verse whose longest normal
colon is the heptasyllable would seem, therefore, just as foreign
to Indo-European metrics as it is to Greek. It is by way of
offering a partial answer to this objection that I call attention
to the second set of facts mentioned at the beginning of this
section (above, p. 61).

The Latin preference for heptasyllables has no parallel in
Greek or Vedic; it does, however, have a very striking parallel
in one other branch of Indo-European, Celtic. Scholars have
long been aware of the resemblance of the Saturnian heptasyllable to a common old Irish metre,[99] but they were forced to
dismiss the resemblance as coincidental so long as it was
assumed, with Thurneysen,[100] that this Irish metre was itself
derived from heptasyllabic lines and half-lines in the rhythmic
Latin hymns of the early Christian church. Recently, however,
the whole question has been re-opened by C. Watkins,[101] who
argues that the old Irish heptasyllable is, along with other Irish

99. See, for example, W. M. Lindsay, *Early Latin Verse* (Oxford 1923),
pp. 9–10.

100. "Zur Irischen Accent und Verslehre," *Revue Celtique* 6 (1883–5),
336–47.

101. "Indo-European Metrics and Archaic Irish Verse," *Celtica* (1963),
218–49. See, especially, 220, 226 and 247–8.

syllabic metres, an Indo-European inheritance largely, if not completely, independent of the Latin forms which Thurneysen believed to be its model.

I am not myself competent to pass judgment on the relative merits of these two views of the prehistory of Irish verse. There are, however, certain obvious weaknesses in the theory of Thurneysen and his followers. For that theory, at least as stated by them, fails to explain (1) why Irish writers should take as their principal model a form that is of only sporadic occurrence in Latin verse of the early Middle Ages;[102] (2) why the earliest attested Latin examples of the form are predominantly from writers who were either Irish themselves or strongly influenced by Irish learning;[103] (3) why in Irish verse the heptasyllable appears in conjunction with a variety of shorter lines (see below, pp. 69–72) in a way that is unparalleled in Latin verse of the early Middle Ages. One suspects, in fact, that Thurneysen's view would not have been so widely accepted were it not for a certain tendency, particularly pronounced in German scholars and their disciples, to assume that the norm of primitive verse is to be found in accentual and alliterative poems like *Beowulf* and the *Nibelungenlied*, and that the isosyllabism characteristic of Romance poetry is always to be associated with development or decadence.[104]

The alternate view, dealing as it does with affinities that are

102. The one important example, Prudentius, *Cath.* 6, is composed in metrical, not rhythmic, heptasyllables.

103. Cf. the verses from Dicuil's *Computus*, the Bangor hymnal, and St Columban and his circle cited by Meyer (above, n. 9), pp. 222–3. These account for all but one of the items in Meyer's list of rhythmic heptasyllables antedating the year 850. To the same early period belong three additional "Irish" poems in rhythmic heptasyllables: the hymn of Oengi mac Tipraite in honor of St Martin of Tours (*Anal. Hymn.* 51.247), the anonymous *Hymnus pro peccatis* (*ibid.* 258) and the *Versus Karoli Imperatoris* attributed to an *Hibernicus exul* (*MGH, Poet. Aevi Karol.* 1.399–400).

104. See the explicit statements to this effect in Wilamowitz, *Griechische Verskunst* (Berlin 1921), p. 22, and E. Kalinka, *Bursians Jahresbericht* 250 (1935), 418.

much more remote and a prototype whose existence is only a matter of inference, cannot be impugned or supported with the same sort of specific argument as can Thurneysen's. But the view is at least a possible and plausible one; and so the parallels between the earliest Latin and the earliest Irish verse deserve a more extensive exposition than they have as yet received.

The basic units of old Irish verse[105] are a longer line of from six to eight syllables and a shorter line of from four to six syllables:

$$(\times) \times \times \times \times \mid \times \times : (\times) \quad \text{and} \quad (\times) \times \times \mid \times \times (\times) \text{ or } \times \times \times \times \mid \times$$

[(|) = obligatory word end; (:) = optional word end; (×) = optional syllable].

As will be seen from these schemata the word arrangements permitted in Irish lines of five and six syllables are, with one exception (× × × × | ×), exactly those allowed in Saturnian cola of the same length: × × × × | × ×, × × × | × × ×, × × | × × × and × × × | × ×. The only thing in these lines which is not paralleled in Latin is the insistence that the shorter lines when hexasyllabic have the cadence: | × × × or | × × | ×. This insistence is probably the result of a desire for a fixed accentual pattern. Exclusion of the form | × | × × from the end of a line means—given the initial stress accent that is regular in old Irish—that the stress pattern of the last three syllables will always be $\overset{\prime}{\times} \times (\overset{\prime}{\times})$.[106] This regularity obviously belongs to a stage in the development of the language when other than purely syllabic considerations have begun to make themselves felt in versification; hence the contrast with Latin practice is no obstacle to deriving the Saturnian and its Irish analogues from a prototype charac- terized solely by a fixed number of syllables and certain pre- ferred quantitative cadences. Similarly, whether the Latin preference for a cadence of the form × – × is an inheritance from the prototype or belongs to the phase in the development of the language when quantity had begun to replace isosyllabism as

105. See, in general, Watkins (above, n. 101), 245–6.
106. Watkins (above, n. 101), 245.

the dominant principle of verse,[107] the absence of anything comparable in Irish is to be expected.

The preferred cadence of the Latin heptasyllable (x – x) differs from that of its Irish counterpart (| x x : x) in the same way and the divergence is susceptible of the same explanation. Otherwise the regular forms of the heptasyllable in the two languages are identical: x x x x | x x x. The Latin variant on this regular form is x x x | x x x x (above, pp. 29–30); the Irish is x x x x x | x x. The former is rare enough that it ought perhaps to be regarded as an anomaly with no historical significance; the latter appears more frequently and is of more dubious explanation. Conceivably it is connected with an octosyllabic form, x x x x x | x x x, which is found occasionally and may reproduce a common ancestor from which the normal x x x x | x x x and the irregular x x x x x | x x will have arisen by processes of, respectively, acephaly and catalexis.[108] By similar reasoning one could derive the regular and irregular Latin forms from a different octosyllabic prototype: (x) x x x | x x x (x). Both hypothetical prototypes, it may be noted, are found in South Slavic verse, whose Indo-European origin has recently been argued by Jakobson and Watkins.[109] But, whatever the explanation for the divergences between the Irish and Latin heptasyllables, these divergences are confined, in both metres, to forms which occur sporadically.

The similarities between the Saturnian and old Irish verse do not end here. Old Irish parallels Latin not simply in its choice of cola, but also in the way it combines these cola into poems.

107. Presumably any inherited quantitative cadence would have been obscured, if not necessarily obliterated, during the period of initial stress accent.

108. So Watkins (above, n. 101), 233–4.

109. R. Jakobson, "Studies in Comparative Slavic Metrics," *Oxford Slavonic Papers* 3 (1952), 21–66. See, especially, 34–5 and 51–5, where octosyllables of the form x x x x | x x x x and x x x x x | x x x are traced back to a common Slavic prototype. Jakobson argues an Indo-European origin only for the Slavic decasyllable, but Watkins extends his analysis to include the shorter line as well (above, n. 101), 211–12.

Shorter cola, for example, may alternate with longer ones to produce a series of distichs. So in

comad cách a | choimded céim      na crich | n-imderb dring

cotlat ina | buailid brú      bid cách | ina crich[110]

we have, with one exception, the metrical pattern of

eorum sectam | secuntur      multi | mortales
multi alii[111] | e Troia      strenui viri.

ubi foras | cum auro      illinc | exibant   (Naevius 5);

and content as well as form suggests the comparison between:

Taurasiam | Cisaunam      Samnio | cepit   (*CEL* 7.6)

and

selaig-srathu | Fomoire      for doine | domnaib.[112]

("He ravaged the valleys of the Fomorians over worlds of men.") Quite as often old Irish repeats a single colon κατὰ στίχον or mingles the colon with related forms in a way which recalls Greek lyric and, more strikingly perhaps, the Arval hymn:

enos Lases      iuvate          x x x x | x x x
neue lue rue      Marmar sins      (x) x x x x x | x x x[113]
incurrere in      pleoris        x x x x | x x x
satur fu      fere Mars        x x x | x x x

110. The lines are isolated by Watkins (above, n. 101), 230, from the old Irish tract on the privileges and responsibilities of poets edited by E. J. Gwynn, *Ériu* 13.5 (1942), 20.

111. For the scansion with hiatus see above, p. 42.

112. From Briccine mac Brigni's Lament for Art, Mess-Delmann (edited by K. Meyer, "Über die älteste irische Dichtung," *SBBerlin* 1913, Nr. 10, p. 6). Cf. E. Campanile, "Note sul Saturnio," *Ann. Scuola Normale Sup. di Pisa* 32 (1963), 191–7, who, however, is concerned only with the bipartite character and propensity for alliteration that are shared by the Saturnian with certain forms of old Irish verse.

113. On the scansion, see above, n. 60.

| | | |
|---|---|---|
| limen sali | sta berber | x x x x │ x x x |
| semunis | alternei | x x x │ x x x |
| advocapit | conctos | x x x x │ x x |
| enos Marmor | iuvato | x x x x │ x x x |
| triumpe triumpe triumpe triumpe triumpe | | (refrain) |

and the only early Latin *carmen* that is well and extensively enough preserved for us to hazard a guess as to its metrical structure:

| | | |
|---|---|---|
| ego tui | memini. | x x x x │ x x x |
| medere meis | pedibus. | (x) x x x x │ x x x[114] |
| terra pestem | teneto. | x x x x │ x x x |
| salus hic | maneto | x x x │ x x x |
| in meis | pedibus | (x) x x │ x x x |

(p. 31 Morel)

With the exception of *advocapit conctos* and the refrain *triumpe* all the cola in these two poems show a trisyllabic cadence preceded by a variable opening (three, four or five syllables).[115] The resulting structure is exactly that of *Fled Bricrenn* 52:

| | | |
|---|---|---|
| tond mairnech | mathrúamdae | x x x │ x x x |
| mórbruth | mborrbíastae | x x │ x x x |
| brisiud múad | mórchatha | ×x x │ x x x |
| con-boing tar écrait | n-écomlund | x x x x x │ x x x |
| allbach mbratha | brógene | x x x x │ x x x[116] |

Much of old Irish verse, is, in fact, very much what Pasquali, proceeding from a comparison of the Arval hymn with the

114. In this and the last line *meis* may be either monosyllabic or disyllabic.

115. The one exception disappears if we assume that *advocapit conctos* recovers an earlier * *advocapit concitos*. The line is certainly one in which the original meaning of *conctos*, "assembled," "summoned together," would be most appropriate.

116. Cited by Watkins (above, n. 101), 231, who gives additional examples of similar verse construction (231–4 and 227–8).

Saturnian, assumed the earliest Latin verse to have been: cola identical with those used in the Saturnian but combined with far greater freedom and variety than the poets of the Saturnian seemed to have allowed themselves.

As is well known, the earliest Latin shares with old Irish not only its most common verse form but also its words for poet (*vates*: OI *faith*) and song (*canere, carmen*: OI *canid*), its conception of the *vates* as a person who combines in himself the roles of poet, seer, and magician,[117] and a series of terms relating to the inherited Indo-European religious usage whose rites and formulae would have been entrusted to the memory of *faith* or *vates* for safe keeping.[118] These facts of linguistic history might in themselves suggest the possibility of a Celtic analogue to the earliest Latin poetry. Comparative metrics and comparative philology are thus compatible here, just as were historical and comparative metrics in pointing to a syllabic ancestor for the second-century Saturnian. Taken together, the two agreements may be more than coincidental. If speculation into the origin of a metre so scantily attested is to be allowed at all, we are justified, I believe, in positing a verse form common to Italic[119]

117. See Watkins (above, n. 101), 214–15.

118. See J. Vendryes, "Les correspondances de vocabulaire entre l'indo-iranien et l'italo-celtique," *MSL* 20 (1918), 265–85.

119. If the Saturnian is an Indo-European inheritance one would expect it to be shared with other Italic dialects, but the Italic Saturnians which have been adduced to date are dubious at best. The most likely examples are two inscriptions from Corfinium (*CEL* 17); cf. Buecheler, "Altitalisches Weihgedicht," *RhM* 33 (1878), 274–6, and "Altitalische Grabschrift," *RhM* 35 (1880), 496. But, if Buecheler's analysis is correct, the high percentage of lines with eight- and nine-syllable cola in these inscriptions (cf. *usur pristafalacirix, sacaracirix Semunu sva, aetatu firata fertlid, afded eite vus pritrome*) indicates that extensive use was made of the equivalence $\times = \cup\cup$, and this in turn would suggest derivation from Latin models of the late second century rather than independent conservation of an Indo-European prototype; cf. Leo (above, n. 1), 68, and Pasquali (above, n. 10), pp. 53–4. The Corfinium inscriptions date from the time of Sulla; much earlier, of course, from the third or fourth century, is the Faliscan *foied vino pipafo cra carefo* (*CIE* 8179). The words may not be intended to form a verse; and, even if

and Celtic, syllabic in character and built up out of the free association of a number of short cola, which was gradually modified in such a way as to give it both the regular stichic structure and the quantitative iambic pattern[120] of the Greek trimeter. No other theory locates the Saturnian so consistently with relation both to the recorded history of Greek and Roman literature and the reconstructed prehistory of Indo-European verse.

they are, the tetrasyllabic second colon would prevent most scholars from classing the line as a Saturnian (see the definition adopted above, p. 10). It is worth noting, however, that old Irish verse uses a tetrasyllabic line both κατὰ στίχον and in alternation with longer sequences (Watkins, [above, n. 101], 238–41), and that there are several sequences in Livius and Naevius which one would be inclined to consider whole verses except for the fact that one colon lacks a syllable of the minimal five:

> Livius 12: atque escas habemus     mentionem
>         36: vinumque quod libabant     anclabatur
> Naevius 40: eam carnem     victoribus danunt
>         41: vicissatim volvi     victoriam
>         58: cum tu arquitenens sagittis     pollens dea

(cf. above, n. 20). It is conceivable that in these lines and in the Faliscan *cra carefo* we have the lone Italic remnants of a colon which underwent a much more extensive development in Irish. But, if this slender piece of evidence is excluded, the existence of an independent Italic tradition of Saturnians remains no more than a hypothesis.

120. This "iambization" of the Saturnian need not have been effected exclusively through the Saturnian–hypercatalectic trimeter equation posited earlier (p. 61). An alternate possibility is that one form of Saturnian came to be felt as a catalectic trimeter with penthemimeral caesura preceded by a single iambic foot: $\times - + \times - \cup - \times \mid - \cup - \cup - -$. This analysis has the advantage of linking the central break in the Saturnian to the more common of the two caesuras in the trimeter or senarius, and of establishing a parallel between the sequence $- \cup \times \mid$ with which the second half of the Saturnian most often opens and the corresponding sequence in those senarii that show penthemimeral caesura and diaeresis after the fourth foot. The metrical pattern to which the syllables between caesura and diaeresis in such lines normally conform is not the $- \times -$ which would be expected in Latin iambic verse but (by virtue of the laws of Jacobsohn and Meyer) $- \cup \times$, just as in the Saturnian.

# The *Menaechmi*: Roman Comedy of Errors

ERICH SEGAL

# The *Menaechmi*: Roman Comedy
## of Errors

P<small>LAUTUS</small> <small>WROTE</small> only one Comedy of Errors. His Greek predecessors wrote so many that Ἄγνοια ("Errora," or more
literarily, "Ignorance"), who speaks the prologue to Menander's
*Perikeiromene*, has often been called the patron goddess of New
Comedy. The *Menaechmi* is generally considered to be early
Plautus, and may well have been an experiment with a theme
which proved uncongenial to the Latin comic poet. For Plautus
usually prefers wit to ignorance, shrewd deception to naive
misunderstanding. Chance, τὸ αὐτόματον, rules the world of
Menander, and things haphazardly "happen to happen,"
ἀπὸ ταὐτομάτου, a condition which Plautus usually mocks.[1]

In a Comedy of Errors we "automatically" laugh at the
bumbling ignorance of characters who are nothing but puppets.
But Plautus' real affection is for puppeteers, manipulators like
Tranio, Palaestrio, Epidicus and Pseudolus, men whose cleverness
leaves nothing to chance, and who flourish in a world where the
source of laughter is not automation, but machination.

The first man to translate it into English saw that the
*Menaechmi* was different. Writing his preface in 1595, William
Warner called the play:

> a pleasant and fine Conceited Comaedie, taken out of the
> most excellent wittie Poet *Plautus*: *Chosen purposely from out
> the rest, as the least harmfull, and yet most delightfull.*

1. Cf. *Miles* 287:

Forte fortuna per impluvium huc despexi in proxumum.

On the roof, I chanced by chance to look down through our neighbor's
skylight.

And there is much stress placed on coincidence in the prologue to this play
(e.g. lines 104, 117 ff.).

It is not "harmfull" because it lacks the very feature that was Roman comedy's prime legacy to the Renaissance: intrigue. It has none of *l'inganno* that was the staple of Italian *commedia erudita*, or the charming roguery that would characterize Jonson's Mosca and Molière's Scapin (not to mention Beaumarchais' Figaro, in a later age). Cedric Whitman refers to this special quality of cleverness in the Aristophanic hero as *ponêria*.[2] Plautus celebrates it as *malitia*.[3] Whatever it be called, it does not appear at all in the *Menaechmi*. Plautus' comedy, though it deals in duplicates, has no duplicity, and, though its heroes are doubles, it has no double-dealing. There is only error, pure, simple...and harmless.[4]

In other respects, however, the *Menaechmi* is a very Plautine creation. Much of it is in that musical comedy style which made its author famous and invited favorable comparisons with Aristophanes (Cicero was not loath to link the two names in praise). Terence, like Menander his paragon, has few (if any) real songs.[5] And, while the *Menaechmi* lacks wit, it has in its place wish-fulfillment, in fact the greatest of all fantasies, that of the surrogate self, the alter ego with no superego, someone

2. Cedric H. Whitman, *Aristophanes and the Comic Hero* (Cambridge, Mass., 1964), pp. 30 ff.

3. Cf. the epilogue to the *Epidicus* (line 732):

Hic is homo qui libertatem malitia invenit sua.

Behold a man who won his freedom by being tricky.

(Except in the one instance [see below, note 8], my Latin text is that of W. M. Lindsay [Oxford 1904]. All translations are my own.)

4. Everyone in the *Menaechmi* wanders in a maze of innocent error. No one is smarter than anyone else; in fact, no one is smart. Even in Menander's *Perikeiromene*, over which the goddess Ignorance presides, the heroine herself is aware that the boy next door is her long-lost brother, though she purposely withholds the information until the last moment.

5. Donatus calls Terentian passages which alternate iambic and trochaic lines "mutatis modis cantica." These do not really qualify as "songs" by Plautine standards. Both Terence and Menander lack the truly lyrical meters which characterize Plautus' celebrated musical moments.

who can indulge his appetite for pleasure without concern for the consequences. Everyone yearns to be "Jack in town and Ernest in the country," but this can only happen in dreams or in "the twin brother of dreams"—as Freud once referred to it—comedy. Plautus presents this happy hallucination in an entertainment which might well be subtitled, *The Importance of Being Menaechmus.*

The two houses onstage represent the conflicting forces in the play. They are not unlike the statues of Artemis and Aphrodite which frame the setting of Euripides' *Hippolytus.* In both dramas, the action takes place in a magnetic field between personifications of restraint and release. It is no mere coincidence that the house of Menaechmus I stands at the exit nearer the forum.[6] The Epidamnian twin is bound by innumerable ties, legal, financial, and social, as well as to a shrewish wife who is constantly "on the job." In fact Menaechmus I describes her behavior as excessive *industria* (line 123), a term which gives almost allegorical overtones to the action of the comedy.

Across the stage, and nearer the harbor whence visitors come, dwells a lady of pleasure aptly named Erotium. Plautus has an affinity for heroines with similarly delicious *redende Namen,* like Philocomasium in the *Miles* and Pasicompsa in the *Mercator.* Terence, on the other hand, seems content to name his ladies Pamphila in play after play.[7] In contrast to the aptly titled

6. Throughout my discussion "Menaechmus I" (occasionally without the numeral) refers to the local Epidamnian twin. "Menaechmus II" is the travelling brother (*né* Sosicles).

7. Plautus himself may have coined these colorful female names. Cf. Friedrich Leo, *Plautinische Forschungen* (2nd ed. Berlin 1912), pp. 107 ff.; Eduard Fraenkel, *Elementi Plautini in Plauto* (Florence 1960, rev. ed. of *Plautinisches im Plautus*, trans. Franco Munari), p. 141. T. B. L. Webster distinguishes between Old and New Comedy in their respective uses of "character names" as opposed to "chance names," *Studies in Later Greek Comedy* (Manchester 1953), p. 13. Webster is referring to *Poetics* IX.5, where Aristotle observes that (New?) comic characters have τυχόντα ὀνόματα, a phrase which may simply mean "fictitious names."

Erotium, Menaechmus' spouse has no name at all; she is merely "matrona." Shakespeare reverses this in his *Comedy of Errors*, contrasting the wife Adriana and a *meretrix* referred to merely as "courtesan."

While Menaechmus I never seems to be in the right place at the right time, he at least knows the right words. His nickname for Erotium (itself a charactonym meaning "pleasure") is *voluptas*. This word is not only an endearment, but *le mot juste* to describe the atmosphere in Erotium's domain, one which contrasts sharply with the *industria* across the stage. Thus when he travels from one side to the other—or at least tries to— Menaechmus is "acting out" the inner direction of the Comic Spirit. The two houses represent *industria* and *voluptas*, Everyday versus Holiday, or, as Freud would describe it, The Reality Principle versus the Pleasure Principle.

We are visiting the town of Epidamnus on a special day, one which Menaechmus has chosen for a festive release from the rules. Such occasions do not come often and, as the parasite Peniculus remarks, today's celebration is much overdue; there has been a long "intermission" (*intervallum iam hos dies multos fuit*, line 104). According to the parasite, when Menaechmus does throw a party, it is a truly gala occasion:

> Ita est adulescens; ipsus escae maxumae,
> Cerialis cenas dat...    (lines 101–2)

> Now here's the way he is: the greatest of all eaters,
> The feasts he gives are festivals of Ceres....

To Peniculus, his patron's entertainments are like those national Roman holidays when banquets are served in the Circus.

At this moment, the hero appears. And Menaechmus I is indeed the protagonist. Plautus focuses on the local twin, giving him the larger and more melodic role, whereas Shakespeare concentrates on the visiting brother. We first meet Menaechmus battling soldier-like against marital aggression; he is a military man fighting domestic restraint (cf. lines 127, 129). Now that he has broken through enemy lines he can celebrate:

> Clam uxoremst ubi pulchre habeamus atque hunc con-
> buramus diem    (line 152)[8]
> Hidden from my wife we'll live it up and burn this day to
> ashes.

His aim, like that of so many Plautine heroes, is *pulchre habere* (or, as elsewhere expressed, *bene habere* or *bene esse*). It is hardly a coincidence that his domestic situation is later described as *male habere*, in fact his wife's behavior to him is SEMPER *male habere* (line 569).

Menaechmus' opening song describes his wife's restrictive actions in no uncertain terms:

> nam quotiens foras ire volo, me retines, revocas, rogitas,
> > quo ego eam, quam rem agam, quid negoti geram,
> > quid petam, quid feram, quid foris egerim.
> > portitorem domum duxi, ita omnem mihi
> > rem necesse eloqui est, quidquid egi atque ago.
> > > > (lines 114–18)

> However often I try to go out, you detain me, delay me,
> > demand such details as
> > Where I'm going, what I'm doing, what's my business
> > all about,
> > Deals I'm making, undertaking, what I did when I
> > was out.
> > I don't have a wife, I've wed a custom's office
> > bureaucrat,
> > For I must declare the things I've done, I'm doing,
> > and all that!

---

8. I depart from Lindsay's text here, preferring the line I have printed, along with Leo and Conrad (Teubner).

It is her behavior, her *industria*, which has driven him out of the house:

> malo cavebis si sapis,
> virum observare desines.
> Atque adeo, ne me nequiquam serves, *ob eam industriam*
> Hodie ducam scortum ad cenam atque aliquo condicam
> foras.    (lines 121-4)

> Watch out for trouble, if you're wise,
> A husband hates a wife who spies.
> But so you won't have watched in vain, for all your
> diligence and care,
> Today I've asked a wench to dinner, and we're going out
> somewhere.

That the playwright himself understood "holiday psychology" is demonstrated by the remarks of Menaechmus' father-in-law later in the play. When the wife sends for him to complain of her husband's vagaries, the old man does indeed get angry— but at *her*. This infidelity is her fault:

> SENEX: Quotiens monstravi tibi viro ut morem geras,[9]
> quid ille faciat ne id observes, quo eat, quid rerum gerat.
> MATRONA:
> at enim ille hinc amat meretricem ex proxumo.
> SENEX:                                         Sane sapit!
> atque *ob istanc industriam* etiam faxo amabit amplius.
>                                                 (lines 788-91)

> OLD MAN: How often have I told you to behave yourself
> with him,
> Don't guard where he's going, what he's doing, what
> his business is.

9. The significance of a woman being *morigera* in Roman life is discussed by Gordon Williams, "Some Aspects of Roman Marriage Ceremonies and Ideals," *Journal of Roman Studies* 48 (1958), 28-9. On the Plautine stage, only Alcumena has this quality (cf. *Amphitruo* 839-42). Ironically, Menaechmus uses this adjective to describe Erotium (line 202).

WIFE:

But he loves a fancy woman there next door.

OLD MAN:                                              He's very wise!
And I tell you, thanks to all your diligence, he'll love
    her more.

In this scene he repeats most of Menaechmus' complaints
verbatim, especially the charge of excessive *industria*.

But, just as the wife is "diligence" incarnate, so the mistress is
*voluptas*, Pleasure personified. When Menaechmus first spies her,
his exclamation emphasizes this contrast. The rhetorical
structure of the line defies adequate rendering into English,
counterpoising as it does *uxor* and *voluptas*, withholding the
verb, and hence the entire meaning, until the last possible
moment. When Erotium comes into view he shouts:

Ut ego uxorem, mea voluptas, ubi te aspicio, odi male!

(line 189)

Oh my wife, my joy, when I see *you*, how I hate *her*!

The antithesis is still more explicit. Just as Erotium is nothing
at all like his wife, so too the day Menaechmus will devote to
her will be totally different from his ordinary agenda. Even the
banquet he orders would underscore—in a special sense for the
Roman spectators—the fact that the usual rules were being set
aside. He asks Erotium for the following bill-of-fare:

iube igitur tribu' nobis apud te prandium accurarier
atque aliquid scitamentorum de foro opsonarier
glandionidam suillam, laridum pernonidam,
aut sincipitamenta porcina aut aliquid ad eum modum,
madida quae mi adposita in mensam miluinam suggerant.
atque actutum.     (lines 208–12)

Please arrange a feast at your house. Have it cooked for
    three of us.

Also have some very special party foods bought in the
    forum:

Glandiose, whole-hog, and a descendant of the lardly ham.

Or perhaps some pork choppettes, or anything along those
   lines.
Let whatever's served be "stewed," to make me hungry as
   a hawk.
Also hurry up.

The desire for "stewed" delicacies is a normal festive
impulse: to get drunk, tie one on.[10] But Menaechmus has been
still more specific. For all the delicacies on his menu and
similar foods *ad eum modum* were specifically forbidden to
Romans by various sumptuary laws. Pliny tells us that this
legislation explicitly forbade the eating of "cenis abdomina,
glandia, testiculi, vulvae, sincipita verrina."[11] Not only do these
outlawed items figure prominently on Menaechmus' *carte du
jour*, but Plautus plays with them verbally, concocting such
comic dishes as *sincipitamenta* from *sincipita* and the absurd
patronymics *glandionida* ("son of glandules") and *pernonida*
("son of ham"). Menaechmus can savor even the words which
describe his breaking-of-the-rules banquet.

In another passage Pliny also recounts how stern Cato—
Plautus' contemporary—constantly inveighed against gastro-
nomic luxury, especially the eating of certain cuts of pork.[12]
In spite of this, or rather because of this, Plautus' characters go

---

10. In the *Casina*, there is a similar call for "inebriated" delicacies by
Olympio, a slave about to be married:

>       propere cito intro ite et cito deproperate.
>   ego iam intus ero, facite cenam mihi ut ebria sit.
>   sed lepide nitideque volo, nil moror barbarico bliteo.
>
>                                                    (*Casina* 744–8)

>       Hurry up and go inside and quickly hurry up,
>   I'll be right in. Prepare a drunken dinner for me.
>   Something fine and fancy. Not your bland barbarian stuff!

There are many parallels here with Menaechmus' request for "stewed"
things, most noteworthy the emphasis on haste (especially line 744, cf.
*Menaechmi* 213 and 215) and Olympio's explicit rejection of ordinary
Roman food (*barbaricum bliteum*, line 748).

11. Pliny, *N.H.* VIII.78.209.          12. *Ibid.* VIII.78.210.

whole-hog in their infringement of these laws.[13] Thus the comic escape from the rules (here dietary) is emphasized by the playwright's calling attention to the very prohibition being violated.

But now that his un-Roman dinner is being swiftly prepared (he is very insistent that they hurry), the hero strangely, inexplicably heads for the forum, not to return until the party is over. The stage is set for a crescendo of errors. The moment that the local Menaechmus exits towards the business district, his twin from Syracuse enters from the harbor. By artful coincidence, the very first word which Menaechmus II speaks is *voluptas* (line 226).[14] He is little aware of the reverberations which this word will have for him, and how apt a description it is of the way of life in this town. For, with the exception of his brother's house, Epidamnus is the ultimate in festive places. His slave Messenio describes its denizens exclusively in superlatives:

> nam ita est haec hominum natio: in Epidamnieis
> voluptarii atque potatores maxumei;
> tum sycophantae et palpatores plurumei
> in urbe hac habitant; tum meretrices mulieres
> nusquam perhibentur blandiores gentium.
> propterea huic urbei nomen Epidamno inditumst,
> quia nemo ferme huc sine damno devortitur. (lines 258–64)

> Now here's the race of men you'll find in Epidamnus:
> The greatest libertines, the greatest drinkers too,
> The most bamboozlers and charming flatterers
> Live in this city. As for wanton women, well,
> Nowhere in the world, I'm told, are they more dazzling.
> Because of this, they call this city Epidamnus:
> For no one leaves unscathed, "undamaged," as it were.

The visiting twin will indeed encounter "voluptuaries," especially the dazzling Erotium, but unlike an ordinary tourist

13. Fraenkel, *op. cit.* in n. 7 above, p. 238 ff., considers the references to pork in Plautus as definite additions by the Roman playwright.

14. It also happens to be the first word which the Braggart Soldier utters when he returns from the forum (*Miles* 947).

on an ordinary day *he* will leave Epidamnus undamaged, since his brother will pay all the bills; *damnum* in its literal sense denotes financial ruin. The boy from Syracuse belongs to a great comic tradition: a lowly stranger who arrives in town, is mistaken for someone else of greater importance, and fulfills the comic dream—everything for nothing, specifically food, sex and money. Xanthias in the *Frogs* is the first of such types in ancient comedy. True to this tradition is Klestakov, Gogol's lowly government clerk who is mistaken for the Inspector General and offered banquets, bribes and a bride. Like Gogol's hero, the travelling Menaechmus has come to town nearly penniless;[15] what happens is too good to be true. A beautiful courtesan calls him by name and invites him to a lavish feast of all the senses, one which his brother has paid for.[16] But, before going inside, he is careful enough to give his purse to Messenio—a final safeguard against *damnum*.

But what Menaechmus II experiences *chez* Erotium is quite the opposite of *damnum*. In fact, he profits in every imaginable way. Having revelled to the fullest and been given a fancy embroidered dress (supposedly to be taken to a seamstress for more improvements), he emerges drunk, garlanded, and amazed:

> Pro di immortales! quoi homini umquam uno die
> boni desistis plus qui minu' speraverit?
> prandi, potavi, scortum accubui, apstuli
> hanc, quoiius heres numquam erit post hunc diem.
>
> (lines 473–7)

> By all the gods, what man in just a single day
> Received more favors, though expecting none at all?
> I've wined, I've dined, I've concubined—and robbed her
>     blind.
> No one but me will own this dress after today!

15. Cf. *Menaechmi* 255–7.

16. We note that Menaechmus II fails to take any cognizance of the fact that he seems to look exactly like someone else with his name—another indication of the low level of intelligence in Plautus' Comedy of Errors.

He then receives some of Erotium's jewelry which, like the fancy garment, was originally stolen by Menaechmus I from his wife.[17] More *damnum* for the married twin, to pay for his brother's *voluptas*.

But what of our protagonist? Where has he been while the day was "burned to ashes" for him? The moment Menaechmus II skips triumphantly offstage, the married twin arrives, singing of his frustration. He enters with a barrage-in-song against the Roman patronage system. The special "Roman-ness" of this particular scene (lines 571 ff.) has often been remarked upon; Eduard Fraenkel heard in it a contemporary Roman's plaint and Professor D. C. Earl has more recently studied its topicality.[18] But whether or not there is a reference to the *Lex Cincia* or any other aspect of *clientela* does not alter the most basic dramatic fact, that just now in the forum, as he was *en route* to Erotium's house, Menaechmus was stopped by a client who forced him to act as his advocate. Molière based *Les Fâcheux* on a similar comic dilemma: a man trying to get to an amorous rendezvous, delayed by assorted blocking characters.[19]

The fate of Menaechmus I demonstrates how inimical are the worlds of business and pleasure. He vociferously regrets being a *patronus*, a man with protective responsibilities towards others. From the Roman standpoint, this was hardly a proper attitude. Polybius tells us that Scipio Aemilianus was considered "un-Roman" by his contemporaries precisely because

17. Cf. Menaechmus I's remark when he steals the dress:

Meo malo a mala abstuli hoc, ad *damnum* deferetur     (line 133)

I've stolen this from hateful her to help bring ruin to me.

18. Fraenkel, *op. cit.* in n. 7 above, pp. 152 ff., D. C. Earl, "Political Terminology in Plautus," *Historia* 9 (1960), 237. See also Raffaele Perna, *L'originalità di Plauto* (Bari 1955), p. 291.

19. Fraenkel (*op. cit.* p. 296) interprets the *Casina* as a conflict between Haste and Delay, a description which serves equally well for Menaechmus' dilemma. One critic sees this as the theme of Molière's comedy in general: Alfred Simon, *Molière par lui-même* (Paris 1957). There is also a *fâcheux* incident described in Terence's *Eunuchus* 327–45: a talkative acquaintance obstructs young Chaerea's pursuit of the girl he has fallen in love with.

he refused to argue court cases.[20] It is tradition, as Horace reminds us, both a pleasure and a duty (*dulce et sollemne*) for a solid citizen *clienti promere iura*.[21] And it is of precisely this solemn obligation that Menaechmus complains; he doesn't want to be a good citizen at all:

> sicut me hodie nimi' sollicitum cliens habuit neque quod volui
> agere aut quicum licitumst, ita med attinuit, ita detinuit.
> (lines 588–9)

> I was just now delayed, forced to give legal aid,
> no evading this client of mine who had found me.
> Though I wanted to do you know what—and with who—
> still he bound me and tied ropes around me.

Citizenship, like marriage, places certain restraints upon a man.[22] Menaechmus has been "tied up" in the forum on business. To emphasize the "tenacity" of these restrictions, Plautus employs three variations of the verb *tenere*. First *retinere* (line 113) in reference to the hen-pecking wife, and here *attinere* and *detinere* (line 589) to describe the clinging client. Both ties prevent Menaechmus from following his instinct, *agere quod licitumst*. In the famous *canticum* which follows, the protagonist realizes that his great mistake was even thinking about the forum on a day like this:

> di illum omnes perdant, ita mihi
> hunc hodie corrumpit diem,
> meque adeo, qui hodie forum
> umquam oculis inspexi meis.
> diem corrupi optumum:
> iussi apparari prandium,
> amica expectat me, scio.
> ubi primum est licitum ilico
> properavi abire de foro.   (lines 596–600)

---

20. Polybius xxxi.23.11–12.        21. Horace, *Epist.* ii.i.103 ff.

22. This is why, according to Freud, marriage was the subject of the first "jokes"; it was the first restriction placed on man. See "Wit and its Relation to the Unconscious," p. 704 and *passim*, *The Basic Writings of Sigmund Freud*, trans. A. A. Brill (New York 1938).

By all the heavens, cursed be he
Who just destroyed this day for me.
And curse me too, a fool today,
For ever heading forum's way.
The greatest day of all—destroyed,
The feast prepared, but not enjoyed,
My love awaits, I know, indeed,
The very moment I was freed
I left the forum with great speed.

Plautus emphasizes the haste with which Menaechmus leaves the commercial center. From business in the forum, he rushes towards pleasure at its polar opposite, across the stage, at the house of Erotium. In this play, and at Rome, the first step in a holiday direction is always—as quickly as possible—*abire de foro*.

Forum and "festivity" are also counterpoised in the *Casina*, a comedy which shares many characteristics with the one we are discussing. Here old Lysidamus, like young Menaechmus, has set aside this special day for merrymaking. But, again like Menaechmus, while he is *en route* to his banquet-of-the-senses, a lawsuit keeps him in the forum. When he finally returns, he has learned a bitter lesson:

> Stultitia magna est, mea quidem sententia,
> hominem amatorem ullum ad forum procedere,
> in eum diem quoi quod amet in mundo siet;
> sicut ego feci stultus: contrivi diem,
> dum asto advocatus quoidam cognato meo;
> quem hercle ego litem adeo perdidisse gaudeo.
>
> *(Casina* 563–9)

It's folly, that's what I would call it, total folly,
For any man in love just to approach the forum,
The very day his love awaits, all fancied up.
That's what I've done—fool that I am. I've ruined the day,
While acting as attorney for a relative.
By Hercules, I'm overjoyed we lost the case!

His *faux pas*, in the most literal sense, was *ad forum procedere*.
For, in Plautine comedy, the funny things can only happen on
the way *from* the forum. This identical situation prevailed in
Plautine Rome, since, on the days when his comedies were
presented, there was no business at all: the theater was packed
and the forum was empty. In fact the *Casina* prologue states
this in no uncertain terms: "the holidays are on...a Haicyon
quiet floats about the forum" (lines 25–6).

Thus, by whatever standards, Roman or Epidamnian,
Menaechmus I has broken the cardinal rule of holiday: he has
gone to business. Forum and festivity are polar opposites, two
completely different ways of life. It is therefore understandable
that Menaechmus I should be tied up with *industria* while his
unattached twin enjoys the *voluptas*. Even when he finally
breaks away from the forum and hastens to cross over to
Erotium's house, the married twin encounters on stage the
greatest *fâcheuse* of all: his wife. Having been warned by the
parasite, the matrona now waits to ambush her wayward
husband. *Industria* literally blocks the road to *voluptas*.
Disaster!

What had promised to be "the greatest day of all" has now
turned out to be the very worst. The entire fabric of Menaechmus'
existence seems torn to shreds. Everyone is angry at him. All
doors are closed to him. Not only is he—to use his own term—
*exclusissumus* (line 697), "the most kicked-out man in the
world," but he is then pronounced insane by a sort of psy-
chiatrist *gloriosus*, ancestor to the quack doctors who appear in
the Saint George plays, a professional whose questions are not
unlike those which Socrates asks Strepsiades in the *Clouds*. And
now several burly *lorarii* are about to drag him off for medical
"treatment." Someone else has acted insanely, but Menaechmus
I must suffer the cure.

How is it possible that one man could get all of the blame and
yet none of the pleasure? This crucial question is finally
answered when the brothers meet face to face. Messenio then
sees the mirror-image of his master "speculum tuum!" (line

1062) and proclaims the same apparent paradox which astounds the Duke in *Twelfth Night*:

> One face, one voice, one habit and two persons!
> A natural perspective that is and is not! (v.i.208–9)

Another of Shakespeare's characters, like Messenio in the Latin play, then cries, "How have you made division of yourself?" In Shakespeare's comedy as well as Plautus', the sudden discovery that the protagonist has a twin brother relieves a situation of potential tragedy. Indeed, there is an ambiguity to the phrase "division of yourself." In a tragic context it could mean, quite literally, schizophrenia. In a comedy, it means twins.

There is a special significance to the identity crisis in the *Menaechmi*. The hero, a married, responsible citizen, desires to go on a wild revel, to break the rules. In point of fact, someone named Menaechmus—someone who looks just like him—does savor all the forbidden delights. But this is *another* Menaechmus, who for one reason or another is not subject to the restrictions which bind the local twin. Without any consequences, Menaechmus II enjoys what is ordinarily illegal: *furtum, scortum* and *prandium* (line 170), stolen goods, stolen love, and an illicit banquet. The travelling twin bears no responsibility for the stolen property. After all, it was freely given to him. He is unmarried, so his fling with Erotium can occasion no domestic repercussions. And, since he is a foreigner, he can enjoy a *prandium* of forbidden delicacies without infringing any local legislation which would restrain his citizen-twin.

The local brother can derive *some* pleasure from this spree— he can enjoy being told about it:

> MEN. II:                Prandi perbene
>    Potavi atque accubui scortum: pallam et aurum hoc
>      abstuli.
> MEN. I: Gaudeo, edepol, si quid propter me tibi eveniat boni.
>    Nam illa quom te ad se vocabat memet esse credidit.
>
>                              (lines 1141–4)

MEN. II:                                    Just terrifically, I've wined and
   Dined and concubined and of the dress and gold I've
   robbed her blind.
MEN. I: Wonderful! I'm glad you had some fun because of
   me, by Pollux.
She invited you to dine because she thought that you
   were I.

The married brother's joy can only be vicarious. But even
here there is a consolation, at least it is completely guilt-free.
While a certain Menaechmus, his mirror image, was revelling
with Erotium, he was busy fulfilling his civic obligations in the
forum—if it was anything like the business district in Rome,
a place dominated from the north by the temple of Janus, that
two-faced deity the Romans worshipped.[23] Since the thought is
not tantamount to the deed, Menaechmus I is, today at least,
totally innocent.

Earlier in the play, at the height of the confusion, the married
brother cries out that all these wild goings-on seem to him like a
dream (line 1047). He does not realize how right he is. For this
comedy is actually the *dream of Menaechmus I,* whose fantasies
have conjured up a surrogate self to indulge in forbidden
pleasures while he himself preserves the outward respectability
of every day. In fact, as the recognition scene demonstrates,
there is really only *one* Menaechmus: the married one. After
this day of errors, this *folle journée,* everything will return to
normal. Identities are properly distributed, and Menaechmus II
must take back his original name—Sosicles. They both will
return to Syracuse, and the family business. *Voluptas* today, but
*industria* tomorrow. The play even closes with an auction
announcement.

If nothing else, the finale of Plautus' one play of errors
reminds us that Menaechmus II does not really exist. Such a

23. Cf. Horace, *Epist.* i.i.54 ff. It is perhaps of interest that Freud, in
the essay cited in n. 22, speaks of "the Janus-like double-facedness of wit"
(p. 739).

man lives only in dreams or in comedy, when responsible citizens invoke an alter ego to let the world slip and succumb to the Pleasure Principle. Forgotten is the Reality Principle, which Freud describes as "ever striving for what is useful and guarding itself against damage."[24] Today in Epidamnus, pleasure has prevailed. And so the brothers can leave this town of *voluptarii maxumi*, this festive spot like Shakespeare's wood outside Athens, where identities are scrambled and lunatics and lovers run rampant.[25] They can depart with everything in order, for, unlike the world of the Reality Principle, there has been no damage. Comedy, which is in essence the triumph of the Pleasure Principle, creates that unique situation wherein joy comes *sine damno in Epidamno*.

24. Sigmund Freud, "Two Principles of Mental Functioning" (1911). The translation quoted is from *A General Selection from the Works of Sigmund Freud*, ed. John Rickman (Garden City 1957), p. 43.

25. My conception of Epidamnus as a "festive place," as well as several other ideas in this essay which are impossible to footnote specifically, owe much to that brilliant study by C. L. Barber, *Shakespeare's Festive Comedy* (Princeton 1959). My approach to the *Menaechmi* in general was greatly influenced by Harry Levin's "Two Comedies of Errors," *Stratford Papers on Shakespeare*, ed. W. Jackson (Toronto 1964), pp. 35–57.

# Imperator histricus

H. D. JOCELYN

# Imperator histricus

THE FIRST CENTURY B.C. had one hundred and thirty comic scripts with the name of Plautus attached. Scholars disputed about which of the scripts really came from the hand of the Umbrian playwright. The authenticity of twenty-one was never challenged[1] and there is no reasonable doubt that these are the twenty-one which survive to the present day in the Ambrosian palimpsest and the so-called "Palatine" codices.[2] The organisation of the lexicon of the third-century grammarian Nonius Marcellus reveals that Nonius used a corporate edition of the same twenty-one.[3] Somewhere in the ancestry of our witnesses lies one or more editions[4] of the individual scripts made according to the method established at Alexandria for the scripts of the classical Athenian tragic and comic poets.[5] The first such scientific edition could hardly have been made before

1. See Gellius III.3.4 (depending on Varro). The dispute seems to have been carried on with the woolliest of aesthetic arguments. Superstition perhaps dictated the choice of twenty-one rather than some other number of "authentic" plays. There are no good positive reasons for thinking that the twenty-one all come from the same hand. For an attempt to detach the *Asinaria* see L. Havet and A. Freté, *Pseudo-Plaute: Le prix des ânes* (Paris 1925), pp. v ff.

2. Some of the scripts are extremely defective. *A* has a little of the *Vidularia*, *B* only the title, *C* and *D* nothing at all.

3. See W. M. Lindsay, *Nonius Marcellus' Dictionary of Republican Latin* (Oxford 1901), pp. 1 ff.; *Philologus* LXIII (1904), 273 ff.

4. Varro (*Ling.* VII.69) and Verrius Flaccus (Paulus, *Fest. epit.* p. 86.27) quote radically different versions of *Poenulus* 530.

5. See F. Leo, *Plautinische Forschungen* (1st ed. Berlin 1895), pp. 1 ff.; Lindsay, *The Ancient Editions of Plautus* (Oxford 1904), pp. 1 ff.; A. Thierfelder, *De rationibus interpolationum Plautinarum* (Leipzig 1929), pp. 1 ff.; G. Pasquali, *Storia della tradizione e critica del testo*² (Florence 1952), pp. 331 ff.; K. Büchner, in H. Erbse *et al.*, *Geschichte der Textüberlieferung* 1 (Zürich 1961), pp. 375 ff.

168 B.C., the year in which the Pergamene philologist Crates visited Rome and gave lectures,[6] that is some sixteen years after Plautus' death.[7] The claim made by Terence in 161, that he did not know Plautus to have adapted the Κόλαξ of Menander,[8] implies that no edition of this play was then available to the public. Even in Plautus' lifetime his scripts were employed by actors without his supervision[9] and doubtlessly suffered alteration at the hands of those who preferred their own to the author's ideas of what was dramatically appropriate. It is unlikely that any editor succeeded in obtaining a Plautine autograph or would have been able to recognise one if he had. Whatever text formed the basis of an edition of a particular comedy was copied in its entirety.[10] Critical signs indicated what parts of the text the editor considered spurious or corrupt. Detailed argument on these matters was set out in a separate volume.[11] Some editors perhaps deliberately conflated scripts from different performances into the one book text.[12] Some certainly conflated earlier book texts into the one.

6. Suetonius (*Gramm.* 2) was wrong to date Crates' visit to 169. The embassy from Eumenes in 168 (Livy XLV.13.12) must have brought him to Rome.

7. 184 according to Cicero (*Brut.* 60).

8. *Eun.* 33.

9. See *Bacch.* 214–15. H. B. Mattingly, however, has argued, *Latomus* XIX (1960), 250 ff., that these verses are a late interpolation.

10. On Alexandrian methodology see G. Zuntz, *The Text of the Epistles: a disquisition upon the Corpus Paulinum* (London 1953), p. 278; Erbse, in *Geschichte der Textüberlieferung* I, 221 ff.; B. A. van Groningen, *Traité d'histoire et de critique des textes grecs* (Amsterdam 1963), pp. 33 ff.; W. S. Barrett, *Euripides: Hippolytos* (Oxford 1964), pp. 46 ff.; Zuntz, *An Inquiry into the Transmission of the Plays of Euripides* (Cambridge 1965), pp. 251 ff.

11. Cf. Pliny, *NH.* XVIII.107 *artoptam Plautus appellat in fabula quam Aululariam scripsit* (*v.* 400), *magna ob id concertatione eruditorum an is uersus poetae sit illius.* There is report of commentaries by Sisenna (first or second century A.D.) and by Terentius Scaurus (early second century A.D.).

12. Whether a serious philologist would have done this seems to me doubtful. The Alexandrians had to deal with scripts that had passed through the hands of booksellers as well as actors. The Romans stood closer in time to their classic dramatists and were perhaps able to get hold of scripts before a book trade had established itself.

This process helped to produce the text of the *Poenulus* which our witnesses present. Two final scenes are transmitted, one ending in iambic trimeters after the classical Greek manner,[13] the other in musically accompanied trochaic tetrameters after the Roman. The prologue contains verses coming unquestionably from more than one theatrical performance.[14] One might assert that the text of the main part of the action is actable as it stands but hardly that every verse comes from the pen of the one poet.[15] Taking up a discussion opened by F. Osann[16] Ritschl argued[17] that everything in the extant prologue postdates 184 B.C. Subsequent scholars have tried to save various parts for Plautus, the conservative extreme being reached in K. Abel's 1955 Frankfurt dissertation.[18] The present paper attempts to re-open the argument from a radically sceptical point of view by considering the allusion made in the prologue to Ennius' adaptation of Aristarchus' tragedy ᾽Αχιλλεύς.

Here is a text of *vv.* 1–58 of the *Poenulus* prologue:

13. Cf. the second *Andria* ending; on this see O. Skutsch, *RhM* c (1957), 53 ff.

14. Verses 121–3 ∼ 124–8.

15. A clear doublet is *vv.* 923–9 ∼ 917–22. Consideration of the degree of interpolation is complicated by the possibility that Plautus conflated two Greek scripts to make the Latin *Poenulus*. On the plot of the extant script see L. Reinhardt, in G. Studemund, *Studia in priscos scriptores Latinos* I (Berlin 1873), pp. 109 ff.; C. M. Francken, *Mnemosyne* 2. IV (1876), 146 ff.; P. Langen, *Plautinische Studien* (Berlin 1886), pp. 181 ff.; Leo, *Pl. Forsch.*, ed. 1, pp. 153 ff., ed. 2, pp. 170 ff.; H. T. Karsten, *Mnemosyne* 2. XXIX (1901), 363 ff.; G. Jachmann, in Χάριτες *Leo dargebracht* (Berlin 1911), pp. 249 ff.; *Plautinisches und Attisches* (Berlin 1931), pp. 195 ff.; E. Fraenkel, *Plautinisches im Plautus* (Berlin 1922), pp. 262 ff. (= *Elementi Plautini in Plauto* [Florence 1960], pp. 253 ff.); B. Krysiniel, *Der plautinische Poenulus und sein attisches Vorbild* (Diss. Munich 1932); *Eos* XXIV (1933/4), 1 ff.; A. Klotz, *PhW* LIV (1934), 289 ff.; W. Theiler, *Hermes* LXXIII (1938), 289 ff.; T. B. L. Webster, *Studies in Menander* (Manchester 1950), pp. 134 ff.

16. *Analecta critica* (Berlin 1816), pp. 147 ff. Osann gave body to an idea that had been in the air at least since the time of Justus Lipsius.

17. *Parerga zu Plautus und Terenz* I (Leipzig 1845), pp. 180 ff.

18. *Die Plautusprologe*, pp. 89–96.

PROLOGVS

Achillem Aristarchi mihi commentari lubet;
inde mihi principium capiam, ex ea tragoedia.
sileteque et tacete atque animum aduortite:
audire iubet uos imperator histricus,
bonoque ut animo sedeate in subselliis,                          5
et qui esurientes et qui saturi uenerint.
qui edistis, multo fecistis sapientius;
qui non edistis, saturi fite fabulis.
nam cui paratumst quod edit, nostra gratia
nimia est stultitia sessum inpransum incedere.                  10
exsurge, praeco, fac populo audientiam.
iam dudum exspecto, si tuom officium scias.
exerce uocem, quam per uiuisque et colis;
nam nisi clamabis tacitum te obrepet fames.
age nunc reside, duplicem ut mercedem feras.                    15
bonum factum †esse† edicta ut bene seruetis mea.
scortum exoletum ne quis in proscaenio
sedeat, neu lictor uerbum aut uirgae muttiant,
neu dissignator praeter os obambulet.
neu sessum ducat, dum histrio in scaena siet.                   20
diu qui domi otiosi dormierunt, decet
animo aequo nunc stent uel dormire temperent.
serui ne obsideant, liberis ut sit locus,
uel aes pro capite dent.   si id facere non queunt,
domum abeant, uitent ancipiti infortunio:                       25
ne et hic uarientur uirgis et loris domi,
si minus curassint, quom eri reueniant domum.
nutrices pueros infantis minutulos
domi ut procurent neue spectatum adferant,
ne et ipsae sitiant et pueri pereant fame,                      30
neue esurientes hic quasi haedi obuagiant.
matronae tacitae spectent, tacitae rideant;
canora hic uoce sua tinnire temperent,
domum sermones fabulandi conferant,

ne et hic uiris sint et domi molestiae.                                    35
quodque ad ludorum curatores attinet,
ne palma detur quoiquam artifici iniuria,
neue ambitionis causa extrudantur foras,
quo deteriores anteponantur bonis.
et hoc quoque etiam, quod paene oblitus fui:                               40
dum ludi fiunt, in popinam, pedisequi,
inruptionem facite; nunc dum occasiost,
nunc dum scriblitae aestuant, occurrite.
haec, quae imperata sunt pro imperio histrico
bonum hercle factum pro se quisque ut meminerit          45
ad argumentum nunc uicissatim uolo
remigrare, ut aeque mecum sitis gnarures.
eius nunc regiones limites confinia
determinabo; ei rei ego sum factus finitor.
sed nisi molestumst, nomen dare uobis uolo                     50
comoediai; sin odiost, dicam tamen,
si quidem licebit per illos quibus est in manu.
Καρχηδόνιος uocatur haec comoedia

*     *     *

Latine Plautus Patruus Pultiphagonides.

*     *     *

nomen iam habetis.   nunc rationes ceteras                     55
accipite.   nam argumentum hoc hic censebitur.
locus argumentost suom sibi proscaenium.
uos iuratores estis.   quaeso operam date.

---

prologus *om. C, uno uersu uacuo*   **4** lubet *B*   hystricus *BCD*   **6** esurientes
*D⁴*: esuplentes *BCD¹*   qui *B*: *om. CD*   **7** edisti *B*   **9** num *B*   **13** qua *T*
**14** num *B*   clamabis tacitum *Turnebus*: clamabista tum *B*: clamabis
statim *CD*   **16** esse *BCD*: uos *dubitanter protuli*   **17** quis *BD*: que *C*
**18** niue *BCD*   **27** curasint *BCD*   reueniant *Bothe*: ueniant *BCD*
**30** pertant *B*: peritent *T*   **32** rediant *B*: redeant *C*: reddeant *D*
**33** onara *cum spat. init. B*: lanora *C*   **36** ad *om. B*   **43** scriblitae *D*:
scribilitae *B*: scriplitae *C*   **47** remigare *B*   sitis gnarures *T*: siti signa
rures *BCD*   **49** eius *codd. Nonii p.* 11.23   factus finitor *B*: finitor factus
sum *Muretus*   **50** nisi molestumst nomen dare *Itali*: nisi molestum si non

mendare *BCD*　　**51** comoediai sin odiost *Gruterus*: comedi ais inodiosi *B*: comediais inodiosi *CD*　　**52** immanu *B*　　**54** Plautus *Itali*: platus *BCD* *ante hunc uersum lacunam statuit Geppert: cf. Cas.* 31–4, *Merc.* 9–10　　**55** orationes *CD* *ante hunc uersum lacunam statui: cf. Trin.* 20　　**57** sibis *B*: scibis *CD*

Until well into the nineteenth century scholars usually thought that the opening verses of this prologue with their allusion to a tragedy by the obscure Aristarchus were a straight literal translation of the opening verses of Plautus' Attic original,[19] the Καρχηδόνιος.[20] The simple-minded view of the relationship between Attic and early Roman drama underlying this notion is no longer fashionable and one need point out only the most obvious signs that we are not dealing with a slavish copy of the Καρχηδόνιος prologue: the mention of the lictor and his rods (*v.* 18), of the palm branch prize (*v.* 37) and of the censor's assistants (*v.* 58), the information about Plautus himself (*vv.* 53–4), the use of a *prologus* to speak the Latin verses.[21] The very form and substance of the first verse, *Achillem Aristarchi mihi commentari lubet*, are not as Greek as they look. It was probably unusual for Menander and his contemporaries

19. See, for example, A. Schöll, *Beiträge zur Kenntnis der tragischen Poesie der Griechen* 1 (Berlin 1839), pp. 485 f.; F. G. Welcker, *Die griechische Tragödien mit Rücksicht auf den epischen Cyclus geordnet* (*RhM* Suppl. 11, Bonn 1839–41), p. 933.

20. Alexis and Menander are credited with a Καρχηδόνιος. On the controversy over which comedy Plautus adapted see W. G. Arnott, *RhM* cii (1959), 252 ff.

21. In Terence's time there was a special costume for the *prologus* (*Hec.* prol. 11, 9). The speaker of the *Poenulus* prologue, called *prologus* by the editorial tradition, seems to have worn no distinctive dress. Euanthius' remark at *De fab.* iii.2 (*tum etiam Graeci prologos non habent more* †*nostrorum*† *quos Latini habent*) probably refers to the relationship between Terence and his particular Greek originals rather than to Greek comedy generally (see Leo, *Pl. Forsch.*² p. 224). There is no evidence, however, that the speaker of a prologue was ever called a πρόλογος either in the Attic theatre or in any scholar's library. In an anonymous comic fragment (*ap.* Demiańczuk, p. 96) there is a discussion of theatrical matters of the type found in the prologues of Plautus' *Captiui* and *Poenulus* but the actor almost certainly wore the garb of Dionysus.

to adduce the name of a tragedy's author as well as its title. Euripides' Αὔγη dealt with a woman who gave birth to a child out of wedlock and identified the child's father through a ring.[22] The fame of this tragedy permitted Menander to give in the final scene of his Ἐπιτρέποντες the following dialogue to Smicrines, the father of an errant daughter, and Sophrone, the nurse:

τί φησιν ἱερόσυλε γραῦ;

'ἡ φύσις ἐβούλεθ', ᾗ νόμων οὐδὲν μέλει ·[23]
γυνὴ δ' ἐπ' αὐτῷ τῷδ' ἔφυ.' : : τί, μῶρος εἶ;
τραγικὴν ἐρῶ σοι ῥῆσιν ἐξ Αὔγης ὅλην,
ἂν μή ποτ' αἴσθῃ, Σμικρίνη.           (*vv.* 764–8)

On the other hand, tragedies and comedies were regularly advertised to second-century Roman audiences with the names of their Greek composers rather than those of the Latin adapters.[24] Indeed, Latin poets perhaps never referred to contemporaries by name and did so only rarely to dead predecessors.[25] Thus aphorisms, regularly assigned to their authors by the Attic

22. On the plot see Wilamowitz, *Analecta Euripidea* (Berlin 1875), p. 189, Th. Zieliński, *Eos* xxx (1927), 33 ff., 416.

23. This verse is frequently quoted in the surviving literature as by Euripides; see fr. 920 N².

24. At *Rudens* 86 the slave Sceparnio describes a storm with the words *non uentus fuit uerum Alcumena Euripidi*, clearly referring to a tragedy the audience has recently seen in Latin form on the stage (see Fraenkel, *Pl. im Pl.* p. 68 [= *Elementi*, pp. 64 f.], *Addenda*, p. 403). At *Eunuchus* 9 and 19–21 a prologising actor describes the behaviour of Terence's rival Luscius with the words *idem Menandri Phasma nunc nuper dedit...quam nunc acturi sumus Menandri Eunuchum, postquam aediles emerunt, perfecit sibi ut inspiciundi esset copia.*

25. Part of the reason would lie in the Greek setting of the plots of comedy; mention of *poetae barbari* was out of place. Social factors also operated. The early poets were immigrants to the Roman community and many were slaves. For a long period they enjoyed little more prestige than did ordinary theatrical workers (on the status of actors see B. Warnecke, *RE* VIII ii [1913], s.v. *Histrio*, 2117, 2125 ff., *NJbb* XXXIII [1914], 95 ff., T. Frank, *CPh* XXVI [1931], 11 ff.). Indeed some of them, Livius Andronicus (see Livy VII.2) for example and perhaps Plautus himself (see Leo, *Pl. Forsch.*² p. 85), were actors.

comedians,[26] are left unattributed in Latin drama.[27] There is accordingly no difficulty at all in regarding the first verse of the *Poenulus* prologue as a reference to a Latin version of Aristarchus' Ἀχιλλεύς. We know that Plautus' younger contemporary Ennius made such a version[28] and have several fragments of this version preserved in the extant literature.[29]

In the same year as Ritschl athetised the whole *Poenulus* prologue E. Klussmann argued[30] that *v.* 3—*sileteque et tacete atque animum advortite*—were verbatim quotations of the script of the Latin *Achilles*. In the first edition of his collection of the fragments of tragedy Ribbeck printed[31] these verses and part of *v.* 4—*audire iubet uos imperator*—as coming from the hand of Ennius. All subsequent editors of the fragments of Ennius' tragedies have accepted this idea. Of editors of the *Poenulus* Goetz–Loewe (1884), Lindsay (1911) and Ernout (1938) have followed Ribbeck,[32] Lindsay adding *v.* 16—*bonum factum* †esse† *edicta ut seruetis mea*[33]—to the alleged quotations. Ussing (1883) and Leo (1896) accepted *vv.* 3–4—*sileteque et tacete atque animum aduortite.* | *audire iubet uos imperator*—as a quotation but rejected *v.* 11.[34]

Ussing's view is the only one at all plausible. The full scripts

---

26. Cf. Com. anon. *ap.* P.S.I. 1175.2 ἐγὼ δ᾽ ἐρῶ [τ]ὸ Σοφοκλέους ἔπος..., Menander, Com. Flor. 69–85 ...ὡς] Καρκίν[ο]ς πού φησιν... Εὐριπίδου τοῦτ᾽ ἐστί....

27. Cf. Plautus, *Curc.* 591–2 *antiquom poetam audiui scripsisse in tragoedia* | *mulieres duas peiores esse quam unam. res itast*; *Truc.* 931–2 *uenitne in mentem tibi quod uerbum in cauea dixit histrio?* | *omnes homines ad suom quaestum callent et fastidiunt.* 28. See Festus, p. 282.9.

29. Cicero, *Verr.* II.1.46 (see schol. Gron. *ad loc.*); Festus, pp. 282.9, 394.33; Gellius IV.17.13; Nonius, pp. 147.18, 166.20, 169.1, 277.23, 472.26; Isidore, *Diff.* I.218. 30. *NJbb* Suppl. XI (1845), 325.

31. Leipzig, 1852, p. 14; see also p. 272.

32. Cf. Fraenkel, *Beobachtungen zu Aristophanes* (Rome 1962), pp. 125 f.

33. Cf. *CQ* XIV (1920), 51.

34. Cf. F. Hornstein, *WSt* XXXVI (1914), 115, n. 2; Abel, *Die Plautusprologe*, p. 145, n. 542; F. Stoessl, *RE* XXIII ii (1959), Nachträge, s.v. *Prologos*, 2370, 2397. Wł. Strzelecki, *Eos* XLIII (1948/9), 155, divided *v.* 11 into two phrases *exsurge praeco* and *fac populo audientiam* which he alleged came from Ennius' version of Aeschylus, *Eum.* 566–71 κήρυσσε κῆρυξ...σιγᾶν ἀρήγει.

of many of the tragedies imitated and parodied by Aristophanes survive and we can see that the Athenian comic poet, while he sometimes quoted two or more verses verbatim at the beginning of a passage of parody, was usually content thereafter to throw brief phrases into paratragic verse of his own making.[35] Menander was even less given to verbatim quotation.[36] We should expect a Roman poet likewise to obey the demands of his dramatic context rather than follow at any great length the exact wording of a tragic passage he happened to remember in passing. The verses *exsurge, praeco, fac populo audientiam* and *bonum factum* †esse† *edicta ut seruetis mea* as a matter of fact spring straight from the discourse the comic poet gives his actor. There is no reason at all to separate them from the verses flanking them and to treat them as quotations of another play.

Acceptance of the verse *exsurge, praeco, fac populo audientiam* as a verbatim quotation indeed raises a serious difficulty. It implies, I think, that a military assembly formed part of the visible action of the *Achilles*. Some of the pieces quoted by the grammarians from this tragedy, however, strongly suggest that the action took place before the tent of Achilles and involved the embassy described in *Iliad* IX. The piece quoted by Nonius in his article on *defendere*, p. 277.23, *serua ciues defende hostes cum potes defendere*, could not be anything but an appeal to Achilles to help the hard-pressed Achaeans. Ribbeck[37] embraced Scriverius' view[38] that Ennius had written two plays about Achilles and proposed that the one dramatised the quarrel between Achilles and Agamemnon at the assembly narrated in *Iliad* II, while the

35. For fairly exhaustive lists of Aristophanes' imitations and parodies see A. C. Schlesinger, *TAPhA* LXVII (1936), 296–314, *AJPh* LVIII (1937), 294–305.

36. See Webster, *Studies in Menander*, pp. 153 ff.; A. Pertusi, *Dioniso* XVI (1953), 27 ff., XIX (1956), 111 ff., 195 ff.

37. *Quaestiones scenicae*, in his first edition of the tragic fragments, p. 272; *Die römische Tragödie im Zeitalter der Republik* (Leipzig 1875), pp. 112 ff. Cf. O. Jahn, *Hermes* III (1869), 191; L. Müller, *Q. Ennius. Eine Einleitung in das Studium der römischen Poesie* (St Petersburg 1884), p. 90; W. Zillinger, *Cicero und die altrömischen Dichter* (Diss. Erlangen 1911), p. 107, n. 4.

38. *Collectanea Veterum Tragicorum Fragmenta* (Leiden 1620), p. 8.

other dramatised the embassy. Vahlen[39] argued that there was one play with two scenes, one at the place of assembly, the other before Achilles' tent. This change of scene is as hard to accept as Ribbeck's two tragedies. The older Athenian tragedians occasionally changed the scene during the course of a play's action;[40] but Euripides, so far as we know, never did, and we should not too readily assume the existence of such changes in plays adapted for the Roman stage. Even the staging of a scene set at a place of assembly is hard to visualise; hard in the theatre of Dionysus at Athens, even harder in a Roman theatre where the flat space in front of the stage was occupied by part of the audience.[41] In extant Attic tragedies the proceedings of assemblies are regularly reported by a messenger;[42] Athena's summoning of an assembly of Athenian notables in Aeschylus' Εὐμενίδες is a special case.

It would not be so very difficult to include *sileteque et tacete atque animum aduortite.* | *audire iubet uos imperator* in a reconstruction of the *Achilles*. Nevertheless *vv.* 3–49 of the *Poenulus* prologue can be interpreted—indeed are best interpreted—without assuming the existence of any verbatim quotation at all. The actor addresses the assembled audience as if he were a magistrate with *imperium* delivering an *edictum*. The formulae of the special language of public administration are solemnly pronounced: 4 *audire iubet uos imperator...*,[43] 11 *fac populo audientiam...*,[44]

39. *Ennianae Poesis Reliquiae*² (Leipzig 1903), pp. cci, 118. Cf. F. Skutsch, *RE* v (1905), s.v. *Ennius*, 2594. Bergk, *Ind. lectt. Marburg* 1844, xi (= *Kl. phil. Schr.* i 225), had argued that there was only one tragedy, distinguished from Livius' *Achilles* by Ennius himself with the title *Achilles Aristarchi*.

40. Aeschylus in his Αἰτναῖαι (fr. 26 Mette) and Εὐμενίδες (230, 488), Sophocles in his Αἴας (873).

41. See Livy xxxiv.44.5, Vitruvius v.7.6.2.

42. Cf. Euripides, *Hek.* 521 ff.; *I.A.* 1543 ff.; *Or.* 884 ff.

43. Cf. Livy ii.7.8 *ibi audire iussis consul laudare fortunam collegae*; Horace, *Sat.* ii.3.77 *audire atque togam iubeo componere* (parody; cf. *Sat.* i.2.37, Fraenkel, in *Festschrift R. Reitzenstein* [Leipzig and Berlin 1931], 121, n. 1, *Horace* [Oxford 1957], p. 82, n. 1).

44. Cf. Rhet. inc. *Her.* iv.68 *iubet aduocari contionem...illi praeco faciebat audientiam*; Livy xliii.16.8 ⟨*cum*⟩ *Claudio obstreperetur audientiam facere praeconem*

16 *bonum factum*[45] †esse† *edicta ut seruetis mea*...[46], 44 *haec quae imperata sunt pro imperio*...[47], 45 *bonum hercle factum pro se quisque ut meminerit*..., 47 *ut aeque mecum sitis gnarures*...[48], 48–9 *regiones limites confinia determinabo.*[49] The general stylisation is reminiscent of the official language: the pleonastic doublets in 3 *sileteque et tacete* and 13 *uiuisque et colis*,[50] the anastrophe of the preposition in 13 *quam per uiuis*,[51] the etymological figure in 44 *imperata sunt pro imperio*,[52] the asyndetic tricolon in 48 *regiones limites confinia.*[53] The phrase in 4 *audire iubet uos imperator* which Ribbeck and others take as a quotation from the speech of a tragic herald may ape an official mode of expression. Nicely parallel would be Cicero's order to Catiline: *exire ex urbe iubet consul*

iussit. In both these passages reference is made to a formal *contio*. The only other occurrences of the phrase (Cicero, *Caecil.* 42, *De orat.* II.325) are metaphorical.

45. Cf. *CIL* VI.31614 *B(onum) F(actum). nei quis intra terminos...ustrinam fecisse uelit*, Suetonius, *Iul.* 80, *Vitell.* 14.

46. *Edicere* and *edictum* were almost exclusively official in use; wherever they occur in comedy mock solemnity appears to have been intended (see *TLL* v ii.63.80 ff.).

47. On imperium see Rosenberg, *RE* IX ii (1916), 1201 ff., H. Wagenvoort, *Roman Dynamism* (Oxford 1947), pp. 59 ff.

48. Cf. *CIL* I² 581.23 *senatuosque sententiam utei scientes esetis* (consuls to men of the *ager Teuranus*, 186 B.C.); *IG* VII 413.3 ὑμᾶς εἰδέναι βουλόμεθα ἡμᾶς κατὰ τὸ τῆς συνκλήτου δόγμα...ἐπεγνωκέναι (consuls to men of Oropus, 73 B.C.); *SEG* IX 8.77 ἵνα πᾶσιν ᾖ γνωστὸν ὧν κηδόμεθα πέμπειν εἰς τὰς ἐπαρχήας διέγνων (Augustus to men of Cyrene, 4 B.C.); Plautus, *Cist.* 521 *meam ut scies sententiam*, *Poen.* 1038 *ut tu sis sciens*, *Trin.* 4 *ne quis erret uostrum*; Terence, *Eun.* 961–2 *at ne hoc nesciatis*, Pythias: *dico edico* (parody).

49. For magistrates with *imperium* assigning land see Livy XXXII.1.6–7.

50. Cf. *CIL* I² 614 *L. Aimilius L. f. inpeirator decreiuit...agrum oppidumqu. quod ea tempestate posedisent, item possidere habereque iousit* (189 B.C.).

51. Contrast Plautus, *Poen.* 1187, Terence, *Phorm.* 28. In the remains of republican drama *per* precedes appellative nouns everywhere except at Plautus, *Stich.* 71 *gratiam per* (A: *a patre* P) *si petimus* (contrast Plautus, *Mil.* 1125, 1200). The official language retained such things as the praetor's *illud quo de agitur* even in Cicero's day.

52. Cf. Lex XII tab. 12.2 *si seruos furtum faxit noxiamue no⟨x⟩it.*

53. Cf. the praetorian formula *do dico addico* (Varro, *Ling.* VI.30), the title *IIIuiri aere argento auro flando feriundo* (Mommsen, *Staatsr.* II 602).

*hostem.*[54] Caesar's habit of referring to himself in the third person in his *commentarii* springs to mind. Self-important personages in comedy regularly issue greetings in the same oblique manner: for example Amphitruo, the triumphant Theban general, addresses his wife with the words *Amphitruo uxorem salutat laetus speratam suam...ualuistin usque?*[55] The spectators of the *Poenulus* are addressed with a relative clause whose verb is in the third, not the second person: 4–6 *uos...et qui esurientes et qui saturi uenerint.* The only close parallels for such a locution in extant Latin are provided by archaic epic and tragedy[56] but it may have been used in the official language. At any rate it could not have come directly from the *Achilles.* Its vulgar substance precludes that.

The situation has the humour of paradox. The prologising actor, probably a person of servile status, certainly one of very low status,[57] gives orders in the manner of a supreme magistrate both to the junior magistrates actually presiding over the festival (*ludorum curatores*) and to the other free citizens composing his audience. Many of his orders are related to things of which even a junior magistrate would find it beneath his dignity to take cognisance.

The actor sometimes forgets momentarily his pose. Instead of getting the herald to call for silence[58] he does so himself. Without much success. Several verses later in the midst of uproar he has to call upon the herald for help. He misuses

54. *Catil.* 1.13.

55. Plautus, *Amph.* 676–9; cf. *Bacch.* 243, *Epid.* 126–7, *Merc.* 713, *Mil.* 900, *Poen.* 685–6, *Trin.* 435–6, 1151–2, *Truc.* 515; Terence, *Eun.* 270–1. See M. Forberg, *De Salutandi Formulis Plautinis et Terentianis* (Diss. Leipzig 1913), pp. 15 ff. For the third person in summonses cf. Euripides, *Hel.* 1168, *Or.* 1226 (contrast 1626, where, however, one of the codices has the third person); Aristophanes, *Ach.* 406. Iuppiter is described as referring to himself in the third person at Plautus, *Amph.* 1065.

56. Cf. Ennius, *Ann.* 620 *uosque Lares tectum nostrum qui funditus curant*; Trag. inc. 35 *Danai qui parent Atridis quam primum arma sumite.*

57. See above, p. 103, n. 25.

58. This was perhaps regular; cf. Plautus, *Asin.* 4.

accidentally the official phrase *imperatori* (*consuli, praetori,* etc.)
*audientiam facere*: what he says—*fac populo audientiam* (11)—can
only mean "see that the people can make themselves heard";
it cannot mean what he wants it to mean, "see that the people
give me ear."[59] The uproar continues. The herald himself shouts
so loudly and for so long that the actor cannot get a word in and
finally has to offer him a double fee to make him sit down.

Every so often the actor deliberately takes account of reality,
of the fact that he is not really in the position of a magistrate
addressing a formal *contio*. He intones the sentence *audire iubet
uos imperator* (4) very pompously, then brings himself back to
earth with the adjective *histricus*.[60] With the somewhat patron-
ising phrase *bonoque ut animo* (5) [61] he assumes again his pose.
He then remembers that his hearers are not standing to attention as at a real Roman *contio*[62] but lounging on seats. Some
crude joking that would ill become a magistrate follows. After
some further by-play with the herald he reassumes the pose
with *bonum factum* †esse† *edicta ut seruetis mea* (16) and a series of
edicts solemnly pronounced in the third person. At *v.* 40 he

59. For the other occurrences of *audientiam facere* see above, p. 106, n. 44.
Fraenkel, *Beobachtungen zu Aristophanes*, pp. 125 f., suggests, without much
apparent confidence, that the dramatist was resurrecting an archaic usage.

60. F. Marx's notion (*SB* Leipzig, Phil.-hist. Kl., LXIII [1911], 46) that
the dramatist had in mind the Roman victor over the Histri of the year 178
and Ennius' portrait of him in the *Annals* seems quite implausible. *Histricus*,
which occurs only here in recorded Latin, must be Plautus' own coinage,
based on \**hister* rather than the regular *histrio* (which provides *histrionius* at
*Amph.* 90 and 152). It was perhaps made in jesting imitation of the official
language (cf. *poplicus, ciuicus, hosticus, colonicus, classicus, bellicus, lustricus*; see
M. Leumann, in Stolz–Schmalz–Leumann–Hofmann, *Lateinische Gram-
matik* [Munich 1926–8], I, p. 229; H. C. Isenring, *Die lateinischen Adjectiva auf
-icus und -ticus* [Diss. Zürich 1955], pp. 8 ff.). There is a more extended parody
of the formation at *Capt.* 78–87: *ubi res prolatae sunt. . .prolatis rebus parasiti
uenatici | [canes] sumus, quando res redierunt, Molossici | odiossicique et multum
incommodestici.*     61. See R. M. Ogilvie on Livy 1.41.5 (Oxford 1965).

62. See Cicero, *Flacc.* 16; Mommsen, *Staatsr.* III¹ 396, n. 3. There seem
to have been attempts on the part of magistrates during the early second
century to prevent the spectators sitting at *ludi* (see Tacitus, *Ann.* XIV.20).

abandons yet again the pose to give some advice to the audience's *pedisequi*, slaves like himself, about where a good snack is to be had. From *v.* 44 to *v.* 49 reality and pretence are more closely linked. Just as a magistrate with *imperium* makes or has made a survey of the land chosen for a *colonia* before making allotments to the *coloni*, so he, the actor, so he declares, will survey the whole of the plot before acting it out in detail with his fellows.

The tone of the language fluctuates with the actor's attitude towards the situation. The phrase *sileteque et tacete* which Klussmann thought to come directly from tragedy has many parallels in tragedy and in those parts of comedy, such as certain types of prologue and musically accompanied scene, whose style approaches that of tragedy. Not only does the second word express the substance of the first[63] but the two are linked by homoeoteleuton and the quite unusual copula -*que et*.[64] *Silere* is an extremely uncommon verb in republican drama[65] and must have possessed a correspondingly elevated tone. *Tacere* on the other hand is one of the commonest of all verbs.[66] Now when one word of a doublet in a republican dramatic script is rarer and more elevated than the other it normally comes second unless the dramatist seeks some special effect.[67] I would suggest

63. Cf., in comic prologues, *Amph.* 11 *concessum et datum*, 16 *aequi et iusti*, 23 *uereri et metuere*, 118 *ueterem atque antiquam*, *Aul.* 4 *possideo et colo*, *Capt.* 47 *compararunt et confinxerunt*, *Men.* 52 *imperato et dicito*, *Merc.* 58 *diffunditari ac didier*; in tragedy Aeschylus, *Choe.* 5 κλύειν ἀκοῦσαι, Ennius, *Sc.* 5 *pugnant proeliant*, 78 *purus putus*, 118 *differt dissupat*, 148 *aecum ac ius*, 148 *expedibo atque eloquar*, 189 *ius atque aecum*, 207 *uerecunde et modice*, 233 *uiduae et uastae*, 237 *mentem atque animum*, 295 *sospitent superstitentque*, 311 *squalam et sordidam*, 337 *profiteri et proloqui*, 361 *delectat ductat*. On the stylistic level of the phenomenon see Fraenkel, *Pl. im Pl.* pp. 356 ff. (= *Elementi*, pp. 344 ff.); H. Haffter, *Untersuchungen zur altlateinischen Dichtersprache* (Berlin 1934), pp. 53 ff.

64. Comedy has this copula quite rarely and then in phrases of some dignity occurring at the ends of iambic and trochaic verses; see *TLL* v ii 887.36 ff.

65. Elsewhere in comedy only at Plautus, *Capt.* 480; Terence, *Phorm.* 778; Iuventius, *Com. pall.* fr. 1.

66. Apart from *tacitus* about 280 times in comedy.

67. Cf. Haffter, *Untersuchungen*, pp. 72 f.

therefore that *tacete* pricks the inflated balloon of *sileteque et*[68] with much the same comic effect as the adjective *histricus* has at *v.* 4, the verb *sedeate* at *v.* 5 and the noun *fabulis* at *v.* 8.

The degree of strictness in the metrical pattern fluctuates similarly. There are far fewer iambuses and resolved feet in *vv.* 3–49 than one normally finds in prologue senarii but they increase perceptibly in number whenever the actor abandons his pose. The alleged quotations of tragedy are fairly strict in metrical pattern but no more so than verses universally believed to come from the hand of the comic poet himself.

If my interpretations are correct, *vv.* 3–49 hang together very nicely. The parody of the magistrate's language resembles what is often found in the mouths of slaves and other persons of low degree in Plautine scripts: one might compare the edicts of the parasite Ergasilus at *Capt.* 791 ff., of the slave Pseudolus at *Pseud.* 125 ff. and of the procurer Ballio at *Pseud.* 143 ff. The particular interests of actors are often referred to in these scripts in such a way as to break the dramatic illusion: keeping to that of the *Poenulus* itself I should draw attention to the scarcely veiled references to the Roman *ludi* at *vv.* 1011 ff. and 1291, the theatrical metaphor at *v.* 581 and the joking asides to the audience by the *aduocati* at *vv.* 550 ff. and 597 ff. and by the slave Milphio at *v.* 920; the most famous cases are of course the anonymous reference to Naevius at *Mil.* 211 ff.[69] and the outright naming of Pellio at *Bacch.* 215.

It has to be admitted that much in verses 3–49 reminds the

---

68. E. Fraenkel's suggestion, *Beobachtungen zu Aristophanes*, pp. 119 ff., that Aristarchus' 'Aχιλλεύς is the ultimate common source of Aristophanes, *Thesm.* 381 σίγα σιώπα πρόσεχε τὸν νοῦν (addressed to a plurality) and *sileteque et tacete atque animum aduortite* is in any case improbable. There is no evidence that Aristophanes ever parodied Aristarchus and, as Fraenkel himself demonstrated, the Greek verse draws upon the formulaic language of the Athenian assembly. Aristophanes could be parodying this language itself (cf. *Ach.* 59, 64, 123) or any contemporary tragedian's use of it (cf. Euripides, *Hek.* 529 ff., *Hik.* 668 ff., *I.A.* 1563 f., *Phaethon* fr. 773.75).

69. See Paulus, *Fest. epit.* p. 32.15, s.v. *barbari.* Cf. Naevius' alleged hit at Scipio (Gellius VII.8.5).

modern reader of tragedy and would do so even without the
pointer given by *vv.* 1–2. But the question is what the author of
*vv.* 3–49 intended with them. My own answer is that he intended parody of a real-life Roman *imperator*, not verbal
quotation nor even parody of a Latinised tragic στρατηγός.
The latter type of parody would certainly be possible, especially
for Plautus, who, unlike his predecessors, seems to have
restricted himself to comedy and perhaps regarded the other
genre as intrinsically absurd. It is not out of the question that
already before the year 184[70] the *Achilles* of Ennius had joined a
repertory of plays frequently performed at the festivals.[71] The
action of the Achilles took place in the Myrmidon encampment
and could have contained a scene in which Achilles gave
instructions to his bodyguard (perhaps the chorus).[72]

It is very likely that Ennius made his Achilles speak with
some of the phrases normally used on formal occasions by
Roman magistrates. The Attic tragedians had available in
choral lyric and epic a poetic vocabulary of a type denied to
the Latin poets who adapted their works; nevertheless they
often put into the mouths of the heroes of Mycenaean antiquity
the stylised formulae of contemporary Athenian public life.[73]
Ennius, much more, it seems, than poets who followed him, was
prone to use the solemn resounding phrases of Roman political,
social and religious ceremony in order to elevate the speech

70. The general character of the *Poenulus* suggests a date well after the
end of the second Carthaginian war and students seem to agree on placing
it quite late in Plautus' career. See K. H. E. Schutter, *Quibus annis comoediae
Plautinae primum actae sint quaeritur* (Diss. Groningen 1952), pp. 119–25.

71. The *Epidicus* appears to have been such a play (Plautus, *Bacch.* 214),
also the *Truculentus* and the *Pseudolus* (Cicero, *Cato* 50; the statement put
into the mouth of Cato probably depends on something in one of the scripts
then attributed by some scholars to Plautus and now lost).

72. Cf. the conversation between Hector and the chorus of camp guards
which opens the extant script of the Ῥῆσος.

73. See Fraenkel, on Aeschylus *Ag.* 830, 950, 1045, 1393; *Horace*, p. 55;
*Glotta* xxxix (1960), 1 ff. (= *Kl. Beitr.* 1 505 ff.); *MusH* xviii (1961), 37,
131 ff. (=*Kl. Beitr.* 1 263, 265 ff.); *Beobachtungen zu Aristophanes*, pp. 119 ff.

of the tragic heroes above that of everyday life and yet in a way immediately perceptible to his audience: I quote, in illustration, *Sc.* 4 *quibus tam concedit hic ordo,*[74] 44–5 *puerum primus Priamo qui foret | postilla natus temperaret tollere,*[75] 56 *mater optumatum*[76] *multo mulier melior mulierum,* 86–8 *quid petam praesidi*[77] *aut exequar, quoue nunc | auxilio exili aut fugae*[78] *freta sim? | arce et urbe*[79] *orba sum: quo accidam, quo applicem?*[80], 92–3 *o Priami domus, | saeptum altisono cardine templum,*[81] 120 *liberum quaesendum causa*[82] *familiae matrem tuae,* 209 *Iuppiter tibi summe tandem male re gesta gratulor,*[83] 260

74. Roman senators regularly referred to their assembled peers with the phrase *hic ordo* (Cicero, *Pis.* 6, 8, 40, 45 *et al.*). Cf. Plautus' parody at *Cist.* 21–3; *decet pol, mea Selenium, | hunc esse ordinem beniuolentis inter se | beneque amicitia utier.*

75. The phrase *puerum...tollere* (cf. Trag. inc. 85; Plautus, *Amph.* 501, *Truc.* 399; Terence, *Andr.* 219, 401, 464, *Haut.* 626–7; Cicero, *Att.* xi.9.3; Horace, *Sat.* ii.5.46 *et al.*) reflects a Roman family ritual wherein the *paterfamilias* picked up from the hearth the child he intended to rear as his own (cf. Augustine, *Ciu.* iv.11).

76. In the political pamphlets of the first century the senatorial supporters of the *status quo* referred to themselves regularly as *optumates* (cf. Rhet. inc. *Her.* iv.45 *et al.*).

77. *Praesidium* could denote the protection which a *patronus* gave his *clientes* (cf. Cicero, *De orat.* i.184).

78. For the legal distinction between *exilium* and *fuga* see Marcianus, *Dig.* xlviii.22.5.

79. Cf. the Fetial oath quoted by Festus, p. 102.11: *si sciens fallo tum me Diespiter salua urbe arceque* (contrast Polybius' translation [iii.25.8] πάντων τῶν ἄλλων σῳζομένων ἐν ταῖς ἰδίαις πατρίσιν, ἐν τοῖς ἰδίοις νόμοις, ἐπὶ τῶν ἰδίων βίων ἱερῶν τάφων) *bonis eiciat ut ego hunc lapidem.*

80. On the *ius applicationis* see Cicero, *De orat.* i.177.

81. Cf. Virgil, *Aen.* vii.174 (the palace of the king of Laurentum); Seneca, *Thy.* 901 ff. (the palace of Atreus). The Roman senate met in places constituted *templa* by the *augures* (see Varro *ap.* Gell. xiv.7.7; Servius auct., *Aen.* 1.446).

82. Cf. Ennius, *Sc.* 129; Plautus, *Capt.* 889; Varro *ap.* Macr. *Sat.* 1.16.18; Suetonius, *Iul.* 52; Gellius iv.3.2, xvii.21.44; contrast Menander, *Dysk.* 842–3, *Perik.* 435, fr. 682.

83. Fraenkel has argued, *Pl. im Pl.* pp. 238 ff. (= *Elementi,* pp. 229 ff.), on Aeschylus, *Ag.* 1387, that Ennius here parodies the prayer offered to *Iuppiter Optimus Maximus* by the triumphing *imperator.*

*multi suam rem bene gessere et publicam patria procul*, 289–90 ... *quin monstrum siet*[84] | *hoc ego tibi dico et coniectura auguro*, 331 *palam muttire plebeio piaculum est.*[85]

The stylistic level of *Poenulus* 3–49 is much above that of other extant prologue verses. The ways of speaking which elevate their tone are ones which pullulate in the remains of third and second century tragedy. Some, like the coupling of two words of similar general sense, are common to the language of tragedy and officialdom. Others seem purely poetical.

The phrase *exerce uocem*, for example, at *v.* 13 has no exact analogues in republican comedy or classical prose. It can hardly mean "train your voice";[86] the actor wants the herald to make professional use of it. The closest parallels are provided by a fragment of Cicero's *Prognostica* (*ap.* Isid. *Etym.* XII. 7.37: *et matutinos exercet acredula cantus*)[87] and two passages of Virgil's dactylic verse: *Georg.* 1.403 *seros exercet noctua cantus*, *Aen.* IX.61–2 *tuti sub matribus agni* | *balatum exercent*. *Exercere* seems to have the sense of *mittere.*[88] It could be that the author of *vv.* 3–49 followed some tragedian in reinterpreting *exercere* etymologically as "release from custody" (*ex + arcere*[89] on the model of *excludere*).

84. Cf. Festus, pp. 122.8, 146.32, s.v. *monstrum*.

85. Cf. Varro, *Ling.* VI.29; Gellius IV.6 on *piaculum*. Contrast Ennius' verse with Euripides, fr. 703 μή μοι φθονήσητ', ἄνδρες Ἑλλήνων ἄκροι, | εἰ πτωχὸς ὢν τέτληκ' ἐν ἐσθλοῖσιν λέγειν.

86. As at Cicero, *De orat.* 1.149; Seneca, *Contr.* I praef. 16; Seneca, *Epist.* XV.8, CXXII.15; Tacitus, *Dial.* 31.1. *Exercere* has the sense of γυμνάζειν or of some metaphorical extension throughout comedy except for a highly coloured passage of the *Amphitruo*: 323–4 *gestiunt pugni mihi.* | *—si in me exercituru's, quaeso in parietem ut primum domes* (in his article on *exercere*, pp. 294.18 – 295.15, Nonius ranges this passage under the meaning *inmittere*).

87. Cicero rewrote this verse of his youthful poem at *Diu.* 1.14 as *et matutinis acredula uocibus instat*.

88. *Vocem mittere* is very common in both classical prose and classical poetry; cf. Rhet. inc. *Her.* IV.60 *citharoedus...si...silentio facto uocem mittat* and the examples collected at *TLL* VIII.1174.75 ff.

89. Cf. Cassiodorus, *Gramm.* VII.204.8 *exercere est ex ex et arcere, ut exercitus qui sub disciplina certa arcetur, unde exercitatio*.

I can find no example of such etymological reinterpretation, in the quite sparse remains of republican tragedy. But the figure is fairly common in both Attic tragedy[90] and classical Latin poetry.[91] The notion that sounds are living things which escape or are released and are trapped by or land in the listener's ear turns up frequently in Homeric epic—*Il.* 1.201 καί μιν φωνήσας ἔπεα πτερόεντα προσηύδα, 3.221 ἀλλ' ὅτε δὴ ὄπα τε μεγάλην ἐκ στήθεος εἴη, 4.350 ποῖόν σε ἔπος φύγεν ἕρκος ὀδόντων—and in Attic tragedy—Aeschylus, *Prom.* 115 τίς ἀχώ...προσέπτα μ' ἀφεγγής, 555 τὸ διαμφίδιον δέ μοι μέλος προσέπτα, *Hik.* 657–8 ἐκ στομάτων ποτάσθω φιλότιμος εὐχά. From the Roman adaptations there can be quoted Ennius, *Sc.* 281 *fructus uerborum aures aucupant* and Accius, *Trag.* 449 *simul ac nota uox ad auris accidit*; from Virgilian epic *Aen.* xi. 380–1 *uerbis,* | *quae tuto tibi magna uolant.* It oftens occurs in Plautine comedy accompanied by extremely pompous modes of expression: note for example *Amph.* 325–6 (Mer.) *uox mi ad auris aduolauit.* (Sos.) *ne ego homo infelix fui,* | *qui non alas interuelli: uolucrem uocem gestito* and *Mil.* 955 *circumspice dum ne quis nostro hic auceps sermoni siet.*

The phrase *te obrepet fames* is a high-falutin variant of *fame moriere* or *fame peribis.*[92] Elsewhere in comedy *fames* is similarly personified only in highly elaborate musically accompanied passages: Plautus, *Pseud.* 350 *hunc fames iam occiderit, Stich.* 341 *quoi misero medullas uentris percepit fames, Truc.* 524 *ne...nos extinxit fames.* The closest parallels are in Attic tragedy: Aeschylus *Ag.* 1641–2 ἀλλ' ὁ δυσφιλὴς σκότῳ | λιμὸς ξύνοικος μαλθακόν σφ' ἐπόψεται, *Choe.* 249–50 τοὺς δ' ἀπωρφανισμένους | νῆστις πιέζει λιμός.[93] The practice of making abstract nouns

90. See L. Kugler, *De Sophoclis quae uocantur abusionibus* (Diss. Göttingen 1905); J. A. Schuursma, *De poetica uocabulorum abusione apud Aeschylum* (Amsterdam 1932), pp. 58 ff., 71 ff.; Fraenkel on Aesch. *Ag.* 149.

91. Cf. Horace, *Carm.* 1.36.18–20 *Damalis...lasciuis ederis ambitiosior;* iv.4.65 *merses profundo: pulchrior euenit.*

92. Cf. Livius, *Trag.* 27, Plautus, *Asin.* 531, *Cist.* 45, *Most.* 1106, *Poen.* 30, *Stich.* 216, 640; Caecilius, *Com.* 219.

93. The Aeschylean verbs nevertheless have little of the colourfulness of *obrepet.*

and incorporalia govern transitive verbs is one of the most striking features of the style of republican Latin tragedy. Where it occurs in comedy it is usually in sung verse and in the company of other devices designed to elevate the style above that of everyday speech.[94] It is very rare in senarii, even in those of prologues, which tend to be a little more elaborate than trimeters spoken by participants in the action.

Apart from *silete* and *gnarures* two words stand out as oddities for a passage of comic trimeters: *occurrite* at *v.* 43 and *uicissatim* at *v.* 46. Instead of *occurrite* one would have expected *accurrite*.[95] *Ob* in the meaning of *ad* seems to have been already archaic in the early second century. The author may have used *occurrite* to pick up *occasio* in the previous verse for the sake of an effect not infrequently sought in early second century comedy but perhaps proper to tragedy; one thinks of Ennius, *Sc.* 245 *Acherontem obibo ubi mortis thesauri obiacent*.[96] The adverb *uicissim* occurs twenty times in comedy, *uicissatim* only here and in elaborate trochaic dialogue at *Stich.* 532. The remains of early epic have *uicissatim* once.[97] It may have been an artificial creation of tragedy.

A number of stylistic features of *vv.* 3–49 occurring singly would be unremarkable: the copula *-que et* in *vv.* 3 and 13;[98] the neologism *histricus* in *vv.* 4 and 44;[99] the odd use of *colere* in *v.* 13,[100] of *temperare* + infinitive in *vv.* 22 and 33,[101] of *remigrare* in

---

94. See Haffter, *Untersuchungen*, pp. 86 ff.

95. Cf. *Amph.* 1069, *Men.* 1054. Acidalius and Ussing wanted to alter the paradosis to *accurrite*.

96. Cf. Leo, *Analecta Plautina* II (Göttingen 1898), p. 33 (= *Ausg. kl. Schr.* I 154).

97. Naevius, *Carm.* fr. 41.

98. See above, p. 110, n. 64.

99. See above, p. 109, n. 60.

100. *Colere*, "*uitam colere*," occurs only here and at *Pseud.* 202 (*canticum*) in republican drama. There are no instances in Caesar and Cicero and only a few in the historians; see *TLL* III.1672.54 ff.

101. Elsewhere in republican drama only at Ennius, *Sc.* 45.

*v.* 47;[102] the nominal phrase *inruptionem facere* in *v.* 42;[103] the prosody of the perfect form *dormierunt* in *v.* 21;[104] the frequent use of asyndetic dicolon—*qui edistis multo fecistis sapientius,* | *qui non edistis saturi fite fabulis* at *vv.* 7–8, *exsurge praeco, fac populo audientiam* at *v.* 11, *domum abeant, uitent ancipiti infortunio* at *v.* 25, *tacitae spectent, tacitae rideant* at *v.* 32, *canora hic uoce sua tinnire temperent,* | *domum sermones fabulandi conferant* at *vv.* 33–4, *nunc dum occasio est,* | *nunc dum scriblitae aestuant* at *vv.* 42–3, *eius nunc regiones limites confinia* | *determinabo, ei rei ego sum factus finitor* at *vv.* 48–9; the frequent use of anaphora—*et qui...et qui* in *v.* 6, *qui...qui* in *vv.* 7–8, *tacitae...tacitae* in *v.* 32, *nunc dum...nunc dum* in *vv.* 42–3, *eius...ei* in *vv.* 48–9; the frequent placing of verbs in front of their subjects—*iubet* in *v.* 4, *sedeate* in *v.* 5, *obrepet* in *v.* 14, *sit* in *v.* 23; the chiastic arrangement of *v.* 25 *domum abeant, uitent ancipiti infortunio*; the alliterative phrases *fite fabulis* in *v.* 8, *inpransum incedere* in *v.* 10, *uarientur uirgis* in *v.* 26, *tinnire temperent* in *v.* 33. Occurring all together in the space of forty-seven senarii they could be argued to have a paratragic effect of the sort indicated by Plautus himself at *Pseud.* 703–7:

(PSEVD.) io te te turanne te te ego qui imperitas Pseudolo
quaero quoi ter trina triplicia tribus modis tria gaudia

102. If *remigrare* has its normal meaning (cf. Plautus, *Epid.* 569, *Persa* 685), the lack of any previous reference to the plot is puzzling. Muretus, however, *Var. Lectt.* xvii 14, compared Cato, *Agr.*, praef. 4 *nunc ut ad rem redeam* and Sallust, *Iug.* 4.9 *nunc ad inceptum redeo*; cf. also Cicero, *Cael.* 6 *ut ad me reuertar*, 37 *redeo nunc ad te Caeli uicissim*. *Re-* is frequently used without the meaning of "back" or "again" in tragedy (Pacuvius 263 *retinere*, Accius 95 *reticere*, 336 *reuisere*, 447 *remanere*) and in passages of heightened style elsewhere (see W. Schoenwitz, *De re praepositionis usu et notione* [Diss. Marburg 1912], pp. 43 ff.). On *re-* compounds in religious language see E. Fehrle, *WSt* xlix (1931), 102 ff.

103. Contrast Plautus, *Amph.* 1048 *intro rumpam in aedis*, *Mil.* 460, *Rud.* 570. A number of such phrases occur once or twice in Plautus (*ascensionem, censionem, collationem, excidionem, legirupionem, reuorsionem, seditionem, suppositionem facere*) and not at all in Terence, who has only the commonplace *mentionem facere*.

104. Such forms occur elsewhere in comedy only at the ends of verses and cola. Their absence from tragedy may be accidental.

artibus tribus tris demeritas dem laetitias de tribus
fraude partas per malitiam per dolum et fallacias;
in libello hoc obsignato ad te attuli pauxillulo.
(CAL.) illic homost.     (CHAR.) ut paratragoedat carnufex.

I should contend nevertheless that the verses make better
dramatic sense when understood as taking off directly the ways
of speaking of a real-life Roman *imperator*. The apparently paratragic elements in their verbal and phrasal style merely under-
line the prologising actor's pomposity; such a person would
have had to use every resource to inflate himself to the size of a
magistrate and so the composer of the verses made him throw
out words and phrases more appropriate to tragedy than to
comedy.

The substance of *vv.* 1–2 will be held to invalidate the whole of
the foregoing interpretation of *vv.* 3–49. It does if the verses
come from the same author's hand. They sound, however, like
the work of someone with more scholarship than theatrical
talent trying to make a point about a text already in existence.
Their tone does not fit with that of the *imperator histricus*.

Osann and Ritschl condemned *vv.* 3–49 as post-Plautine. The
signs of lateness which they saw in the references to *subsellia* at
*v.* 5 and the *palma* at *v.* 37 are probably not really there. The
metaphorical language used at *Trin.* 706—*facile palmam habes:
hic uictust, uicit tua comoedia*—suggests that early second century
audiences were acquainted with competitions for actors if not
for poets.[105] The accounts of conservative opposition to the
building of a permanent stone theatre given by the classical
historians need not be interpreted to mean that there were no
fixed seats of any kind for early second century spectators.[106]

---

105. Plautus, *Amph.* 69 has been suspected. For actors' competitions in the
first century see Cicero, *Att.* IV.15.6. The ivy of Dionysus was the symbol of
victory at the Athenian festivals (see Olck, *RE* v [1905], s.v. *Epheu*, 2838),
not the palm of Apollo (see Steier, *RE* xx i [1941], s.v. *Phoenix*, 401). One
cannot therefore talk of heedless translation of the Attic original.

106. See P. Fabia, *RPh* xxi (1897), 11 ff., W. Beare, *CR* LIII (1939), 51 ff.

On the other hand it is wrong to argue, as Abel does,[107] that the mention of the lictor's rods in *v.* 18 guarantees an early date, i.e. one preceding the passing of those *leges Porciae* which forbade the flogging of Roman citizens by the magistrates. There is no suggestion in the *Poenulus* prologue that anyone but the actors and stage hands was in danger of having the rods put about him. Whether or not actors were of servile status,[108] it is pretty certain that the authorities could deal with them in ways they would hesitate to apply to citizens of the upper classes.[109] Part of the humour of the *Poenulus* actor's pose is that he imagines that he is removing for the moment one of the hazards of normal theatrical life. Osann and Ritschl were wrong to say that *vv.* 3–49 could not be Plautine. Still there is no good reason for going to the opposite extreme and saying that they must be Plautine.

Verses 55–8 certainly come from a different hand from the one which composed *vv.* 3–49. Here there is a drastic change of metaphor. The prologising actor is no longer an *imperator* presiding over the survey of land to be divided among *coloni*. He is merely a private citizen presenting an account of his property to the censors' assistants.[110] The members of the audience now have the superior position.[111] The account of the plot given in *vv.* 59–120 has a tone befitting the nervous citizen under examination by the censors rather than the imperious magistrate; one notes the ingratiating gossip at 62–3, the servile insolence of 80–2, and the cautious plea for a favourable hearing at 116–17.

The information about the Greek comedy underlying the *Poenulus* script given in *vv.* 50–4[112] looks as if it was inserted at

107. *Die Plautusprologe*, p. 89.     108. See above, p. 103, n. 25.
109. See Plautus, *Amph.* 81–5, *Asin.* 946, *Cist.* 785.
110. On the *iuratores* see Mommsen, *Staatsr.* II¹ 362.
111. Nevertheless the *iuratores* have to come to the theatre to examine the actor and his *argumentum*. Ordinary citizens went to the *Campus Martius* or the *Forum* for examination.
112. C. E. Geppert (edition of *Poenulus*, Berlin 1864) rightly marked a lacuna after *v.* 53 in which the name of the Greek comedian and perhaps a

the time when scholars were taking an interest in the early plays. The mention of the Latin poet's name looks equally late. Comparatively few of the eighteen prologues which attach to Plautine scripts do this and at least two of those which do[113] contain indisputable signs of scenic interpolation. We possess the prologues that were delivered at performances of Terence's comedies during Terence's own lifetime. The prologists spoke of Terence in the third person without actually naming him. In fact none but the names of dead poets are mentioned: i.e. those of Naevius, Plautus, Ennius and Caecilius. The hated Luscius Lanuvinus remained as anonymous as Terence himself. Osann[114] and Ritschl[115] were surely right to condemn such passages as this one and *Asin.* 9–12, *Cas.* 30–4, *Men.* 3, *Merc.* 9–10, *Mil.* 86–7, *Pseud.* 1–2, *Trin.* 8–20, *Truc.* 1–3, *Vid.* 6–7.

Verses 1–2, *Achillem Aristarchi mihi commentari lubet;* | *inde mihi principium capiam, ex ea tragoedia*, have always been taken to come from the same hand as *vv.* 3–49.[116] I should separate them from the latter verses and treat them as of the same character as *vv.* 50–4, i.e. as a semi-learned addition of the time when interest in the comedies of Plautus revived in the Roman theatre.[117] Academic students of Attic comedy liked to point out where their author had a passage of tragedy in mind;[118] so too did those of Roman comedy.[119] They recognised most

literal translation of Καρχηδόνιος would have been mentioned. It seems to me necessary to mark a further lacuna after *v.* 54 to contain a reference to the title *Poenulus* (cf. *Trin.* 20). *Patruus* is best taken as one of the *tria nomina* of the Latin playwright.

113. *Casina* and *Pseudolus*.

114. *Anal. crit.* pp. 161 ff.

115. *Parerga*, pp. 233 ff.

116. Fabia, *RPh* xxi (1897), 24, argued that such a reference to the *Achilles* could only have been made during Ennius' lifetime.

117. Terence mentions Ennius with Naevius and Plautus as being the classical poets of the contemporary (comic?) stage at *Andr.* 18.

118. Cf. the scholia to Aristophanes, *passim*.

119. Cf. Donatus, Ter. *Eun.* 590. The paucity of such remarks probably reflects an actual tendency of Terence to avoid parody of the other genre. A body of Plautine scholia might have a very different appearance.

easily, of course, an opening verse or group of verses.[120] Ancient writers were even more anxious than moderns to begin a work in an impressive and memorable way.[121] Beginnings certainly stuck in the readers' minds; wherever we have a number of ancient quotations of a play the great majority come from near the beginning.[122] Writers wishing to refer to another literary work often referred to the opening words of the text[123] rather than to the title given at the end of the roll or inscribed on the σίλλυβος. The composer of *vv.* 1–2 may have himself observed an accidental similarity between *vv.* 3–49 and something in Ennius' version of Aristarchus' 'Αχιλλεύς or he may have been aware of a contemporary scholar's observation. What the similarity alleged was it is now impossible to say. The words *inde mihi principium capiam, ex ea tragoedia* could be interpreted not only as "I shall open this play with an exact quotation of the *Achilles*"[124] but also as "I shall open this play with a speech like one in the *Achilles*."[125]

Many current interpretations of the word *commentari*—

120. Cf. Schol. Arist. *Thesm.* 1065.

121. For rhetorical treatises see A. E. Douglas, *CQ* LIV (1960), 68; for mathematical treatises Wilamowitz, *Hermes* XXXV (1900), 33; for legal works, F. Schulz, *History of Roman Legal Science* (Oxford 1946), p. 187, n. 3.

122. See Zillinger, *Cicero und die altröm. Dicht.* pp. 78 f.

123. Cf. Theocritus XIV.30; Cicero, *Fin.* 1.5; Propertius II.24.2; Ovid, *Trist.* II.261, 534; Persius, 1.96; Martial IV.14.13. Library catalogues seem to have listed the opening verses of poems as well as their titles; see E. G. Turner on Ox. Pap. 2455, part XXVII (London 1962), pp. 32 f.

124. *Ex ea tragoedia* is epexegetic of *inde*; for similar redundancy cf. Plautus, *Poen.* 78 *illic...in illisce aedibus*, Lucretius III.862 *in eo tum tempore*. For *principium capere* cf. Rhet. inc. *Her.* 1.6, Seneca, *Dial.* VII.8.4. For the use of *inde* with this and similar phrases cf. Ennius, *Sc.* 248, Ovid, *Fast.* III.125–6, Seneca, *Dial.* VII.8.4.

125. For *principium* as "dramatic prologue" cf. Suetonius, *Vit. Ter.* 3 *Adelphorum principium Varro etiam praefert principio Menandri*; Apuleius, *Socr.* 24 *ut Accius Vlixen laudauit in Philocteta suo in eius tragoediae principio*. Stoessl argues, *RE* XXIII ii (1959), Nachträge, s.v. *Prologos*, 2370, that, where the *Achilles* is concerned, the comedian refers to something other than a prologue scene. General considerations would support the conventional view.

"*scribendo imitari*,"[126] "imitate,"[127] "*afferre*"[128]—not only make
the interpolated verses sound quite intolerably pedantic even in
the context of the orthodox interpretation of *vv.* 3–49 but leave the
usage isolated in the remains of ancient Latin. Ussing's "*in
memoriam reuocare*" and Ernout's "remettre en mémoire" are
much more credible. One could, however, take *commentari* as
actors' jargon, as the equivalent of "apply the mind to,"
"study," "con" (i.e. with a view to acting a role), and secure
some continuity between *vv.* 1–2 and *vv.* 3–49. The prologist
would have spoken *vv.* 1–2 as an actor who had frequently
played the leading role in Ennius' adaptation of the 'Αχιλλεύς.[129]
A parallel usage of *commentari* is indirectly evidenced from the
schoolroom: Plautus, *Truc.* 735–8 *litteras didicisti: quando scis,
sine alios discere* | *—discant dum mihi commentari liceat* (Itali:
*argentarilliceam* codd.), *ni oblitus siem.* | *—quid erit interea magistrae*
(Buecheler: *magister* codd.), *dum tu commentabere?* | *uolt illa itidem
commentari. —quid? —rem accipere identidem.*[130] However the
switch from actor-scholar to actor-general at *v.* 3 offers as much
difficulty to dramatic interpretation as the switch back to
actor-scholar at *v.* 50 and that to actor-private citizen at *v.* 55.

CONCLUSION

The now orthodox view of the verses given to the prologising
actor in the extant script of the *Poenulus* is that with the exception of one or two here and there they all come from the same
hand which composed most of the rest of the script, i.e. that of
Plautus himself. My analysis suggests that the true situation is
much more complicated. Verses 3–49 come from a poet of
considerable skill and imagination; 55–120 from a second poet

126. So Forcellini–de Vit. Muretus claimed (*Var. Lectt.* xvii 14) to have
seen a manuscript with *mihi imitari* instead of *mihi commentari*.

127. So Lewis and Short, Riley, Nixon, Duckworth.

128. So Bannier, *TLL* iii 1864.19.

129. For Roman actors performing in both tragedy and comedy see
Cicero, *Orat.* 109.

130. Cf. Plautus, *Cist.* 509 and Leo's note.

who may have possessed equal powers of imagination but did not think it necessary to display them in writing prologue verse;[131] 1–2 and 50–4 from yet a third poet, one with more scholarly knowledge than dramatic sense. It is not necessary to identify any of the three with Plautus himself. Ritschl's blanket condemnation may be a just one. Still the comic effects sought in *vv.* 3–49 are such as are frequently sought in passages of the twenty-one *comoediae Varronianae* which no one has ever thought of athetising. In any case what our tradition presents as the prologue of the *Poenulus* is an editor's conflation of several acting scripts.[132]

131. Verse 79 puts the date of composition before the destruction of Carthage (146 B.C.).

132. C. O. Brink, A. T. Cole, C. M. Dawson, G. Luck and O. Skutsch have given me help in the writing of this paper. No one but myself should be blamed for the general line of argument.

# Nine Epigrams from Pompeii
## (*CIL* 4.4966–73)

DAVID O. ROSS, JR.

# Nine Epigrams from Pompeii
## (*CIL* 4.4966-73)

IN 1883 our knowledge of one genre of Latin poetry was roughly doubled: fragments of nine epigrams, three of which were substantially complete, were found scratched on the outside wall at the west entrance gate of the Small Theatre in Pompeii and were recognized almost immediately as examples of pre-neoteric, amateur verse inspired by Hellenistic epigram, a genre represented until then only by the five epigrams of Aedituus, Licinus, and Catulus (Morel, *FPL*, pp. 42-3, 46). A faint note of enthusiasm can be detected in the words of those who read and studied the *graffiti* at the time, but since then the epigrams have again been almost universally forgotten, not only by Lovers of Poetry (whose lack of enthusiasm may be freely pardoned), but even by historians of Latin literature[1] seeking to reconstruct this important, though dark, area of poetic development. It would seem worthwhile, then, to sketch a history of the epigrams since their discovery, to present the text in a purer form than that which can easily be had today, and to discuss briefly the importance of these fragments and their place in the development of Latin poetry.

1. The few literary historians who grant more than a passing reference to these epigrams have often confused what little was originally clear about them. H. Bardon (*La littérature latine inconnue* II [Paris 1956], pp. 226-7) does give the text of the first, but mentions it in a Neronian context, assigns it to the wrong location (the house of a later Tiburtinus), and says nothing more; there is no mention of them in his full discussion of the epigrams of Aedituus, Licinus, and Catulus. (Bardon's extraordinary lapse can be traced to a careless reading of della Corte's study of the Pompeian Tiburtini.) My own attention was first drawn to these epigrams by a reference by W. B. Sedgwick ("Catullus' Elegiacs," *Mnem.* 3 [1950], 64—an extremely suggestive study).

## I

Sogliano, in his original publication of the *graffiti* in 1883,[2] relates how Mau had drawn his attention to certain letters scratched on a wall of the Small (Covered) Theatre, built at the time of Sulla, and how they had uncovered the rest of these *graffiti* by removing the wall of the later gladiatorial school (dating not before the time of Claudius) which had been built over them; the *graffiti* had then been taken to the Naples Museum for further study. The transcription originally published by Sogliano was, he says, from his own apograph, though he had had the benefit of comparing it with Mau's.

Considerable credit must be given to Buecheler, who, in the same year, recognized both the nature and the importance of these poems.[3] He too had Mau's help, and quotes from a letter some of Mau's comments on the difficulties both he and Sogliano had had in reading certain letters of the *graffiti*.[4] At the same time Baehrens' attention was attracted by the discovery, and he saw fit to make his own restorations of the first epigram.[5] Buecheler's publication in his *Carmina Latina Epigraphica* (nos. 934–5) in 1897 reproduced his earlier restorations with additional comment, but his text was still based mainly on Sogliano's first transcription.

Buecheler's original enthusiasm was hardly contagious, nor did his insights, tucked away in the sombre gloom of that monument of nineteenth-century *Wissenschaft*, find a receptive audience. In 1908 another Pompeian, F. C. Wick, discussed the epigrams at length, torturing Latinity to no other purpose, it seems, than to explain what Buecheler may or may not have had

2. *Not. d. Scavi* 1883, pp. 52–3.

3. "Pompejanisch-Römisch-Alexandrinisches," *Rh. Mus.* 38 (1883), 474–6.

4. *Loc. cit.* p. 474, n. 1. Mau's remarks to Buecheler will be cited here as Mau (1883).

5. (*Fleckeis.*) *Jahrb. für Phil.* 127 (1883), 798.

in mind when he restored the text.[6] In one way, however, Wick's precedent has been binding: the poems have since been considered sacred territory for epigraphers alone, where *grammatici* have regarded themselves as the *profani*.

Next on the stage is Mau, who re-entered in 1909 to publish his own text, with a careful and faithful (it would appear) copy of the original letters ("litterarum formas ut potui expressi"), in *CIL* 4.4966–73: his own apograph, he in turn notes, had been corrected by Zangemeister. The plot thickens, and new interest is added by noting how Mau's new publication (or is it really Zangemeister's?) often differs from Sogliano's original, and sometimes even from Mau's own (as he communicated to Buecheler) almost twenty-five years before.

Another long intermission precedes the next act, which takes place around 1930. The actors are again Pompeians and epigraphers, whose deeds need not be chronicled here in any detail. The text of three of the poems was presented by della Corte and an attempt was made to establish the poet, a man who signed himself Tiburtinus, in an old Pompeian family.[7] Magaldi[8] reprinted della Corte's text, provoking a certain amount of indignation from his reviewer Ribezzo,[9] who in turn supplied his own restorations after calling Magaldi's verses "prebücheleriani", an epithet of impossible validity, indicating, however, the curious muddle created by those few concerned with the epigrams at that time. Meanwhile the three more nearly complete epigrams had been republished in *CIL* (1². 2, nos. 2540 a, b, c) in 1931 by Lommatzsch, whose text is a strange conflation including one new, but unassigned, suppletion.

6. "Vindiciae Carminum Pompeiorum," *Atti della Reale Acc. di Arch., Lett., e Belle Arti* 25 (Naples 1908), II, 216–18.

7. *Pompei: I Novi Scavi* (Pompeii 1930), pp. 78–9; *I MM. Lorei Tiburtini di Pompei* (Pompeii 1932), pp. 19–21.

8. "Le inscrizioni parietali Pompeiane," *Atti della R. Acc. di Arch., Lett., e Belle Arti*, n.s. 11 (Naples 1929–30), II, 156–7.

9. *Riv. Indo-Greco-Italica di Filologia, Lingua, Antichità* 16 (1932), Fasc. I–II, 106.

Degrassi has recently published his text of three of the epigrams,[10] but (perhaps wisely) made no attempt to clarify the tangle of suppletions and restorations; his *apparatus* is deceptively simple, and unhelpful.

This review has seemed necessary for several reasons. First, no one again may be able to consult the original *graffiti*: they seem to have disappeared.[11] Mau's copy is thus the closest one can get to the original, but even this can be used only with certain reservations. Yet it seems doubtful, judging from the obvious difficulty recorded by those who first studied the *graffiti* in making out certain crucial letters (or even in deciding if at certain points any letters at all were to be seen), that even direct consultation would serve any purpose, even a negative one. It is necessary, then, to examine carefully every available bit of evidence we have concerning the state of the original *graffiti*, to make sure that certain assumptions continually made about them are valid, and to search the words of those who worked with the originals for any indication that their published assertions might conceal some doubt or hesitation about what they actually saw on the wall. Finally, every text of the epigrams so far published is based on certain false reconstructions: no editor after Sogliano and Mau perhaps realized what the original state of these *graffiti* must have been, and consequently most suppletions appear either too strict or too free. It will be of some use, then, to attempt to describe fully the state of the original text at each point, *in usum editorum*, in the hope that the obvious importance of these epigrams will attract the attention of literary historians once again.

10. *Inscriptiones Latinae Liberae Rei Publicae* II (Florence 1963), no. 1125, 312–13.

11. No editor after Mau claims to have seen the original *graffiti*. Sogliano definitely stated that he and Mau had moved them to the Naples Museum, and perhaps they are still in some storage room there; I have been unable to find out if this is so. Prof. Carlo Giordano, now in charge of *graffiti* at Pompeii, has kindly informed me that they have been lost for at least twenty years.

## II

The text of all the epigrams follows: only what may be read with certainty is offered. The text is followed by a discussion of what must have been the original arrangement of the epigrams on the wall and of the placement of the signature "Tiburtinus." I then offer, for each epigram, a line-by-line analysis of any difficulties in assuming the remains of certain letters, a complete (it is hoped) catalogue of suppletions and restorations, and whatever comment seems necessary for those who would supply and restore for themselves. In pointing out certain trivial mistakes or misreadings by Sogliano, Buecheler, and Mau my criticism will seem captious and unnecessary: my purpose in so doing, however, is to stress the caution with which we must use their reports, which are now, after all, our only source for the text of these poems.

1. *CIL* 4.4966 ( = *CLE* 934):
   ...t[?]ui me oculei pos⟨t⟩quam deducxstis in ignem
   ...vim vestreis largificatis geneis
   ...non possunt lacrumae restinguere flam⟨m⟩am
   ...cos. ?.incendunt tabifican⟨t⟩que animum
   TIBURTINUS EPOESE ( = *CLE* 935.13)

2. *CIL* 4.4967 ( = *CLE* 935.1–2):
   ...veicinei [vesci nei?] incendia participantur
   ...flammam tradere utei liceat

3. *CIL* 4.4968 ( = *CLE* 935.3–6):
   ...bus per vic......[a]morem
   ...etur dei........⎫
   ...cios  .........⎬ .?.stost
   ...h[?]uc ........⎭ t

4. *CIL* 4.4969 ( = *CLE* 935.7–10):
   ...n ore d[?]...
   ...sumat aut ea va...
   ...sumpti opus est a...
   ...udam aut ei[?]...dai...

5. *CIL* 4.4970 (= *CLE* 935.11–12):
   ...habere aiunt eum...que locare
   ...vi...um...deo condere uti liceat

6. *CIL* 4.4971 (= *CLE* 935.14–16):
   sei quid amor valeat nostei, sei te hominem scis,
   commiseresce mei, da veniam ut veniam

7.
   flos veneris mihi de

8. *CIL* 4.4972 (= *CLE* 935.17–20):
   caesia sei n...
   sei parvom p...
   es bibe lude...
   nec semper...

9. *CIL* 4.4973 (= *CLE* 935.21–3):
   solus amare v...
   multa opus sunt s...
   quod nesceire dare...

*Arrangement and signature*

Only Mau (1909) indicates (clearly though indirectly) how
these epigrams were grouped on the wall: the first five were
inscribed in one column (note also that the beginning of each
line of these five epigrams is damaged), and the last four in
another column, the top of which was to the right of the fourth
epigram of the first column. It is necessary to get a clear picture
of this arrangement, for on it depends the question of the
signature TIBURTINUS EPOESE. Sogliano, and hence Buecheler,
considered that it followed the fifth epigram, but Mau (1909)
placed it after the first and noted, " *Tiburtinus epoese* (pro
ἐποίησε) haud dubie ad hoc carmen pertinet, a quo non recte
diviserunt Sogliano et Buecheler." Lommatzsch, who may
possibly have seen the original (though he makes no claim to
have done so), notes about the signature simply "a dextera,

litteris maioribus," and places it, with Mau, after the first. It can therefore be inferred that the signature stood at the top of the second column (which led Sogliano to record it after the fifth epigram), but had originally been intended to accompany only the first epigram, to the right of which it was placed. The question is of some importance (see below). Mau was certainly right in restricting the signature to the first epigram: it did *not* stand after the fifth (though one can now see why Sogliano, for convenience, so listed it, and why Buecheler in turn assumed from Sogliano's listing that it did); it stood well above the epigrams of the second column (which began on a line with the fourth epigram of the first column) and so cannot be taken with the last four epigrams; and further, just because of its rather confusing relation to the *group* of epigrams, we can infer that it must have been written to accompany the first epigram before the inscriber had thought of adding the other eight epigrams (its position would not have been confusing when only one epigram stood on the wall).

### Comments on the text

Before discussing specific problems and readings in each line, it may be helpful to paraphrase the content and comment on the relationship of the first two epigrams. Restoration will of course depend upon the interpretation of the remains of each line, which in turn will often depend on how one feels the gaps should be filled, a vicious circle allowing no easy or convincing way out. However, the words of the first epigram dictate the following paraphrase (with the basic possibilities for restoration indicated):

> After you, my eyes, led me forcibly into the fire of love,
> You pour down your cheeks the full force of your
> [*either* tears to extinguish the fire you
> kindled (*as Baehrens*), *or* fire (*as Ribezzo*);
> *or the line may be restored to mean* you do
> not supply tears in sufficient quantity to

> put out the fire (*as della Corte after a*
> *suggestion of Buecheler*)].
> But tears cannot put out this flame,
> [and even they] burn...and waste my spirit.

The second epigram (as will be argued more fully below) seems to be an answer to this, and a simple one: "Neighbors share their fires: why don't you do likewise?" The text as we have it allows numerous possible variations of this answer, but the basic sense must remain the same.

*1, line 1:* Mau, in his letter to Buecheler (1883), admitted that he had not seen the crossbar of the first *t*; Sogliano had recognized it, however, and, after Mau had expressed his doubts, had verified it, and Mau later (1909) printed the *t* without comment. Mau's original doubt about the *t* is, however, sufficient reason to allow the possibility of another letter, perhaps an *i* or even an *s*. In addition, if this letter were a *t*, it would be the only one in all of the nine epigrams formed with a long vertical stroke (if Mau's copy can be trusted in such detail), a stroke almost always representing a long *i* and occasionally a short *i*.[12] Though this letter has always been printed as a *t*, editors may feel justified in restoring an *i* (or even an *s*).

Buecheler's *quid fi*]*t?* has always been accepted as a probable suppletion, but *aedi*]*tui* Baehrens, *atta*]*t* Ribezzo.

*1, line 2: vim* appears certain. Preceding this are the traces of three letters, though according to Mau (1883) Sogliano had at first not seen any trace of the first two of these letters and had recognized (and published) them only after Mau had pointed them out. (It is important to note this, as only one publication[13] indicates just how unclear these three letters must have been—so unclear as to have at first completely escaped Sogliano.)

12. *t* is always formed with a short vertical stroke, the only exception being the initial *t* of the signature *Tiburtinus*—but this is a somewhat different matter.

13. Lommatzsch, sensibly, gives in his *CIL* transcription no indication that any letters are to be seen before *vim*.

Sogliano's original publication thus prints NAD VIM, with no indication of the state of the first two letters, and Mau described (to Buecheler, 1883) these three letters, "erst N und nicht IV, dann obere Stücke wie von A und cursivem *d*, dann sicher VIM." Yet later (1909) Mau retracted only his opinion about the third of these letters ("tertium enim signum potest esse B, non D, cuius scriptor noster constanter aliam formam exhibet"), and, though he expressed doubt about the others ("ceterum haec tria signa admodum detrita et incerta sunt"), there is no indication just how unclear these letters must have been. Consequently some editors have felt constrained to restore, as Buecheler did, *no]n ad vim*; and others, relying on Mau (1909), would have to deal with the impossible combination NABVIM. Furthermore, Sogliano (and consequently Buecheler) noted slight damage just before *vim*, indicating even less certainty about the letters preceding *vim*. Thus, here again editors should no doubt feel free to restore as they want, taking no account of what Sogliano or Mau claim to have seen.

*no]n ad vim* Buecheler (though "Lieber würde ich Z. 2 geradezu *aquam* haben, aber die Vorlage zwingt nun einmal zu sehen, dass man mit der 'Gewalt' fertig wird," and Mau (1909) remarks, "Expectaveris, ut recte monet Buech., *non acuam*, vel simile quid"); *lymphae] vim* Baehrens; *non acq]uam* della Corte, after Buecheler; *ignis] vim* Ribezzo.

*1, line 3:* No difficulties. *verum]* Buecheler; *vanum:]* Baehrens.

*1, line 4: hae]c os* Buecheler; *tun]c os* Ribezzo. After *os* there was a damaged surface where Mau could not determine if any letter had been (1883, "zwischen s und i beschädigte Stelle, nicht zu constatiren, ob da etwas stand"); if Mau's copy (1909) may again be trusted in this detail, there is no room between *os* and *incendunt* for anything but a single, narrow letter. Della Corte, however, read *ossa* in his text, poetically very attractive but epigraphically an unlikely restoration.

*2, line 1:* The difference between *vesci nei* and *veicinei* is epigraphically slight, an i and an s being both formed by a long

vertical stroke, the double curve of the s often being very slight.
Sogliano (and thus Buecheler) read *vesci nei*, and Mau (1909)
noted, "et ita ego quoque descripseram; *veicinei* scriptum esse
vidit Zangemeister," and printed *veicinei* without further
comment. With these two possibilities no certain restoration is
possible. *Illud agant*] *vesci, ni* Buecheler;[14] *hi* ["h.e. *oculi*"] *si
sunt*] *vesci, ni* Wick; *accurrunt*] *veicinei* Lommatzsch (?), simple
and attractive; *sic nobis*] *veicinei*, della Corte.

   *2, line 2: tu cura*] Buecheler; *igniferam*] della Corte.

   *3, line 1:* Mau's copy shows three vertical strokes before *bus*,
but no one has ever pretended to read them as letters. [*a*]*morem*
has been restored by all.

   *3, line 2:* The trace of a letter before *etur* (Buecheler (*CLE*),
"prima littera incerta, curvata dextrorsum") was taken as a *d*
by both Buecheler and Mau.

   *3, line 3:* Sogliano (and Buecheler) transcribed the beginning
of the line ...*o*...*cios*..., but, though Mau's copy shows the illegible remains of three letters before *cios*, he prints...*ocios*...as his
text: it seems unnecessary to retain the first *o* at either position.

   *3, lines 2–3, 3–4:* Sogliano transcribed *intaestost* (?) at the end
of the second line, and *t* at the end of the third; and so Buecheler
(*CLE*, who noted, however, "extrema non recte lecta, *in
triviost* sim. postulatur"). (Mau mentioned the uncertainty of
their positions, and printed them as the endings of the third and
fourth lines of the epigram, as seems more likely from his copy.)
*stost*, however, are the only letters we can now accept with
certainty: the first two letters of Sogliano's *intaestost* fall where
Mau's copy clearly shows a huge hole in the stucco, and therefore could never have been seen by Sogliano, while his third
letter (*t*) quite clearly appears in Mau's copy as an *n*; Mau, on
the other hand, though his copy shows ...*naestost*, prints *n in
istost* (?) as his text. This is the most serious discrepancy between
those whose word we now have to accept, and should indicate

   14. Further suggestions for suppletion are given by Buecheler, *CLE* 935.

caution (and at the same time free restoration whenever there is similar doubt or disagreement elsewhere).

*3, line 4:* Mau prints, and his copy indicates, *huc*; Sogliano and Buecheler *iuc*.

*4, line 1:* Two letters remain after *ore*. Sogliano read them as *d* and the trace of an *n*, which Buecheler took to be *da̧* (*CLE*, "quasi inperfecta *n* post *d*, *datur* aut *diu* aut aliud opus est"). Mau's copy would suggest that the form of the first of the two letters is a *d* and that the second was illegible, but in his text he prints them as *ap* (?), another indication of somewhat questionable procedure on his part.

*4, line 2:* This line may be taken as a further warning for those who read the epigrams only in the *CLE*. Buecheler there notes first, "*sumat, u* incertam esse indicat Sogl.": Sogliano transcribed *sumat* with no indication of any doubt, nor does Mau's copy indicate any unclarity about the *u* (had Sogliano communicated privately with Buecheler, mentioning doubts which do not appear in his published transcription ?); then Buecheler says, "post *eava* incipit velut *m* littera, *vana*?" Besides the obvious contradiction in this statement and suggestion, Mau's copy shows that what Sogliano transcribed as part of a possible *m* is the barest particle of a stroke disappearing into the gap in the stucco.

*4, line 4:* Buecheler tentatively restored *nudam* for *udam* at the beginning of the line. *ei* is doubtful (Sogliano transcribed *e* and the lower part of a vertical stroke, which Buecheler in *CLE* printed *ii*). Sogliano's transcription and Mau's copy both show a letter preceding *dai* which may be read as either an *n* (so Buecheler, *CLE*) or *u* (so Mau's text).

*5, line 1:* Of the *eum* read by both Sogliano and Mau, Buecheler said, "fortasse *num*[*mos*."

*5, line 2:* Buecheler (*CLE*) suggested either *video* or *studeo* as a restoration for *deo*.

*6, line 1:* Buecheler (*CLE*) notes, 'hiatum tolleret *novistei* aut *te esse h.* aut inversio extremorum," all of which is epigraphically unsound and poetically unnecessary (see below, note 20).

*6, line 2:* Sogliano (and therefore Buecheler) read *mihi*; *mei* is clearly to be read in Mau's copy.

*7:* Sogliano rightly recorded this as the first line of a separate epigram.[15] Mau's copy does not show that the stucco of the wall is broken off after the beginning of the line; the inscriber thus simply (though strangely) left the line incomplete, as if he had been interrupted while writing up another epigram, or had been composing directly on the wall when inspiration failed him.

*8, line 1: sei n*. . ., very clear in Mau's copy, was transcribed by Sogliano as *selin*. . .; he questioned the *l*, however, and printed the *i* as a small raised letter (which is actually the dot indicating word separation). Buecheler (*CLE*) interpreted this rightly. We can only wonder (and must keep in mind) how this clear sequence of letters (clear at least in Mau's copy) was so misread by Sogliano (especially as *sei* followed by the dot occurs at the beginning of the next line, where he read it correctly).

*9:* Buecheler (*CLE*) interprets, "solus amare valet qui scit dare multa puellae."

### III

It is time now to justify the preceding length and detail by outlining the nature of the epigrams and their importance for the literary historian. The following observations may appear too brief, though I hope they will not seem irrelevant. I hope to expand and support these points at greater length elsewhere in a fuller discussion of amateur epigram at Rome.

15. His division, ignored by all editors after Buecheler, is certainly right (cf. Mau's copy, in which the third line begins considerably to the left of the preceding two lines and is written with larger letters). Sogliano notes, "la mia numerazione si fonda unicamente sulla distanza materiale dei graffiti, quando non è possibile tener dietro al concetto." The preceding couplet certainly gives the impression of being a complete epigram in itself. We should thus properly speak of nine epigrams, not eight (as Mau's *CIL* numbering would have it).

The epigrams (or at least the first) are undoubtedly early. Though they may have been scratched on the wall at any time between the building of the Small Theatre (under Sulla) and the Claudian (?) construction of the wall of the gladiatorial school by which they were covered, the orthography, according to Mau (1909) indicates the earlier years of this period. Buecheler referred to the final -*s* of *largificatis*, to phonetic forms, and to the lexical forms *largificare* and *tabificare* when he placed them in the Sullan–Ciceronian period. Precise archeological dating is impossible, but not entirely important: what should concern us is the place of these epigrams in the development of Latin poetry, and this, fortunately, other considerations make clear enough.

Who was responsible for these epigrams? The first has been signed by a Tiburtinus, but need this mean (as has always been assumed) that the poet and the inscriber were one and the same? Mau (1909) states that all the epigrams were inscribed by the same hand, an assertion never challenged. This may well be so, but even a casual glance at Mau's copy shows great variation in size of the letters from one epigram to another; and, as we can tell from Mau's copy of *CIL* 4.4971, the epigrams in the second column followed no neat left-hand margin. Perhaps, then, even if the same hand is responsible for all the epigrams, they need not have all been written up at the same time. We may imagine the inscriber returning to the wall on different occasions, adding to what he had written previously as inspiration moved him. In support of this we can mention again the inference drawn above from the position of the signature: the signature, belonging only to the first epigram, seems to have been written when only the first epigram stood on the wall and before the inscriber had conceived the idea of adding an answer (and the other epigrams) to it.

It has been assumed, by Buecheler and others, that the second epigram is an answer to the first. This assumption can be taken one step further: a second poet answered the epigram of the first. This suggestion, at least, may be more likely than to imagine a single poet writing an obvious retort to his own epigram. The very fact that the first epigram is signed is strange, an unusual circumstance in that most of those, ancient as well as modern, who write *graffiti* prefer anonymity. It is therefore entirely possible, and even probable, that the inscriber copied the first epigram onto the wall, noted the author's name beside it, and then afterwards, moved by a happy inspiration, provided his own answer to it, leaving this unsigned; and at different times subsequently added further efforts of his own. The work of two poets may be seen: Tiburtinus, an ancestor of the old Pompeian family, known about town as the local laureate, author of the first epigram; and the anonymous inscriber of all nine, author of the last eight, who made this wall his own "poets' corner."

This convenient hypothesis can easily degenerate into romance: anyone who has stood at the gate of the Small Theatre next to which the epigrams had been inscribed can imagine Pompeian theatre-goers entering for a performance and glancing at the wall to see what new efforts had been added by the inscriber, now a local celebrity. But the hypothesis can explain more than the simple facts that the second epigram is a retort to the first and that the first is signed with the name of the poet: the first epigram is demonstrably different from the others, both older and more literary.

It was the first epigram, and the first only, for which Buecheler produced parallels from Hellenistic epigram: the theme of fire and the poet's eyes has its source in *A.P.* 12.91 and 92.[16] The epigram is obviously an elaborate conceit based on a motif common in Hellenistic epigram, and Buecheler was right when he compared it also with the five epigrams of Aedituus, Licinus, and Catulus; the theme of the fire of love, for instance, is the motif for the second epigram of Aedituus (p. 43 Morel), and the even more elaborate conceit of Licinus (p. 46 Morel),

---

16. *A.P.* 12.91 is now reprinted by Gow and Page in *The Greek Anthology: Hellenistic Epigrams* (Cambridge 1965) as Polystratos 1, and *A.P.* 12.92 as Meleager CXVI; cf. also *A.P.* 5.226 (Paulus Silentiarius). Other occurrences of the theme may be found.

for both of which other Hellenistic epigrams have been cited as sources. Clearly Tiburtinus was familiar with collections of Greek epigrams[17] and consciously tried to reproduce them in Latin.

For the other epigrams no Hellenistic sources are obvious:[18] the second poet seems to have relied more on native Latin elements (such as the word-play *da veniam ut veniam*) than on Hellenistic conceits: his retort to Tiburtinus' conflation of motifs appears less concerned with further elaboration in a Hellenistic manner than with a fairly simple statement in terms of the native Latin cliché of the *flamma amoris*; and in the other poems, as far as we can judge, there is little indication of Hellenistic inspiration. Two explanations are possible: the second poet was less literary, less concerned with Hellenistic epigram; and may well have been writing somewhat later, at a time when the first Latin excitement with the reproduction of Hellenistic epigram had passed and the form had become established and adaptable to more native taste and expression.

Two general points may be made in conclusion. First, the Tiburtinus epigram, though so thoroughly Hellenistic in its inspiration, is in no sense a translation: its motif, fire and the poet's eyes, is a conflation of several Hellenistic originals which may not even have been direct models for the poet. The poem is an imitation in spirit, a reconstruction, rather than a direct and meticulous copy. The second point follows naturally enough from this: there is no attempt to reproduce any of the stylistic niceties of the originals. Besides the "unpoetic" lexical features remarked by Buecheler (*tabificare, largificare*) and the pre-neoteric licence of the final -*s*,[19] none of the stylistic and technical

17. What collections were available at what times need not concern us here, but it is no longer valid to consider the *Garland* responsible for a sudden Latin interest in such poems. (See Gow and Page, vol. 1, p. xvi, "...the belief once held that he [Meleager] was the first anthologist is no longer tenable. Papyrus scraps of anthologies of sufficiently early date make it plain that he had predecessors.")

18. Any such assumption, of course, must remain as inconclusive as the fragments are incomplete.

19. Besides *largificati*(*s*) *geneis*, also 9, line 2, *multa opu*(*s*) *sunt*....

refinements introduced by the neoterics are found in these epigrams.[20] Though a rough dating may be suggested by these observations, it is far more important to realize that these efforts, while being literary in their interest in the themes of Hellenistic epigram, are outside any tradition of serious Latin poetry of their time. They, like the epigrams of Aedituus, Licinus and Catulus, are the work of amateurs and dilettanti not concerned with any development of style or technique.

The tradition established by the first discovery and interest in Hellenistic epigram was more widespread, and lasted longer, than is now realized; and certain important traces of it remain in later Latin poetry. The nine epigrams from Pompeii are of unique importance in reconstructing and understanding this tradition, for they represent what must have been an extensive body of amateur love poetry, based loosely on, and having as its first impetus, Hellenistic epigram, but technically (and therefore poetically) rough in the eyes of later literary Romans, a source of embarrassment to such as Antonius Julianus (Gellius 19.9), but too important a tradition for poets at the time of Cicero to ignore. Amateur verse, so vast a part of it necessarily second-rate, fortunately (for the reputation of Latin poetry) disappeared, but its disappearance should not lead to the assumption that it never existed or was altogether unimportant for those more gifted and serious craftsmen who wrote at the same time or later.

20. The amateur quality of the verse—that is, the lack of concern for the development of poetic style—can be seen in such metrical features as the elision of a long vowel before a short vowel (*me oculei* in the first epigram, and *sumpti opus* in 4, line 3), the general frequency of elision, and the hiatus *te hominem* (6, line 1), which reflects colloquial usage (as in Plautus) and indicates that the poet was little concerned with the metrical practices which had even then become established for hexameter verse. Other stylistic features then being evolved in serious poetry, such as characteristic patterns of word order, are conspicuous by their absence and need not be detailed here. These epigrams, however, are remarkably similar to those other of Aedituus, Licinus, and Catulus in their "unpoetic" stylistic character as well as in their Hellenistic inspiration.

# *Obscura de re lucida carmina*: Science and Poetry in *De Rerum Natura*

ANNE AMORY

# Obscura de re lucida carmina: Science and Poetry in De Rerum Natura

THE scientific portions of Lucretius' poem, that is, those passages which deal most explicitly and argumentatively with technical matters, are often disparaged, or at least tacitly ignored. At best they are tolerated for the sake of the proems and the "digressions." As Bailey puts it in the introduction to his edition:

> It has often been said that Lucretius has two styles, one the free style of the poet, in which he rises above the argument and writes sheer poetry, the other on a far lower plane, where the poet is hampered by his philosophy and the philosophy by his verse.[1]

Bailey himself argues that "there are not in fact two styles; the one is only the heightening or intensification of the other,"[2] but his argument is perfunctory and has certainly not prevailed against the general feeling among commentators and common readers alike that the technical parts of the De Rerum Natura are less interesting than the "poetic" passages.[3]

The consensus that Epicurean philosophy constitutes an intrinsically unpoetic subject is perhaps derived from a famous

1. Cyril Bailey, *Titi Lucreti Cari De Rerum Natura*, 3 vols. (Oxford 1947), I, 168. Henceforth this edition will be referred to simply as Bailey.

2. Bailey, I, 168.

3. Just to give one example out of many, J. Wight Duff, *A Literary History of Rome* (New York University Paperbacks 1960), p. 218, remarks: "The unpoetic is partly inherent in [Lucretius'] matter...Prosaic phrases of inferences and transition [recur] with wearisome insistence...Worse still there are long dreary flats." The same attitude can be found even in specialized studies of Lucretius; see e.g. Raymond V. S. Schoder, "Poetic Imagination versus Didacticism in Lucretius," *TAPA*, 76 (1945), xxxix.

passage in which Lucretius himself seems to say that his poetry is, in the modern cliché, merely the sugar coating on the bitter pill of his science. In his own image, he touches everything with the charm of the Muses just as doctors, when they try to give nasty wormwood to children, first smear the rims of the cup with honey. This simile occurs towards the end of book I, embedded in a longer passage in which Lucretius explains his aims. Since the passage is long, it is usually paraphrased or merely referred to, but we will have occasion later to refer to it in detail, so I quote it in full:

> Nunc age quod superest cognosce et clarius audi.
> nec me animi fallit quam sint obscura; sed acri
> percussit thyrso laudis spes magna meum cor
> et simul incussit suavem mi in pectus amorem
> musarum, quo nunc instinctus mente vigenti          925
> avia Pieridum peragro loca nullius ante
> trita solo. iuvat integros accedere fontis
> atque haurire, iuvatque novos decerpere flores
> insignemque meo capiti petere inde coronam
> unde prius nulli velarint tempora musae;            930
> primum quod magnis doceo de rebus et artis
> religionum animum nodis exsolvere pergo,
> deinde quod obscura de re tam lucida pango
> carmina, musaeo contingens cuncta lepore.
> id quoque enim non ab nulla ratione videtur;        935
> sed veluti pueris absinthia taetra medentes
> cum dare conantur, prius oras pocula circum
> contingunt mellis dulci flavoque liquore,
> ut puerorum aetas improvida ludificetur
> labrorum tenus, interea perpotet amarum             940
> absinthi laticem deceptaque non capiatur,
> sed potius tali pacto recreata valescat;
> sic ego nunc, quoniam haec ratio plerumque videtur
> tristior esse quibus non est tractata, retroque
> vulgus abhorret ab hac, volui tibi suaviloquenti    945

carmine Pierio rationem exponere nostram
et quasi musaeo dulci contingere melle.   [1.921–47]⁴

In interpreting this passage, it is easy to distribute the
emphasis wrongly, to overlook, for example, the force of *cuncta*
in *v.* 934 (see below pp. 152–3), or to attach too much importance to *primum* and *deinde*, as Bailey does in his note on this
passage, where he comments that Lucretius' "poetry is of
secondary importance and is *only* [italics mine] an attraction to
secure attention."⁵ The division which Lucretius appears to
make between his content and his form has encouraged those
whose interests are primarily philosophical, like Bailey, to
extract the message from the poem without letting more than
their lips be touched by the sweet coating of yellow honey.
Literary critics, meanwhile, have turned their attention to those
passages in the poem which might be called the rims where the
honey is thickest, appreciating the poetry, and ignoring the
message.

But the first half of the passage makes it clear that for
Lucretius his poetry is not merely ancillary to his philosophy,
as the wormwood-and-honey simile might by itself suggest.
His love of the Muses, his sense of being a great poet breaking
fresh ground, are obviously genuine, and his poetic ambitions
are as strong as his missionary zeal. As we shall see later
(below, p. 164), some of the language which he here uses
of himself and poetry, he uses elsewhere of Epicurus and
philosophy.

There are of course many who have not been misled into
regarding the poetry and philosophy in Lucretius as separate.
For example, in a penetrating and sympathetic study of
Lucretius, M. D. C. Tait remarks that Lucretius

> is one of the great poets of all literature. For the *De Rerum
> Natura* is not simply a scientific treatise with a moral,
> written in metrical form. Nor is its poetry incidental,

4. Verses 926 through 947 are repeated verbatim in IV.1–22.
5. Bailey, II, 757.

scattered here and there among scientific arguments to make them more attractive.[6]

But general appreciations have seldom received the support of a detailed study of the text; most critics have contented themselves with a few references to Lucretius' "startling imagery" and "the vivid naturalism of [his] descriptions."[7] There is also an understandable tendency to dwell on the more human and tractable parts of the Epicurean theory which Lucretius expounds—ethics and anthropology, for the most part.[8]

The plain fact, however, is that the bulk of the poem's scientific material is what we may call "physics." This may not interest modern classical scholars or amateur readers, but it must have interested Lucretius; poets do not spend three-fourths of their time working material which bores them or which they consider an unpromising subject for poetry. Nor can we say that Lucretius, having set himself the task of expounding Epicureanism in order to lessen the terrors of life, was forced to include even parts of the theory which neither interested him nor stirred his poetic impulses. For there were at least three main areas of Epicurean thought which Lucretius touched on, but did not deal with exhaustively. These are the *Canonice*, or rules of investigation; the moral theory; and thirdly the gods. It is hard to avoid the conclusion that Lucretius wrote at such length and in such detail about physics because it was precisely this part of Epicureanism which seemed to him most meaning-

6. M. D. C. Tait, "Lucretius," *University of Toronto Quarterly*, 2 (1932), 37. Cf. also C. H. Herford, "The Poetry of Lucretius," *Bulletin of the John Rylands Library* (Manchester 1917), pp. 271–2; and D. E. W. Wormell, "The Personal World of Lucretius," *Lucretius*, edited by Donald R. Dudley (New York 1965), pp. 46–7. (Henceforth this collection of essays will be referred to simply as Dudley.)

7. Tenney Frank, *Life and Literature in the Roman Republic* (University of California Paperback 1956), p. 245. Frank too, like Tait, says, *loc. cit.*, that "the poetic quality of [*De Rerum Natura*] is in no sense 'purple-patch' work," but he discusses Lucretius too briefly to document this assertion.

8. As Frank, for instance, does, *op. cit.* pp. 237–43.

ful, important, and interesting. Moreover, a careful reading of
the passage quoted above suggests that it is just these technical
details, this *obscura res*, which aroused his poetic impulses most
deeply.

We need not attempt a complete definition of the role of
Epicurean physics in the whole poem to understand the process
by which Lucretius turns his *obscura res* into clear song. If we
examine in detail almost any short section of the poem, we can
learn much about the way in which Lucretius expounds his
philosophy and sweetly spoken verse and touches it all with the
sweet honey of the Muses. The passage which I have chosen is
richer and more complex in its implications than many of the
passages which Bailey calls "arid."[9] But it is merely a question
of patience to demonstrate that the use of language and the
significant connections between scientific content and poetic
quality which are visible in the passage about to be discussed
operate elsewhere throughout the whole poem.

Again, I quote the whole passage for reference, though it is
long:

> Nunc age iam deinceps cunctarum exordia rerum
> qualia sint et quam longe distantia formis
> percipe, multigenis quam sint variata figuris;                335
> non quo multa parum simili sint praedita forma,
> sed quia non vulgo paria omnibus omnia constant.
> nec mirum; nam cum sit eorum copia tanta
> ut neque finis, uti docui, neque summa sit ulla,
> debent nimirum non omnibus omnia prorsum                      340
> esse pari filo similique adfecta figura.
> praeterea genus humanum mutaeque natantes
> squamigerum pecudes et laeta armenta feraeque
> et variae volucres, laetantia quae loca aquarum
> concelebrant circum ripas fontisque lacusque,                 345

9. Bailey, 1, 169; he does not seem to realize that the adjective tacitly
contradicts his contention (in the passage quoted on p. 145 above) that
Lucretius does not have two styles.

et quae pervulgant nemora avia pervolitantes;
quorum unum quidvis generatim sumere perge,
invenies tamen inter se differre figuris.
nec ratione alia proles cognoscere matrem
nec mater posset prolem; quod posse videmus                350
nec minus atque homines inter se nota cluere.
nam saepe ante deum vitulus delubra decora
turicremas propter mactatus concidit aras
sanguinis exspirans calidum de pectore flumen.
at mater viridis saltus orbata peragrans                  355
quaerit humi pedibus vestigia pressa bisulcis,
omnia convisens oculis loca si queat usquam
conspicere amissum fetum, completque querellis
frondiferum nemus adsistens et crebra revisit
ad stabulum desiderio perfixa iuvenci,                    360
nec tenerae salices atque herbae rore vigentes
fluminaque illa queunt summis labentia ripis
oblectare animum subitamque avertere curam,
nec vitulorum aliae species per pabula laeta
derivare queunt animum curaque levare:                    365
usque adeo quiddam proprium notumque requirit.
praeterea teneri tremulis cum vocibus haedi
cornigeras norunt matres agnique petulci
balantum pecudes: ita, quod natura reposcit,
ad sua quisque fere decurrunt ubera lactis.               370
postremo quodvis frumentum non tamen omne
quidque suo genere inter se simile esse videbis,
quin intercurrat quaedam distantia formis.
concharumque genus parili ratione videmus
pingere telluris gremium, qua mollibus undis              375
litoris incurvi bibulam pavit aequor harenam.
quare etiam atque etiam simili ratione necessest,
natura quoniam constant neque facta manu sunt
unius ad certam formam primordia rerum,
dissimili inter se quaedam volitare figura.      [II. 333–80]

Lucretius has just been discussing the constant motion of atoms; at the beginning of our passage he turns to the question of shape. Verses 333–41 are an introductory statement, a sample of the "unpoetic" passages in the poem. Certainly the words are not highly colored. But they contain several interesting pieces of language in them, pieces which Lucretius used often and deliberately, and whose force we are apt to overlook until we notice just how often. First there are the imperatives, *nunc age* and *percipe*. These are two of the small sleeve-plucking words by which Lucretius continually reminds us that he is saying something he cares about and wants the reader to understand clearly. Poets seldom indulge in such direct ways of capturing the reader's attention, but in Lucretius the very directness of his imperatives reminds one of the principle that attentive observation is the prerequisite of scientific knowledge, while their frequent repetition eventually gives them some of the poetic effect of a refrain.

Then there is the parenthetical *uti docui*, one of a great number of reminders and predictions which run through the poem, and which indicate that Lucretius sees the system as a whole and wants the reader not only to see what is being presented to him at the moment, but also to remember that the facts and phenomena of the system bear a certain relationship to each other which it is important to keep in mind.[10] The interrelation of facts is crucial not only for Epicurean physics but for any scientific investigation; a long poem must also have its parts disposed in a comprehensible pattern. Like the recapitu-

10. *Uti docui* occurs at least four more times: 1.539, II.1050, III.520, v.364. The alternative *quoniam docui* occurs: 1.265, 951; II.478, 522; III.31; IV.26, 45, 752; VI.43. Among the other reminding phrases are: *iam supera... ostendimus ante* [1.429]; and *quoniam...repertast* [1.504]. Admonitions and predictions of what Lucretius will discuss include: *expediemus* [II.183]; *ut noscere possis* [1.90]; *invenies...videbis* [1.450]; *licet hinc cognoscere* [II.143]; cf. the images of surrender, like *victus fateare necessest* [1.625], and passages like 1.921 (quoted p. 146 above) and 1.1114–17. B. Farrington, "Form and Purpose in *De Rerum Natura*," Dudley, pp. 19–34, argues well that Lucretius' injunctions are throughout addressed primarily to Memmius, but admits, p. 34, that the audience of general readers should heed them too.

lations of past action and predictions of the future that we find
in the Homeric epics, Lucretius' reminders of what he has shown
and anticipations of what he will show give his poem an order
which is satisfying emotionally as well as intellectually.

Next there is the fortunate circumstance that Latin has
relatively few single nouns for such concepts as relationship,
quality, extent, multiplicity, etc., so that Lucretius had to resort
to the indirect question. Syntactic preferences are important in
any long poem, and gradually the clusters of indirect questions
in *De Rerum Natura* become as much a poetic device as a
Homeric formula. For one thing they contribute to the alliteration which is such a marked feature of Lucretius' style, since
most interrogative words in Latin begin with *qu-* as do also most
of the causal particles. This coincidence contributes to the sound-
pattern which is one of the most distinctive features of Lucretius'
poem,[11] but it is also the chance which he, like any good poet,
makes flower to choice.

The crucial fact which Epicurean physics grasped is that the
qualities of the objects around us depend on the quantitative
relation of the parts which compose them. The parts themselves
are quality-less; it is only their relation to each other which is
important. This is what Lucretius expresses with his *qualia*s,
*quanta*s, and *quo*s. Furthermore, the fact that the difference in
what these words signify is brought about by a change of few
letters expresses in itself one of the important principles in
Epicurean theory, that a small change in the atomic constituents
of any thing brings about a change in the visible qualities, and
Lucretius often reminds us of this principle.[12] In the same way,
the different causal and interrogative conjunctions, by their
similarity of sound, reinforce on a sensuous level the abstract
principle that all the multiple phenomena of nature are governed
by a few basic causal relations.

11. See P. Friedländer, "Pattern of Sound and Atomistic Theory in
Lucretius," *AJP*, 62 (1941), 16–34 and Rosamund E. Deutsch, *The Pattern
of Sound in Lucretius* (Bryn Mawr 1937).

12. E.g. 1.196 ff., 823 ff., 912 ff.; 11.688 ff., 1013 ff.

Finally, the repetitions of *multum, omne, cunctus,* and *copia* are significant both poetically and scientifically. In themselves and for most Latin poets these are abstract words, colorless and common. But for Lucretius they are magic words (as "every" is for Blake, or "all' for Milton, or "things" for Wallace Stevens), because he was profoundly aware of the multiplicity, the fullness of the universe. Much the same attitude lies behind the fantastically detailed explorations of modern science: wonder at the very great number of entities, at their range in size, and at the variety of their shapes. It was not the common attitude of antiquity, which preferred to see the generic similarity of things and believe in the essential sameness of their substance. But Epicurean physics grasped clearly the discrete nature of the physical world, and it is not hard to see that Lucretius found this way of thinking deeply congenial to his poetic impulses.[13]

If now we look back at the passage in which Lucretius enunciates his poetic purposes (p. 146 above), we see that some of the language there, in what Bailey calls "exquisite verses, which have always been recognized as a *lumen ingeni*,"[14] is similar to that in the "arid" beginning of the passage from book II. It too begins *nunc age* and admonishes the reader to pay attention (*cognosce*). It uses indirect questions and causal clauses, not so thickly, but certainly noticeably. And it now appears that *cuncta* is a more emphatic word, if we consider the rest of the poem, than it first appeared to be in an isolated quotation.[15] If Lucretius says that he will touch *cuncta* with

13. This kind of statement is hard to prove without extended documentation, but any attentive reader of Lucretius is usually struck by the qualities of fullness and multiplicity in Lucretius' descriptions of the world around him. Compare, for instance, Horace's spare allusiveness to a picnic, Odes II.3.6–14 with Lucretius' brief but much lusher accounts of similar scenes in II.29–33 and v.1392–1404.     14. Bailey, II, 757.

15. Frequency alone does not illuminate the emotional color of words in a poet, but it is significant that *cunctus* appears 54 times in Lucretius and only 5 times in all of Horace. For references see J. Paulson, *Index Lucretianus* (Leipzig 1926) and Lane Cooper, *Concordance of the works of Horace* (Washington 1916).

poetic grace, he does not mean that he will embroider the work as a whole with a few splendid passages here and there, but that every detail, perhaps for him every word and letter, will have an aroma from the sweet honey of the Muses.

Let us return and look more closely at the second passage, from book II. Lucretius first states an abstract atomic principle, that atoms vary in shape, *vv.* 340–1, then goes on to the visible phenomena of the world, which occupy the bulk of our passage in verses 342–76. It might be debated whether Lucretius here offers analogies or examples of the principle stated in *v.* 341, but I think the point is that they are not quite one or the other.[16] The transitional word is *praeterea*, which is additive, not analogical like *velut*, *sicut*, etc.; nor is it quite the appropriate word to introduce a first example. The passage becomes more definitely analogical, but there remains a certain ambiguity about the matter for reasons which will emerge eventually (see below, pp. 166–7). In any case, we have a series which has begun in atomic terms, but continues with visible objects in the world which have all the secondary qualities, such as color and emotion, that the atomic end of the scale lacks.

This whole section, from 342 to 376, therefore has an intellectual relevance, both explicit and implicit, to the atomic

16. Bailey, II, 859, calls the passage "an appeal to the analogy of experience," but notices the difficulty here and in his note on *praeterea*, II, 860. Tait, *op. cit.* 37–8, remarks generally that Lucretius' use of analogy is "a distinctive feature...which gives full play to his remarkable powers of observation and description," but he makes no specific application. Frank, *op. cit.* p. 245, notices this passage among others as one of poetic power used "in the service of inductive logic," remarking that "[Lucretius'] pictures will always be found to derive from unusually accurate observations of nature so that they may serve their purpose as the starting points of the induction, or, when induction was impracticable, as a basis for some significant analogue. They are so indelibly presented that the argument which they carry cannot be forgotten." Gavin Townend, "Imagery in Lucretius," Dudley, p. 101, observes that "the visible world is accordingly relevant to the atomic structure in two ways: from observable processes we can infer general laws concerning the nature of unseen matter, and at the same time these processes are themselves examples of the laws in operation."

argument. Simultaneously it has connections with a surprisingly large number of the major emotional themes of the
poem, so that, if we analyze the passage in some detail, if we
look attentively at the ways in which both the argument and
the emotional themes are deployed, we can learn something
concrete about the techniques by which Lucretius infuses
poetry into his scientific material.

The explicit argument, with some implied steps in parentheses, runs somewhat as follows: not all atoms are alike in
shape, for there is an infinite number of them (and so it is unlikely that they should all be like each other). Men, beasts,
birds (of whom, or which, there is a large, though not infinite,
number) differ from each other even when they are of the same
species and therefore appear superficially alike. All these, plus
grain and shells, have different shapes, much as atoms do, for
they are all, including atoms, a result of natural creation and
are not shaped to one pattern.

This explicit argument is not entirely satisfactory,[17] but the
lack of logical precision allows Lucretius to express what is
really important to him, namely the underlying thought. This
runs as follows: atoms are infinite in number and varied, but
not infinitely varied, in shape. We know this by a combination
of observation of visible phenomena and inferences drawn
logically from these phenomena. This proves that the composition of the entire universe is of a piece, and this is a very
comforting thing to think—or fact to know—because it allows
us to operate in relation to the true nature of things as familiarly
and safely as we are accustomed to operate in relation to the
apparent nature of things which we see and feel around us.[18]

17. Bailey, for example, remarks uncomfortably, II, 859, "his arguments
are not as happy as usual."

18. For contemporary expressions of this feeling see almost any issue of
*Scientific American*; e.g. François Jacob and E. L. Wollman, "Viruses and
Genes," *Sc. Am.* 204 (June 1961), 93: "Almost everyone now accepts the
unity of the inanimate physical world. Physicists do not hesitate to extra-
polate laboratory results obtained with a small number of atoms to explain
the source of the energy produced by the stars. In the world of living things

In short, this passage serves the argument on two levels, first as one step in a series of detached statements expounding the Epicurean system of physics, and secondly as yet another piece of evidence for Lucretius' claim that an understanding of the true nature of things will free men from fear. Part of the poetic effect of these lines depends precisely on the complexity of their connection with the philosophical arguments of the poem. The same is true of almost all sections of argument, illustration, and analysis; and to appreciate fully the art of Lucretius the reader must constantly bear in mind the importance to him of both his explicit arguments and his underlying thoughts.

But the poetic effect of these lines depends even more obviously on the fact that they are interlocked with much of the human, emotional material in the poem—the parts dealing with superstition, fear, especially the fear of death, life, reproduction, love, and the problem of certainty. There are, for example, a number of similarities between our passage and the famous proem to the first book, which begins:

> Aeneadum genetrix, hominum divumque voluptas,
> alma Venus, caeli subter labentia signa
> quae mare navigerum, quae terras frugiferentis
> concelebras, per te quoniam genus omne animantum
> concipitur visitque exortum lumina solis:                    5
> te, dea, te fugiunt venti, te nubila caeli
> adventumque tuum, tibi suavis daedala tellus
> summittit flores, tibi rident aequora ponti
> placatumque nitet diffuso lumine caelum.
> nam simul ac species patefactast verna diei                  10
> et reserata viget genitabilis aura favoni,
> aeriae primum volucres te, diva, tuumque
> significant initum perculsae corda tua vi.
> inde ferae pecudes persultant pabula laeta

a comparable unity is more difficult to demonstrate; in fact it is not altogether conceded by biologists. Nevertheless, most students of bacteria and viruses are inclined to believe that what is true for a simple bacillus is probably true for larger organisms, be they mice, men, or elephants."

et rapidos tranant amnis: ita capta lepore           15
te sequitur cupide quo quamque inducere pergis.
denique per maria ac montis fluviosque rapacis
frondiferasque domos avium camposque virentis
omnibus incutiens blandum per pectora amorem
efficis ut cupide generatim saecla propagent.     [I. 1–20]

There are differences of detail and proportion between the
two passages, of course; but the important point is that the
theme of reproduction, which might go unnoticed in II.342–8 if
we regard these lines only as a piece of atomic argument, is infused into these lines by the verbal similarities to the first proem,
which is unmistakeably concerned with this theme. Seven words
are common to the first proem and our passage from book II: *pecudes, laeta, ferae, volucres, concelebro, generatim,* and *perge.*[19] In addition, different words are used to describe similar things: *armenta*
in II, *pecudes* in I; *laetantia loca aquarum* and *fontisque lacusque* in II,
*mare, amnes, fluviosque rapaces* in I; *nemora avia* in II, *frondiferasque
domos avium* in I. Moreover, both passages have images of rapid
motion, though in II it is the fish swimming (*natantes*) and the birds
who flock fluttering (*pervulgant pervolitantes*) which produce the
images, while the *armenta* who frisk and swim rivers (*persultant,
tranant amnis*) in I, only gather peacefully to drink in II.

That the theme of the regeneration of life is one of the most
important and complex elements in the *De Rerum Natura* is
obvious from its position and treatment in the first proem. It is
there closely connected with Venus, who is elsewhere related to
or merged with *Natura creatrix* or *gubernans.* This personification
of a force for order in the universe puts Epicurean physics in a
less purely scientific light than that in which we would otherwise
see it. Lucretius nowhere deals with the logical implications of this
personification, but the emotional necessity for an escape from a
completely mechanistic view of life is comprehensible both

19. There are of course striking variations in which words are applied to
what things; e.g. *pecudes* (clarified by *squamigerum*) means fish in II. Note also
the presence of a characteristically Lucretian compound in both passages:
*navigerum* in I, *squamigerum* in II.

intellectually and emotionally, and the results of this particular solution are visible throughout the poem.

We need not here explore all the complexities of the relation between Lucretius' Venus and Epicureanism.[20] It is perhaps sufficient to observe that the identification of Natura with Venus has at least three effects: it brings the natural world into close relation with *voluptas*, the center of Epicurean ethics; it fuses various mythological connotations with the science in the poem;[21] and it furnishes Lucretius with a means of dealing with the emotion of love. These ideas—love, pleasure, peace, a governing Nature, the reproduction of life—are firmly knotted in the first proem; from there a complex strand runs throughout most of the poem, sometimes tightly woven, sometimes so loose that only one or two threads are visible. At the other end of the strand, both emotionally and in the structure of the poem,[22] are fear,

20. See E. E. Sikes, *Lucretius: Poet and Philosopher* (Cambridge 1936), pp. 117–23, and especially J. P. Elder, "Lucretius 1.1–49," *TAPA*, 85 (1954), 88–120.

21. For example, Lucretius makes use of the fact that Mars is Venus' husband or lover, not only in the first proem, but throughout the poem in all the images of war and struggle of various kinds, atomic as well as human; he uses these images as counterpoints to the images of peace and union. The mythological relation between Mars and Venus in the first proem enables him to lend a kind of Empedoclean Love/Strife organization to his picture of atoms, thus giving him some poetic advantage—without compelling him to depart from strict Epicurean theory. See Elder, *op. cit.* 114–19; Bailey, II, 723 ff.; Wormell, *op. cit.* pp. 39–41; and W. S. Anderson, "Discontinuity in Lucretian Symbolism," *TAPA*, 91 (1960), 11–19.

22. The contrast between the bright opening and dark close of the poem has been commented on since Giussani; see Bailey, III, 1724, and Tait, *op. cit.* 36. Many incline to the view that this is a result of the supposedly unfinished condition of the poem; others favor the even more supposititious influence of a manic-depressive psychosis of Lucretius. Elder, *op. cit.* 93, n. 10, argues that Lucretius "intended, deliberately, to end with the depressing picture of the plague, contrasting so violently with the first and sixth proems, in order to move men into conversion through the time-honored method of frightening them into 'true religion'." Indeed all the books have bright beginnings and dark closes, with the exception of V, which ends on an ambiguous note; it seems probable that such contrasts were a deliberate poetic device.

superstition, war, death, and the degeneration of life. All this is crudely stated here, but the play of these ideas throughout the poem is very subtle, whether they appear directly, as in the proem to book I, or indirectly, as in the passage from book II, where Venus is not explicitly mentioned but is suggested by the similarities to the first proem which we have noted.

Nor is Venus the only divinity who haunts the list of analogies or examples in II.342–8. We have already mentioned a few verbal similarities between the opening lines of the passage from book II and Lucretius' statement of his poetic purpose (see above, pp. 146 and 153–4). The second section too, that is II.342–8, contains at least two echoes which evoke the Muses:[23] the birds which flit around the actual *nemora avia* recall Lucretius himself as the poet exploring the pathless tracts of the Pierian Muses.[24] Similarly, the real watering places in II.345 reflect the metaphorical virgin springs of poetry from which Lucretius drinks in I.926. We cannot here divagate into a detailed comparison of the verbal and imagistic similarities between the first proem and the passage on poetry, but it should be noticed that water is one of the chief connections, for Lucretius associates water with creative force, whether physical or artistic,[25] and he habitually uses the same imagery for poetic creation and for

23. The Muses and Venus are associated for Lucretius, to judge from his appeal to Venus to inspire his verse [1.24 ff.] and his invocation to Calliope as *hominum divumque voluptas* [VI.94]; cf. Elder, *op. cit.* 112 and 118.

24. Bailey translates *avia* as "distant" in both 1.926 and II.346, which is unfortunate because this translation disguises, as "pathless" does not, an important point—that the motion of visible things, like birds, corresponds to the constant, random motion of the atoms. It is clear from Lucretius' usage of *avius* that the principal connotation of the word is that of moving in various directions rather than along a track or path; see especially v.396, where it is used of the motion of the sun's chariot under Phaethon's uncertain control. Cf. Callimachus, *Aetia, prologue* (Pfeiffer, frag. 1), a parallel which Professor Christopher Dawson brought to my attention.

25. The connection between water and physical creation is obvious in nature and is exploited by Lucretius in such passages as the first proem and 1.250 ff. That between water and artistic creation we have observed in 1.927–8 (p. 146 above); cf. 1.412–13.

physical reproduction.[26] Thus the prominence of water in
II.342–8 immensely enriches the suggestiveness of the apparently
literal list of analogies (or examples), since water is intimately
associated with two of the major non-scientific themes of the
poem, Venus and poetry.

At line 347 of the passage from book II, Lucretius invites us
to take a representative of any species. We will find, he proceeds,
that different individuals of the same species differ among
themselves in shape, for otherwise mothers and offspring could
not distinguish each other, as we see they do, just as men can
tell each other apart. This brings us to *v.* 351, and here, from
352 to 365, Lucretius appears to abandon his atomic argument
in favor of a touching vignette of a mother cow looking for
her calf, who has been sacrificed. Actually the illustrative point
is not obscured: though all calves may look alike, they are not,
since the mother will not mistake any of the others for her own;
in the same way, atoms differ from each other. But the scene is
expanded far beyond what would be necessary if the atomic
argument were the sole consideration, and it carries emotional
overtones which link this passage with other non-scientific
themes in the poem.

One of the most important of these themes is that of religion.
In book I Lucretius warns the reader not to think that Epicureanism is impious, but instead *Religio* itself: *quod contra
saepius illa | religio peperit scelerosa atque impia facta* [I. 82–3]. He
goes on, in a famous and eloquent description, to adduce the
example of the sacrifice of Iphigenia by her father. Iphigenia's
sacrifice was extraordinary and barbarous; that of heifers was
standard and indeed generally regarded as a sign of piety, but
in book II Lucretius encourages us to view the sacrifice of this
particular calf as another *impium factum*. For the sacrifice of the
calf is not just stated, but described; the description is not so

26. One of the most constant images is that of *lumina*, which Lucretius
uses not only of physical creation, as in the famous Ennian phrase, *in
luminis oras*, but also of his poetry, as in 1.144. Cf. Anderson, *op. cit.* 2, n. 4,
and Elder, *op. cit.* 109–11.

extended as that of Iphigenia's sacrifice, but the phrases *delubra decora* and *turicremas...aras* make us visualize the whole scene, so that the next line, which describes the calf breathing out a warm river of blood from its heart, comes with a jolt. Then the grief of the mother cow is dwelt upon at such length and so vividly that the passage has much more emotional force than it would have if Lucretius had confined himself to a simple statement that a cow whose calf has been killed will not content herself with another. For the atomic argument the calf does not need to be sacrificed on an altar; it could just as well have been killed accidentally, or even just lost, but Lucretius chooses instead a situation which allows him to attack religion. A similar side-swipe at the evil effects of religion occurs in other passages of atomic argument.[27]

Yet another theme important throughout the poem is recalled in II by the background of flourishing fields, trees, and rivers. These are extraneous as far as the atomic argument is concerned, but they provide a natural and appropriate *mise en scène* for the cow, and increase the poignancy of her loss by the contrast between her desolation and their abundance. Moreover, even more sharply than the fish and birds, waters and groves in *vv.* 342–6, the details in the vignette of the cow recall the first proem. The same sense of the fullness and urgency of nature is present in both passages, as well as some verbal echoes. *Pabula laeta*, with its double connotation of joy and fertility,[28] is common to both passages. Other less exact similarities include: *frondiferum nemus | frondiferasque domos avium; virides | virentes; flumina summis labentia ripis | rapidos amnes, fluviosque rapaces.*[29]

But perhaps the most striking similarity between the first

27. Townend, *op. cit.* p. 109, briefly discusses the relation of the sacrifice of the calf to that of Iphigenia. For other instances of anti-religion argument see, e.g., II.1090, 1104, 1153–6; III.776–83; v.1194 ff.

28. See Anderson, *op. cit.* 9–10, though he does not seem to realize fully that the meaning "fertile" is a real denotation of *laetus*, not just an overtone.

29. The rivers in the mother cow passage also may recall the picnics which illustrate the right kind of Epicurean pleasures and friendship in II.29–33 and v.1395–6, perhaps even more closely than they do the rivers in spate of the first proem. Cf. on *pingere*, pp. 164–5 below.

proem and our passage is the unusual and vivid way in which animals are not merely invested with human emotions, but driven by them. Both passages show animals moving under the strong compulsion of some emotion: desire in I (*perculsae corda tua vi, capta lepore*); and grief in II (*orbata peragrans, desiderio perfixa*). Animals play a curiously prominent and impressive role in the whole poem, and a systematic study might be interesting.[30] The ordinary outlook of antiquity tended to be man-centered; even pastoral poetry does not humanize animals in the way that Lucretius is prone to do.

Part of Lucretius' interest in animals seems to be psychological, for he transfers to them some troublesome emotions which he seems to be unable to deal with in direct relation to human beings. This is true, for example, of physical passion. In the animal realm, as in the first proem, love appears as a benignant aspect of *Venus genetrix* regenerating the world, but at the end of book IV, where human beings are involved, love is bathed in a malevolent, some say even pathological, glare.[31]

---

30. One finds scattered recognitions of Lucretius' interest in animals. For example, Wormell, *op. cit.* p. 62, notes "His extraordinary sympathy for and understanding of the animal world and of children...—he was attracted to them as to something natural and unspoilt, but he also had a natural affinity with young growing creatures." But Lucretius seems just as interested in grown and in savage animals as in small and domestic ones. A thorough and systematic study of animals in *De Rerum Natura* would I think prove illuminating in general and would especially clarify such vexed passages as v.1308 ff. on early man's use of wild animals in war, which Bailey, III, 1529, calls "perhaps the most astonishing paragraph in the poem." Although K. L. McKay, "Animals in War and ΙΣΟΝΟΜΙΑ," *AJP*, 85 (1964), 124–35, is substantially right in arguing that the passage is not so strange as all that if we remember the *venationes* that were held at Rome in the first century B.C., one can hardly attribute all the slightly strange wild-animal passages in the poem to that source. J. H. Waszink, "La Création des animaux dans Lucrèce," *Revue Belge de Philologie et d'Histoire*, 42 (1964), 48–56, is too specifically about v.791–820 to shed much light on animals in general.

31. The unusual vehemence of Lucretius' feelings about love has of course often been discussed; see e.g. J. Logre, *L'Anxiété de Lucrèce* (Paris

Another vexed center of emotion for Lucretius is death—our fear of it, the physical process, and our emotions when bereaved of those we love—together with destruction on a more universal scale.[32] The theme of death then is also infused into a piece of relatively minor atomic argument by the grief of the mother cow for her dead calf.

Another part of Lucretius' interest in animals is the result of certain features of Epicurean theory. For one thing, Epicureanism stressed observation of the world around one, and animals, before the advent of modern industry and the horseless carriage, were naturally a ubiquitous feature of the world. In addition, the atomic theory presented the universe both as a series of objects and as a conclave of forces, in which all phenomena, from atoms, to inanimate objects, to plants, to animals, to man, to the earth, to the heavenly bodies form an interconnected chain. All are composed of atoms, and so all are basically the same, in spite of enormous variations in qualities and size.[33]

The chief force in the universe is restlessness, motion, or what modern science calls energy. The atoms move continually and blindly; and all the things which are composed of atoms move.[34]

---

1946), pp. 217–38. It has often, in my opinion, been exaggerated. If one makes allowances for Epicurean precepts about avoiding *taraché*, for the usual intensity of Lucretius, and for the subject itself, about which other poets too are vehement, the end of book IV does not seem as peculiar as some have claimed. The reasonableness of IV.1192–287, for instance, is often overlooked.

32. In book III Lucretius devotes a great deal of space to the folly of grief as felt by humans, but he seems to accept the grief of the mother cow with equanimity, just as passion among animals does not disturb him as much as it does in the human realm; cf. Elder, *op. cit.* 94.

33. This is essentially the Epicurean principle of *isonomia*. Bailey, I, 57, II, 888, etc., interprets this only as equilibrium or equal distribution, but Townend, *op. cit.* Dudley, p. 101, formulates the principle more accurately when he remarks that Lucretius' analogies are "assisted by the clearly asserted Epicurean principle of isonomy whereby the nature of the universe was held to be essentially uniform throughout,...[even] at different levels of magnitude." McKay, *op. cit.*, finds no clear reference to *isonomia* here.

34. The question of movement is discussed at length at the beginning of book II, just before our passage; cf. n. 24 above.

But man and the animals can pursue some object, and the language describing the cow's wandering search for her calf suggests another theme which is important in the poem. The cow is described as *peragrans*, the same word which Lucretius used about himself in the passage on his poetic purpose (see above, p. 146). In another passage he says that Epicurus voyaged in mind throughout the whole universe—*omne immensum peragravit mente animoque* [1.74]. I am not suggesting that the cow is intended to appear as a searcher for truth comparable to Epicurus in his philosophy or Lucretius in his poetry, but, on the principle noticed in the last paragraph, the cow's search forms the lower end of an interconnected series of searches which culminates in Epicurus' mental survey of the universe.

At verse 367 Lucretius returns to his argument, restating the main point that atoms are not all alike in shape, and adducing further illustrations. He does this in a series of graded steps; first lambs and kids, each of whom knows his own mother. These four verses actually do all that is necessary for the argument; the illustration of the calf could have been similarly compressed. Even in the brief statement in verses 367–70, however, the parenthetical phrase *quod Natura reposcat* calls up *Natura gubernans* and thus *Venus genetrix*, and thereby connects these lines as well as the preceding ones (*vv.* 342–66) with the first proem.

Next Lucretius moves to grain and shells—inanimate objects which are superficially even more alike than animals, but which upon close observation are found to differ. In these six verses (371–6) the functions of poetry are served not so much by the indirect introduction of emotional elements, as in the passage about the mother cow, but rather by concrete imagery. The grain and the shells themselves are not described, but Lucretius adorns the shore on which the shells rest with the metaphorical phrase *telluris gremium*, with the descriptive adjectives *mollibus*, *incurvi*, and *bibulam*, and with the expressive verbs *pingere* and *pavit*. These words convey a concrete image, and the picture which they present may seem a purely incidental adornment, but some of them are used in other passages that are connected to the significant emotional themes of the poem. For example the phrase *telluris gremium* calls up the passages in which Lucretius, arguing that nothing is completely destroyed, but only broken down to its constituent atoms, which are then reused to form something new, describes how the rain which the father sky casts into the lap of our mother earth is transformed into crops and trees which nourish in turn both man and the animals:

> postremo pereunt imbres, ubi eos pater aether
> in gremium matris terrai praecipitavit;
> at nitidae surgunt fruges ramique virescunt
> arboribus, crescunt ipsae fetuque gravantur;
> hinc alitur porro nostrum genus atque ferarum. [1.250–4]

This passage in turn has some connections with the first proem, in which Mars casts himself into the lap of Venus (1.32–4).[35] The verb *pingere* calls up another notable passage in which Lucretius describes the recreations of early man which include a picnic when the season paints the green grass with flowers— *anni | tempora pingebant viridantis floribus herbas* [v.1395–6]. I am not suggesting that the single verb *pingere* infuses into the seashell passage any significant amount of the Epicurean ethical theory about friendship and pleasure which operates in the description of the picnic. The poetic effect of the seashell passage depends more, I think, on its membership in a group of many remarkable passages in which Lucretius describes earth, the abode of man, in terms which are both poetically fresh and vivid and at the same time scientifically exact (in the Epicurean scheme).[36]

35. The resemblance is strongest in the lines just after those I have quoted, that is in 256–61.

36. Recently Richard Minadeo, "Three Textual Problems in Lucretius," *CJ*, 63 (1968), 241–6, has argued that Lucretius' full treatment of the earth, the abode of man, is the answer to the promise of v.155 to prove *largo sermone* that the abodes of the gods are unlike ours. Whatever one thinks of the argument, he does emphasize a point which is sometimes not fully appreciated, that *De Rerum Natura* is one of the most magnificent poetic evocations of earth as man's abode that has ever been written, a worthy counterpart to Dante's picture of the other world that is the abode of the soul.

Before we leave the descriptive part of the passage from book II, it may be remarked that Lucretius has taken an incidental, and very probably wholly instinctive rather than conscious, care to round the passage with two images that are related in kind. It opens at verse 342 with fish, for all practical purposes, since the verbally colorless *genus humanum* is immediately overwhelmed by the striking phrase *mutaeque natantes* | *squamigerum pecudes*. Live fish are not mentioned again, but Lucretius ends his description with the evocative images of the shells on the seashore which we have just been discussing. This kind of slight, subtle shaping of an argument according to poetic rather than intellectual considerations is constant in the poem, and the poetic effect of *De Rerum Natura* depends more on this habit of Lucretius than is sometimes recognized.

In the last four verses, 377–80, Lucretius completes the circle of the atomic proposition by making the analogical character of the preceding section more definite in the phrase *simili ratione*. As we have observed before, however, (see above, p. 154), it is not important to decide whether Lucretius uses the visible world as an analogy or as an example of his scientific theory. The point is rather that the atomic theory offers an explanation of the world which is partly one with the phenomena it seeks to explain. It subsumes all phenomena in a rational, abstract scheme and at the same time it forms one end of a continuum from the invisible to the infinite.

This situation may not be ideal from a philosophical point of view, but it has certain advantages for Lucretius as a poet. The general structure of the poem is overtly didactic, discursive, and logical.[37] It is clear that a large part of Epicureanism's appeal to Lucretius was precisely the rational structure which it offered. But at the same time he is also moved by a non-rational, or perhaps better an infra-rational, connection between the

37. See, however, C. Bailey, "The Mind of Lucretius," *AJP*, 61 (1940), 278–91, in which he elaborates Büchner's observation that Lucretius has "a habit of holding over or suspending a thought or concept through an intervening digression" (Bailey, I, 165).

atomic world of Epicurean physics and the visible world of the earth and what inhabits it. It is this connection which enables him to form the structure and progression of his poem according to emotional and imagistic considerations as well as logical ones.

In the passage from book II, the sheer presence of the illustrative material is occasioned by a logical necessity—that of the atomic theory. The order in which it is put is a scientific, categorical one; five main species of life are given to choose from: man, fish, domestic animals, wild beasts, and birds. Then a descending series of the cow, other domestic animals, grains, and shells is superimposed on the first scheme. But, within this scientific framework, the proportioning of the material is dictated by other considerations, which are poetic. The incident of the cow takes up the most space, for reasons which have been discussed (see above, pp. 160–61). The other animals and the landscape occupy most of the rest of the passage because they are essential elements in one of the major themes which dominates the entire poem—the fertility of the earth (see above, pp. 157–9).

What has been said so far does not exhaust the significance of this passage in the context of the whole poem, but I have tried to show in some detail how the scientific argument and the poetic effect sometimes work together and how sometimes elements which are not strictly necessary for the argument are introduced, or expanded, to provide an emotional complexity. Most of the devices by which Epicurean physical theory is expressed poetically throughout the *De Rerum Natura* are exemplified in this passage. Many of the observations which we have made about this passage can be applied, *mutatis mutandis*, to the rest of the poem, so that, although we have examined only a passage of less than fifty verses, we are in a position to draw some general conclusions about science and poetry in *De Rerum Natura*.

For Lucretius, I believe, the basic sources of the connection between science and poetry were somewhat as follows. First, the alternation of space and matter. The world is, or at any rate appears to be, composed of objects moving through or located in space. Epicureanism offered a system which corresponded essentially to the nature of things as they appear to be—in contrast to, for instance, the Empedoclean system. Secondly, multiplicity. Lucretius, unlike many people, saw the vast number of different kinds of things that there are in the world. Furthermore he looked closely enough to observe, as the passage from book II has shown, that there are differences even between things and creatures of the same kind. And the atomic theory provided a multiple substructure to match the visible world, whereas most other ancient attempts to explain the nature of matter did not. Thirdly, the assumption of continual motion. One can prefer to look at what stationary objects there are or seem to be in the world. Or one can look at things from a stationary aspect. Or one can pretend that there is a changeless and peaceful realm somewhere towards which this world should strive. Lucretius, in spite of his orthodox profession of desire for *ataraxia*, obviously preferred to see things as restless; indeed he was probably incapable of seeing them otherwise. It is this part of Epicurean physics which attracts him most powerfully, and no small part of his poetic impact resides in the verbs by which he describes the motion of everything in existence, from the smallest atom to the universe as a whole.

Lucretius succeeds in making a satisfactory poetic whole of his apparently unpromising material partly because of the completeness of the explanation of the world offered by Epicureanism, but mainly because the elements of Epicurean theory—fullness and space, multiplicity and motion—are facts of which he must always have been deeply aware in the world around him.[38] We, who tend to separate science and its ways of thinking from the major part of our everyday lives, do the poem a serious injustice if we assume that for Lucretius also the "scientific" and the "poetic" views of the world were different, even opposed.

38. Pierre Boyancé, "Lucrèce et la Poésie," *REA*, 49 (1947), 88–102, concludes that Lucretius was a poet *because* he was an Epicurean, but does not discuss in any detail what features of Epicureanism were especially congenial to the poetic impulses of Lucretius. Cf. R. F. Arragon, "Poetic Art as a Philosophic Medium for Lucretius," *Essays in Criticism* 11 (1961), 371–89.

# Catullus 64 and the Heroic Age

LEO C. CURRAN

# Catullus 64 and the Heroic Age

IN POEM 64[1] Catullus has encapsulated a great deal of the heroic world within the space of four hundred lines: two relatively brief moments of time (the meeting and wedding of Peleus and Thetis and Ariadne's awakening on the shore of Dia) are filled out by flashback and prophecy so that the range of reference extends from the first voyage in history to near the end of the Trojan War. The poem becomes an epitome of the whole age of heroes, and its central meaning is defined by the poet's attitude to that age and by his conception of its relationship to his own period. Set against the heroic period, in a moralizing epilogue, is a highly colored vision of Catullus' own times (397–408). The theme of degeneration through the ages goes back to Hesiod, but Catullus dispenses with the older poet's first three ages in order to make a two-member contrast. Once gods mingled with men. So, in the primary instance in the poem, they came to the wedding of Peleus and Thetis. So Jupiter attended sacrifices made to him, Bacchus led his worshippers at Delphi, and Mars, Minerva, and Diana encouraged their favorites in battle. Now, *spreta pietate*, man's guilt is so great that the gods will no longer join him in bodily form. The epilogue is not an afterthought. The contrast of ages balances the address to the heroes in 22 ff. and asserts the fundamental antithesis of the poem.[2]

1. I shall refer to the following works by author's name only: W. Kroll, *C. Valerius Catullus* (3rd edit. Stuttgart 1959); A. L. Wheeler, *Catullus and the Traditions of Ancient Poetry* (Berkeley 1934); L. Richardson, Jr., *Poetical Theory in Republican Rome* (New Haven 1944); F. Klingner, *Catulls Peleus-Epos* (*Sitzungsb. Bayer. Akad. Wiss.* 1956, 6); M. C. J. Putnam, "The Art of Catullus 64," *HSCP* 65 (1961); C. J. Fordyce, *Catullus* (Oxford 1961).

2. But, as I shall argue, fundamental as this antithesis is, to recognize it is not by any means to exhaust the meaning of Catullus' poem. He invites us to go far beyond the basic antithesis. The following scholars give full weight

Although the epilogue's list of the crimes of modern man is not to be taken as a police report, there is no reason to doubt either its reference to Rome or the reality of Catullus' disaffection with the life around him. He was disillusioned with politics and politicians. He did not witness the horrors of civil war that Virgil and Horace did, but enough had happened in the part of Roman history through which he lived to confer at least an initial credibility upon the old myth that men were living in an Age of Iron. Finally, Catullus was a man whose own candor filled him with contempt for the sham, pretence, and affectation around him, in life, in manners, and in art, and a man whose capacity for love and friendship seems to have rendered him singularly vulnerable to betrayal.[3]

to the epilogue, but all exaggerate its importance at the expense of other elements in the poem. R. Waltz (" Caractère, sens et composition du poème 64 de Catulle," *REL* 23 [1945], 92–109) believes that the epilogue is the key which contains the unifying idea of the poem: nostalgia for a Golden Age when gods mingled with men. L. P. Wilkinson (*Entretiens sur l'antiquité classique. Tome II. L'influence grecque sur la poésie latine de Catulle à Ovide* [Vandœuvres–Genève 1956], p. 54) speaks of the "symbolic and topical significance" which it gives to the poem and the poet's desire to express his depression over "the decadence of the contemporary world." Klingner (p. 18), pointing out the correspondence of 22 ff. with the references at the end of the poem to the present relationship between god and man, says the former virtually contains the essence of the poem in lyric form. Putnam (see especially pages 197–8) emphasizes the epilogue, but exaggerates the specifically autobiographical element.

   3. Putnam's interpretation is based upon an even greater and more specific relevance and applicability of the poem to Catullus' own life: the poet is dealing directly, although under the guise of symbols, with his own experience. "Lesbia and the poet's brother are...very much involved in the story as it unfolds. In a word, poem 64 shows Catullus writing of himself in the figures of Ariadne and Aegeus, and of the way he had hoped his relationship with Lesbia would evolve in the story of Peleus and Thetis. With the present disguised under symbolic forms, it is true autobiography..." (p. 167). However, I find it difficult to accept Putnam's extremely literal allegorical interpretation of the poem. The emotional and imaginative unity which Putnam rightly believes 64 to share with the rest of Catullus' work derives rather from the fact that the poet is sympathetically involved

But Catullus was no naive preterist. His attitude towards the heroic past is complex and ambiguous. His expression of it in this poem takes the form of a hierarchy of antitheses, most of which turn out under closer examination to be more like statements of identity than of contrast. The poem is animated and enriched by the resulting tension: tension between antithetical pairs, with their surface disparity overlying a profound similarity, between wonder and disenchantment, between idealization and realism.[4] The striving for antithesis expands into other areas and determines important features of the poem even on the strictly formal level. The structure is itself an elaborate tissue of carefully wrought balances and contrasts.[5] The same tendency can be seen operating in as small a unit as the individual line: the poet exhibits a remarkable fondness for verse-types in which a noun and its adjective enclose the line or in which pairs of nouns and adjectives are arranged in parallel or in chiasmus.[6]

The basic antithesis of the poem, that between the age of heroes and the contemporary world, is immediately qualified

in the lives and situation of the characters he is creating and is not merely indulging in formal literary exercise or demonstrating his expertise in a fashionable kind of poetry. It is a measure of the seriousness and depth of his involvement that he should, as Putnam's parallels and comparisons demonstrate, constantly use of his characters the language and imagery he uses in his personal poems of his own experience.

4. As my argument will show, I have in mind something more disciplined and intellectual than what Klingner sees as a striving for *poikilia* (p. 79) and something more precise than his idea of the relationship of the two stories as the union of opposites (reversed mirror images, p. 70) in a new harmony (p. 72).

5. The "Chinese box" structure has been amply charted and diagrammed by others. For the present purposes it is not necessary to concern ourselves with minor differences in division and arrangement. There is agreement in the recognition of an elaborate system of balanced and contrasted structural members.

6. Fordyce's (p. 275) figures are 27 lines of the enclosing type, e.g. 54 *indomitos...furores*, and 58 lines of the parallel or chiastic type, e.g. 7, 39, 42, 46.

for, within the heroic world, the picture Catullus paints for us is far from uniformly bright. He is concerned not only with the story of Peleus and Thetis, but also with the story of Ariadne. He forces us to consider the two stories together and to observe the light they cast on each other by inserting one within the other. "Insertion," in fact, characterizes the formal relationship of the two stories, but the connection is more than a matter of external form. It is restated in visual terms in the description, both at the beginning and end of the insert, of the way in which the coverlet bearing the Ariadne story embraces within its folds the marriage couch of Peleus and Thetis. The contrast between the two stories, so intimately joined on both the formal and visual levels, gives rise to tension within the heroic vision itself. The manner of insertion thus becomes more than a mere technical device of structure: it creates meaning.[7]

One is the story of divinely sanctioned marriage, the other a story of human betrayal. The wedding of Peleus and Thetis is attended by the gods, its fruitfulness is guaranteed by the Parcae themselves, and its issue will be the greatest warrior of all time. In the other story, Theseus abandons Ariadne and causes his father's death; Ariadne herself has conspired in the killing of her brother and left home and family. (A family, incidentally, with a good many skeletons in its closet, including human sacrifice, the monstrous Minotaur, and the unnatural lust of Pasiphae that produced it. It is beginning to sound not unlike the catalogue of crimes with which Catullus later charges his own generation.[8] Cf. 403, where *mater substernens se impia* suggests Pasiphae's arranging herself in her Daedalic contraption.)

7. Richardson (p. 33) identifies references to couches as a recurrent unifying device, citing lines 47–51, 86–90 ("Ariadne first sees Theseus in her father's palace, and we find in the mention of the couch of the young girl an irony which is meaningful in the light of what we already know"), 163 ("This is part of Ariadne's wish to be with Theseus even if only as his slave, a curious antithesis to the happy marriage of Thetis and Peleus..."), and 265–6.

8. Cf. Richardson (pp. 55 f.), who compares 149–51 with 398 and remarks, "The sin [of 398] is curiously like that of which Ariadne accuses herself."

The barrenness of the union of Theseus and Ariadne is pointedly contrasted with the glorious fertility of the marriage of Peleus and Thetis. The former is not even a proper marriage at all, a point insisted upon by Ariadne's bitterly sarcastic dwelling upon the language of marriage: *coniunx* (123), *conubia laeta, optatos hymenaeos* (141), *conubia nostra* (158), *coniugis an fido consoler memet amore?* (182). Lines 86–90 contain motifs from wedding songs,[9] and lines 117–20 are a parody of the bride's departure from her own family.[10] Catullus goes out of his way to apply the language of reproduction to Ariadne, ironically, in order to make her experience a grotesque travesty of motherhood. She conceives, but it is not a child: *cuncto concepit corpore flammam* (92). She gives birth: [sc. *querellae*] *nascuntur pectore ab imo* (198). In describing her breasts, Catullus calls them *lactentis* (65), a word suggesting the nursing breasts of a mother as much as their color.[11]

A principal means of asserting the contrast between the Peleus and Ariadne stories is to be found in the role of nature, particularly the sea. Since both myths involve voyages, references to the sea are inevitable, but Catullus goes so far as to make it a major character in the poem, expressing several quite different attitudes towards its changing moods.[12] In the Peleus story the sea is a thing of beauty, first serene, then wondrous and magical. In our first glimpse of it in the opening lines it is clear and peaceful: *liquidas...undas* (2). The oars of the Argonauts gently sweep its level surface: *caerula uerrentes abiegnis aequora palmis* (7). It is innocent and inexperienced: *rudem* (11). The magical aspect of the sea is rendered by a combination of personification, metaphor and paradox. The ships are pine trees "swimming" through its waves (2). The

9. Cf. Klingner (pp. 82 f.), who compares 61.21–5, 56–9, 62.21–3, 39–41.

10. The recurrent motif of the couch also plays a role here; see the remarks of Richardson quoted above in note 7.

11. Cf. the breasts of Thetis and the other Nereids in 18.

12. Richardson recognizes the sea as a recurrent, unifying motif (pp. 34, 55), but does not discuss its several aspects.

paradox of trees swimming in the water is intensified by calling
the men on the ship "trees" (*robora*, 4) and restated in the
juxtaposition of *abiegnis* and *aequora* (7). There is implied
personification in *palmis* (7), a metaphor from another form of
travel in *currum* (9), and wit in *imbuit Amphitriten* (11).[13] The ship
not only "swims," but "runs" (*decurrere*, 6, actually said of the
men on the ship) and "flies" (*uolitantem*, 9). The personification
of the ship is matched by the personification of the sea, although
*Neptuni* (2) may seem at first to be little more than a faded
application of the sea god's name to his element. When the sea
is fully personified in 11, it is significant that it is now a female
deity and a sister of Thetis, whose epiphany along with the
other Nereids is imminent.

In line 12 action and the motion of the sea begin to increase.
Now it is ruffled by the wind and plowed by the ship's prow:
*rostro uentosum proscidit aequor* (12). *Proscindere* is the technical
term for the first plowing, and *aequor* is a word used for plain as
well as sea: man not only makes the trees of the mountain
forest swim, but also plows the sea like a new field. Next the
waves are churned by the oars and whiten with foam: *tortaque
remigio spumis incanuit unda* (13). The gradual increment in
movement and agitation (as well as the personification introduced in *Neptuni* and *Amphitriten*) reaches its climax when the
sea actually comes to life by taking on human form. The
sudden emergence of the Nereids further enhances the magical
quality of the sea, and the very word order in lines 14 ff.
re-creates the stages as they miraculously take shape. In the
splashing white foam, something unspecified came to the
surface (*emersere*). At first one could see no more than a white
turbulence (*candenti...gurgite*). Then faces could be discerned
(*uultus*). They were sea creatures (*aequoreae*), a wonder (*monstrum*), the Nereids! They continue to rise until their bodies
project from the white swirl of which they are at once part and

13. Catullus is, of course, using *imbuit* in its figurative sense; the wit lies
in the literal meaning of the word, for it is in fact the ship which is *imbuta*
and not the sea.

personification. (I have of course misconstrued *monstrum*, but the word order encourages us to regard the strange apparition as as much a *monstrum* as the Argo, and lines 16–17 make this explicit.) Wonder confronts wonder, as the Nereids gaze at the first ship and as the Argonauts gaze at the nymphs.

The most important nymph is, of course, Thetis; and, when the poet identifies her, the wonder he shares with the awestruck Argonauts forces him to break into highly excited language (19–21).[14] After the praise of the heroes of old, the poet reverts to the close association of Thetis with the sea, which is presented as a whole family of personifications, Thetis herself, her grandmother Tethys, and her grandfather Oceanus.

In the Ariadne story we see a different aspect of the sea. For one thing, after the concentration on its visual splendor in the Peleus story, we now *hear* it for the first time, as the breakers crash on the shore of Dia: *fluentisono...litore* (52). Voyaging becomes more violent: the Argonauts had *swept* the waves with their oars, but in his guilty haste Theseus *beats* at the sea with his: *fugiens pellit uada remis* (58). For Ariadne the sea is not an object of beauty nor is it humanized by means of charming personifications. Its shore is the scene of her betrayal and her lament, and it is the picture of Ariadne on the shore while Theseus sails away that opens and closes (with the addition of the coming of Dionysus) the section of the poem devoted to her. (This picture also constitutes an important structural link: her first appearance on the shore sets her against the sea background of the voyage of the Argonauts and the meeting of Peleus and Thetis; her second leads up to the great sea simile of 269 ff.)

For Ariadne the sea is barren and hostile:

> unde aciem in pelagi uastos protenderet aestus,
> tum tremuli salis aduersas procurrere in undas. (127 f.)

14. And with some learned verbal wit. Catullus' reader had to know the Greek word τίτθη to understand the expression *nutricum tenus* (18). Having reminded the reader of this word, the poet then plays on its sounds in *Thetidis...Thetis...Thetidi* (immediately following in 19–21) and in *Thetis...Tethys* (a few lines later in 29–30).

Less important references to the sea have the effect of keeping the theme of its hostility to Ariadne alive in the reader's mind. In 167 it is a measure of the distance between her and a Theseus who cannot hear her cries, in 174 he is the *perfidus nauita*, and in 179 Ariadne speaks of the *ponti truculentum...aequor*, where *aequor* reminds us of the peaceful sea at the beginning of the poem. More interesting is the passage in 154 ff. where Ariadne questions Theseus' humanity. She at first speculates on the possibility of his mother's having been a lioness, but soon finds the only suitably monstrous parent to be the sea itself in its various unpleasant manifestations. In the first of the two lines devoted to the sea as Theseus' mother, the way in which he is imagined as having been spewed forth violently from the foaming waves vividly recalls the very different emergence of the Nereids from the sea in the Peleus story.[15]

So much is the sea Ariadne's enemy, the sea upon which Theseus came to Crete and which now keeps her from him and from home, that water and its motions become a metaphor for her sufferings: *magnis curarum fluctuat undis* (62);[16] the waves play with her clothing (67), which is itself *fluitantis* (68); *qualibus incensam iactastis mente puellam | fluctibus...* (97 f.); she *pours forth* her complaint (125, 202). The water imagery should be considered in connection with the familar fire imagery which is used of her love for Theseus. Both fire and water thus conspire to torment her.

Not just the sea, but all of nature is hostile to Ariadne. The

15. The charge of inhuman parentage goes back to Homer (*Iliad* 16.33 ff.). (Cf. Wheeler [p. 145], who shows how Catullus' version of the theme differs from others in the multiplication of instances.) What is significant here is the repeated and varied reference to the sea. Contrast the use of the same motif in Catullus 60.1–2, where the lioness is followed not by multiple references to the sea, but by a Scylla whose monstrous shape completely overshadows her connection with water. In Homer the sea (ironically Patroclus is made to substitute the sea for the sea-nymph Thetis) is followed by rocks.

16. Putnam (pp. 171–2) discusses the wave imagery and says that at 62 it becomes "internal."

winds carry away the empty promises Theseus had made to her (59). The mountains around her are jagged and threatening (126). Wild beasts and birds will tear her body apart (152). In 164 ff. she complains in vain to breezes that can neither hear nor answer her:

> nec missas audire queunt nec reddere uoces.

All nature conspires in its silent menace:

> omnia muta,
> omnia sunt deserta, ostentant omnia letum.   (186 f.)

Nature plays a very different role in the Peleus story. For Ariadne the silence and loneliness of the landscape are parts of her terror and suffering. The landscape of Thessaly, the fields and farms, are deserted too, but in joyful celebration of the royal wedding (38 ff.). The loneliness of Dia is contrasted with the repeated mention of *throngs* in the other story. The inhuman, savage character of the island is contrasted with the marks of human civilization and society in Thessaly (e.g. the palace with its furnishings, the agricultural pursuits abandoned for the wedding) and with its vegetation (gifts of flowers and trees will make a lush bower for the bridal pair). The winds were hostile to Ariadne, but the breezes of Thessaly are beneficent and life-giving:

> aura parit flores tepidi fecunda Fauoni.   (282)

So great is the violence of nature that Jupiter himself must restore order to it, and his response to Ariadne's prayer significantly takes the form of an assertion of his control over sea, land and heavens:

> annuit inuicto caelestum numine rector;
> quo motu tellus atque horrida contremuerunt
> aequora concussitque micantia sidera mundus.   (204 ff.)

The long simile of the sea at dawn to which the departure of the human guests from the wedding feast is compared (269 ff.)

makes the transition from the violence of the Ariadne story
(which has just risen to a crescendo of frenzy in the description
of the Bacchic revel) to the serenity of the wedding and restores
the original vision of the sea as a thing of beauty. Its language
recalls both of the earlier roles of the sea, the magical and the
violent, reconciling them in a splendid image of order and peace.
The sea is of little thematic interest after the long simile of
269 ff., but water imagery in another form is of significance, as
we shall see when we turn to the Song of the Parcae.

I have spoken of the Ariadne story as the darker side of the
heroic age, and light imagery serves in a minor way to differenti-
ate the two stories. Although the only explicit references to
darkness in the Ariadne story are the two instances of the word
*caecus* (197, 207), light, in particular the word *lux*, plays a not
insignificant part in the Peleus story. In four cases it means
"day" or "light of day," and the choice of this word bathes in
brilliance the days involved: that on which Peleus first saw
Thetis (16), the wedding-day (31, 325), and the morning after
the wedding-night (376). In 44–6 the splendor of the palace is
described in terms of light, and light (*luce* again) is the climax
of the simile of the sea at dawn (275).

Within the Ariadne story itself there is one element of
positive contrast, for it does, after all, have a happy ending in
that Dionysus is coming to rescue Ariadne. But what we are
shown is not the meeting of Ariadne and the god, not the joy
and glory he brings her, but only his outlandish and barbarous company. We leave the Ariadne story to the wild strains
of the Bacchantes, beside themselves in the same hysterical and
potentially destructive frenzy that Catullus evokes in that
disturbing *tour de force*, the *Attis*. This terrifying scene and the
picture of the betrayed Ariadne are what linger in the mind,
not her deliverance.

So far, then, my analysis has shown that the poet so arranges
his material as to invite us to consider three interlocking antithetical pairs which qualify each other in a complex way. First,
the heroic past is set against the decadent present. Second, this

opposition is undercut by the disparity within the vision of the heroic age between the story of Peleus and the story of Ariadne. Third, there is within the latter story a further contrast, barely developed, between Ariadne the victim of betrayal and Ariadne the bride of a god. It will be noted that the Peleus/Ariadne antithesis tends to deny the validity of the past/present antithesis and to suggest at least the possibility that similarity may be as relevant as dissimilarity. Consideration of the Peleus story will reveal that it, too, contains within itself elements of contradiction and that the antithetical relationship between the Peleus story and the Ariadne story also breaks down under closer examination. The marriage of Peleus and Thetis at first seems to be the positive, joyful counterpart of the unhappy experience of Ariadne, but the situation is actually more complicated. Catullus goes out of his way to bring in the less pleasant aspects of the Peleus story by means of direct statement, allusion, and suppressions of detail so violent that they call attention to what is being glossed over.

Before discussing the Peleus story itself, I should like to reconsider briefly the function of the coverlet and to mention some of the many links of vocabulary and imagery joining the two stories. Mention has already been made of the emphasis Catullus places on the way in which the coverlet with the Ariadne story enfolds the marriage couch of Peleus and Thetis. The device does more than connect the two myths. It is highly significant that this covering, emblazoned with its picture of discord and desertion, should embrace within its folds the most prominent physical object in the poem and the concrete symbol of the union of Peleus and Thetis. It would be difficult to imagine a worse omen for the success of the marriage than the fact that the couch is thus literally enshrouded in a covering of such sinister import. As for the verbal links, one cannot always tell when they are intended to heighten the contrast and when they are intended to point up the ironic similarities, but the latter effect is certainly there and plays its part in the undermining of the antithesis.

Both Peleus (19) and Ariadne (86 ff.) are victims of love at first sight. The fire of passion enflames Peleus (19), Ariadne (91–3, 97), and Dionysus (253).[17] Theseus has a *cupiens animus* (145) and *cupidae mentis* (147); Peleus is the *cupido marito* (374). *Optatae luces* (31), *optatos amores* (372), and *optata* (328) anticipate and pick up Ariadne's bitter *optatos hymenaeos* (141).[18] The *filum* (377) passed around Thetis' neck as a test of the success of the wedding-night recalls the *filum* Ariadne gave to Theseus (113). The Parcae are also spinning a *filum* (317), and there are other links between these figures and Ariadne. The lament of Ariadne and their song constitute a balanced pair in the structure of the poem, and there are several verbal echoes of the description of Ariadne in the song: *clarisonas...fudisse...voces* (125) and *clarisona...voce...fuderunt* (320 f.),[19] *tegmina* (129) and *subtegmina* in the refrain, *ante pedes* (67) and *ante pedes* (318).

In 87 ff. Ariadne's beauty as she falls in love is compared to the myrtle and to flowers, a description which is echoed in the gifts of Chiron for the bridal couple (281 ff.): compare *odores, flumina, aura, distinctos,* and *colores* in the former passage with *fluminis, aura, flores, indistinctis,* and *odore* in the latter. The tree simile applied to the falling Minotaur is recalled by the trees Penios carries as wedding gifts: note especially the repetition of *radicitus* (108 and 288). Ariadne and Polyxena are both *praeda* (153 and 362). Similar phrases are used of the victories of Theseus and Achilles: *prostrauit corpore* (110) and *prosternet corpora* (355).

To turn to the marriage of Peleus and Thetis itself, Catullus has chosen for his paradigm of harmony between god and man a story in which the heroine was violently opposed to the union and had to be tricked and wrestled into it. As far back as Homer, Thetis marries Peleus πολλὰ μάλ' οὐκ ἐθέλουσα (*Iliad* 18.434), and her unwillingness is a constant feature of the later versions of the myth. Another frequently occurring detail is the serious

17. Cf. Richardson, p. 56.
18. Richardson (p. 56) compares 20, 31–2, 140–1, and 328–9.
19. Richardson (p. 63) compares 52, 125, 263, 320.

quarrel with Peleus over her somewhat bizarre methods of infant care. It might be objected that the marriage was so familiar as an exemplar of human happiness and union with the divine that no poet could use the story in the way in which I am arguing that Catullus did, especially a poet who turned Thetis into a willing participant. One can answer in the first place that Catullus is extremely independent and original in his handling of the myth.[20] Indeed his placing of the Voyage of the Argonauts *before* the marriage and his declaring Thetis willing in the opening lines of the poem are a clear announcement to the reader not to expect the story to be handled in a traditional manner. It must also be remembered that mythological figures and stories do not possess an inviolable existence independent of the individual works of literature in which they are embodied. A poet's treatment of a myth is subordinate to his artistic end in composing a particular poem on a particular occasion, and sometimes he has other than purely artistic ends in mind. A brief examination of some of the other versions of the Peleus story will reveal that the most glowing tributes to its happiness are conditioned by the artistic and other purposes of the works in which they occur. Ellis, in his introduction to the poem, provides a useful collection of the more laudatory references to Peleus and to his wedding. Probably the most enthusiastic celebrations of the marriage are to be found in Pindar, in whose odes Peleus appears eight times. In six of these odes—and they are the six in which the praise is most elaborate—the victor for whom it was composed was from Aegina, of which island Pindar engagingly confesses (in *Isth.* 6.19 f.) that, whenever he

20. Gustav Friedrich (*Catulli Veronensis Liber* [Leipzig and Berlin 1908], pp. 318 ff.) emphasizes Catullus' *Souveränität* in his treatment and lists the deviations from the tradition. See also Wheeler (pp. 123 ff.), who, against Friedrich, rejects the idea that Catullus "invented or dealt arbitrarily with the main points of the tale" and believes that he must have had authority for his details in "later Greek literature which is lost to us." Even if Wheeler is right, the choice of variant details made by Catullus is as significant for the meaning of his poem as free invention would have been.

comes to it, he cannot resist praising the Aeacidae.[21] Pindar's attitude, therefore, is more than a little conditioned by deference to Aeginetan local patriotism. And even in Pindar the less pleasant aspects of the story are not entirely absent: in *Isth.* 8.25 ff. there is the clear implication that Thetis is palmed off on a mortal because she is a source of strife among gods and would be too dangerous a mate for one of them. He is also aware of the wrestling match which constituted Peleus' courtship of the unwilling goddess (*Nem.* 3.35 f., 4.62 ff.). In *Nem.* 5.14 ff. Pindar pointedly glosses over the unpleasant story of how Peleus and Telamon killed their half-brother. Finally, in *Pyth.* 3.87 ff. Peleus appears, along with Cadmus, not only as a type of great human happiness, but also as one of suffering (because of the loss of his only son). Euripides is also cited by Ellis, and two passages in the *I.A.* require brief comment. The first (701 ff.) occurs in the context of Agamemnon's attempt to persuade Clytemnestra of the advantages of a marriage between Iphigenia and Achilles; in the second (1036 ff.) the chorus's praise of the marriage of Peleus and Thetis is designed to heighten the contrast with the impending sacrifice of Iphigenia.

From the examination of these passages in Pindar and Euripides it can be seen that the happiness of Peleus and Thetis was not so much an unalterable constant as an element which was sometimes enhanced in order to suit certain aims of the poets telling the story. The happiness was not so unalloyed that it precluded others from concentrating on the darker side of the myth. This, we shall see, is what Catullus did after his initial introduction of the theme.[22]

21. He was not always so disposed elsewhere. See *Paean* 6.118 for a slur on Peleus' grandson Neoptolemus made while he was writing for the *Delphians* and his apology for it to the offended Aeginetans in *Nem.* 7.61 ff.

22. It is worthwhile to remember that, whatever Peleus' marriage stands for, Thetis is also a paradigm of profound mourning. (Cf. Callimachus, *Hymn to Apollo* 2.20–1, Plautus, *Truc.* 731, Ovid, *Amores* 3.9.1.) In view of the central role of the sea in 64 as discussed above, we should remember that Thetis is also the sea. Her name is used in Latin poetry to stand for it, and

One device Catullus employs to cast a shadow on the marriage is allusion to the story of Jason and Medea. By beginning the story with the participation of Peleus in the Argonauts' expedition and by going so far as to have him first meet Thetis on that very voyage (perhaps an invention of his own, for only here is he not already married before he leaves for Colchis), he places us from the beginning in the context of the Jason–Medea story and inevitably reminds us of all of its betrayal and treachery. The connection is reinforced by the echoes of the *Medea* of Ennius and of Euripides in the opening lines[23] and by the way in which Ariadne in her lament is modelled upon Euripides' and Apollonius' treatment of the heroine. The motif of ordinary mortals bringing gifts to the wedding seems also to be an allusion to the latter version.[24]

The wedding of Peleus and Thetis is supposed to be a signal instance in Catullus' poem of how gods mingled with men, yet the poet lays special emphasis on the fact that the human and divine guests attend in shifts and do not in fact mingle with each other. The tactful withdrawal of the human guests before the arrival of the divine is emphasized by a long simile which is framed by explicit references to their leaving:

> sanctis coepit decedere diuis    (268)
>
> linquentes...discedebant    (276 f.)

The other guests appear only after still further specification of the parting of the human guests: *quorum post abitum* (278). One wonders what to make of the word *linquentes* in a passage which places so much stress on the departure of the mortals. *Linquere* and *relinquere* are used with particular frequency in the Ariadne story and in such a way that they lose their colorlessness and become loaded words. Their occurrence in 35, presumably in

at the beginning of our poem we saw her take shape from its waters. The varying aspect of the sea can thus be taken as a commentary on the contradictory character of Thetis herself.

23. Cf. Kroll, *ad loc.*, and Klingner, pp. 5 f.

24. See Apollonius 4.1139–98 and Klingner, p. 30.

the corrupt 287, and perhaps in 213 is innocent and therefore does not concern us. Three instances refer literally to Theseus' desertion of Ariadne (123, 133, 200) and one figuratively (59, *linquens promissa procellae*). They thus essentially define Theseus' crime against Ariadne, and, with poetic justice, *liquere* is used of his forgetting his father's instructions (240). In harmony with Catullus' point that Ariadne is not altogether innocent, two cases involve her own betrayal of her father (117, 180). By the time the words are used in 276 (and 299), the notion of "leaving" has decidedly dark connotations.

Look at the list of divine wedding guests. It ends with the only two gods who did *not* attend. In Homer (*Iliad* 24.63) and Pindar (*Nem.* 5.21 ff.), Apollo is present at the wedding,[25] but Catullus sees fit to use (or invent) a version in which the god's hostility to Achilles dates back before the hero's birth. A guest who does come, although not in other versions, is Prometheus, that symbol of defiance and cosmic discord, still bearing the marks of the suffering he endured in the dispute with Jupiter. His presence, with scars that are reminders of divine strife, strikes a discordant note in a celebration of harmony.[26] Special emphasis is placed on the attendance and rather forbidding appearance of the grim Parcae, working away at their *aeternum laborem* amid the gaiety of the wedding (contrast the cessation of all human labor in Thessaly earlier). This is the only version in which it is these rather uncongenial goddesses who sing the wedding-song. The most vivid touches of realism in the poem concern the

25. For the ambiguous role of Apollo as prophet of the greatness of the son of Peleus and Thetis and as his killer, see Klingner, pp. 15 ff.

26. J.-P. Boucher ("À propos du carmen 64 de Catulle," *REL* 34 [1956], 190–202) regards this passage as one of the places where the "vivacité de la sensibilité du poète ne va pas...sans inconvénient:...ce nom évoque vigoureusement la silhouette d'un supplicié attaché à un rocher, ce qui provoque une gêne dans cette atmosphère de bonheur." Putnam (pp. 191–2) observes that the appearance of Prometheus disturbs "the bliss of the wedding" and "somehow breaks the enchanting spell," but one cannot accept his autobiographical explanation, which sees Prometheus as Catullus (by way of Attis).

Parcae, viz. their appearance, the details of their work, and the slight touches of earthiness appropriate to a real Roman wedding at the end of their song. This realism is a further warning that we are not to look upon the Peleus–Thetis story as uncritical idealization.

It might be objected that, whatever else is to be said about the marriage of Peleus and Thetis, it did at least produce Achilles. But Catullus' Achilles is a distinctly ambiguous figure. Long before we actually see him, allusions are made to some of the less happy parts of his story. When Catullus describes Thetis rising from the sea with the Nereids, who can forget that, when Homer presents this scene in *Iliad* 18.35 ff., the Nereids are mourning the Patroclus who died because of Achilles and the Achilles who will die soon himself? His death will be a prominent part of the prophecy of the Parcae, an ironic choice of subject for the song sung to felicitate his parents at their wedding. When Ariadne says of Theseus in the passage already discussed in connection with the sea, *quod mare conceptum spumantibus exspuit undis*, who can forget that she is echoing the words of Patroclus in *Iliad* 16.33 ff. when he reproaches Achilles for his heartlessness towards the Greeks? In the Song of the Parcae itself, he fights at Troy for the *periuri Pelopis...tertius heres*, a form of reference which serves both to throw an unfavorable light over the whole Trojan War and to remind us that duplicity has been a feature of the Age of Heroes for some time. (*Tertius heres* suggests the bloody succession of the House of Atreus and *periuri* the treacherous preliminaries of Pelops' marriage). Achilles is a figure of savage brutality who will drench the plains of Troy in blood, as the Parcae tell us, and choke the Scamander with corpses. The river Scamander joins the sea in the complex of water images which we have already seen to be of central importance. Sea and river are both water, but their obvious similarity is not in itself sufficient to justify our seeing any essential connection between the two in the metaphorical economy of the poem. But the poet himself makes the connection by treating Achilles' effect upon the river as a

nightmarish reversal of elements of the original vision of the sea
as an object of beauty. The most impressive element of that
splendid vision was the materialization of the Nereids amid the
waves. Now the beautiful bodies of the nymphs rising from the
waves are replaced by the corpses of the victims of Achilles
choking the waters of the Scamander.[27] This grim detail is the
major feature of the reversal, but there are others which help to
convey the point. In the earlier passage, the whiteness of the
foaming waters was emphasized, as they began to take on the
color of the Nereids' flesh; now the waters of the Scamander are
red with slaughter. The breasts of the Nereids, breaking through
the surface of the water, are replaced by the withered and
bruised breasts of the mothers mourning the men Achilles has
killed, a connection tightened by the use of *nutricum* for the
Nereids' breasts. There is a larger pattern discernible here,
which goes beyond the stock reference to a standard gesture of
mourning women. The allusion to breasts involves a central
concern of this poem, the motherhood that is spectacularly
successful in Thetis' case and at once denied and ironically
attributed to Ariadne. It is significant that a song celebrating
the motherhood of Thetis should dwell upon the disastrous
effect her son's birth and life will have upon other mothers
and their sons. Finally, the reversal of the vision of the
sea also involves the agricultural metaphor: the sea was
"plowed" by the Argo and now Achilles is a "reaper" of
corpses.[28]

27. The grisly unnaturalness here picks up that of the "swimming trees"
of the opening lines.

28. Klingner (pp. 24–5) calls the emphasis Catullus places on Achilles'
bloodiness a contrast or *Gegenthema*, but does not seem to recognize its larger
relevance in undercutting the Peleus–Thetis story. Putnam (pp. 192–5)
gives full weight to the bloody brutality of Achilles and to Catullus' lack of
sympathy for him. More persuasive than the autobiographical identifications
Putnam offers by way of explanation is the following: "Though Achilles is
associated with the glorious marriage of Peleus and Thetis, nevertheless the
brutality of his actions somehow helps bridge the gap between the ideal/past
section of the poem and the real/present. He is a part of the heroic age, yet

The crowning glory of Achilles in the prophecy of the Parcae is the slaughter of Polyxena on his burial mound (362–70). She collapses like a sacrificial animal, falling under the blow of the two-headed axe, a simile which casts a shadow on the reference in lines 387 ff. to Jupiter's coming in person in the old days to witness sacrifices of a hundred bulls. The sacrifice of Polyxena extends the irony of the effect Thetis' motherhood will have upon other mothers. The prophecy which takes up most of the wedding-song of the Parcae itself ends in an allusion to another "wedding," for Polyxena was sacrificed in order to provide a "bride" for the dead Achilles.[29] There is a verbal link between Achilles' reception of his "bride" and Peleus' reception of his (*excipiet* [364] and *accipiat* [373]), and the reference to Polyxena's virginity is also a standard element in the description of brides. Her virginity and mock-marriage also associate her, negatively, with the theme of motherhood: like Ariadne she is denied the fertility of a Thetis. The vision of Polyxena as a bride lingers on like an after-image into the final stanza of the Song of the Parcae, for there Thetis is not the great goddess of the sea, but a young girl whose mother and nurse show a very human concern for the success of the wedding-night and have a charmingly quaint device for resolving their anxiety. One is tempted to see deliberate ambiguity of reference in the last two stanzas of the Song of the Parcae, especially in line 372: *quare agite optatos animi coniungite amores*. The sudden transition to the

the brilliance of his deeds is tainted by a certain unheroic quality" (p. 195). It is the thesis of my paper that there is more to the dark side of the Peleus story than the behavior of Achilles and that the poem, in the end, denies the existence of a "gap," at least of a moral kind, between past and present. Putnam himself seems to approach this point of view when he says, "...the sadness which the reader feels in the Song of the Fates is deliberately made explicit [*sc.* by means of verbal echoes in 397–9], for it also, like the lament of Ariadne, is a commentary on the evils of the times" (p. 195). Compare also what he says in connection with Achilles on p. 168: "The ideal is never reached, even in the union between Peleus and Thetis, which to ancient authors was above all others the most perfect."

29. See Kroll and Fordyce at 362.

second person plural can at first be taken as an apostrophe to Achilles and Polyxena, reinforcing the idea of the sacrifice as a kind of marriage, rather than as a direct address to Peleus and Thetis. The apostrophe would be, of course, bitterly sarcastic. The ambiguity which I suspect exists here is preserved by the negative form of the statements in 376–80.

The contrast between Polyxena's "snowy limbs" and her blood, drenching Achilles' tomb, provides a shocking climax for what otherwise might seem to be a purely decorative use of color. Throughout the poem Catullus has been pairing red and white; now we see that this is not mere ornament but a preparation for the final and most powerful statement of the color contrast. The blood drenching the tomb seems further to constitute a final transfiguration of the water imagery. We are, I think, justified in making this connection because of the way in which Catullus associates by verbal link the blood-stained river and the blood-stained sepulchre:

> *alta tepefaciet* permixta flumina *caede*   (360)

> *alta* Polyxenia *madefient caede* sepulcra   (368)[30]

We have passed from the sea's white foam of the opening lines, to the river stained red with gore, to a horrifying final vision of the pouring of an innocent girl's blood over the tomb of a ruthless killer. The fusion here of what we may call the "fluid" imagery (to include sea, river and blood) and the color contrast of red and white serves to throw the strongest possible emphasis on the Polyxena passage and to make up in visual intensity what the Song of the Parcae lacks in length as a complement to the long section on Ariadne.

At this point I should answer the possible objection that a disapproving reaction to the Achilles passage represents an anachronistic imposition of alien values and sensibilities upon

---

30. Putnam (p. 194) comments, "The tomb is as lofty as the river is deep...." To which he adds (p. 204, n. 62), "With *alta madefient* of l. 368 cf. *alta tepefaciet* of l. 360." He also compares *aceruis* in 359 with *coaceruatum* in 363.

the heroic point of view. Of course this attitude disturbs us, but it was an accepted, indeed glorified, part of the heroic code: the greater the killer, the greater the hero. Catullus simply adopts heroic values for the purposes of his poem. But, even if Homer or his heroes could accept such a simple view of life (and in fact they did not), after Euripides and after the Alexandrians no poet, least of all a sophisticated and urbane poet like Catullus, could describe such conduct from an uncritical point of view. We can be confident that Catullus regarded Achilles' brutality as we would.

The savagery of Achilles is the final and most explicit expression of contradiction within the Peleus and Thetis story. The contrast between its bright and dark elements parallels that between it and the Ariadne story and, in turn, that between heroic past and evil present. It would be a pedantic and, in the end, fruitless exercise in logic to try to determine how much each of these polarities remains intact under the influence of the others. The ultimate result of the interweaving of antitheses seems to be an implicit statement of essential similarity. Catullus' response to the past is thus complex. The nostalgia and the admiration for the heroes of old is undeniably present, although I have said little about this aspect of the poem in my paper. But the idealism is strongly qualified by a recognition of the discordant, the destructive and the tragic. To take the Achilles passage as only one example, there is tension between simple heroism and a more civilized sensibility, between admiration for the hero and awareness that he was just a very efficient killer. Catullus' attitude is a combination of a nostalgia for the glamor of the heroic world with an ironic realization that it is only an irrelevant dream. Transcending the fundamental antithesis in the poem, that between the heroic past and the degenerate present, is a vision of a tragic constancy in human nature, stated in mythological terms, which contradicts the antithesis and reveals evil and suffering lurking beneath the surface of the brilliantly enamelled picture of the Age of Heroes. Myth becomes a metaphor for the present, an unpleasant present but, as the poem as a whole declares, it was never any better.[31]

31. T. E. Kinsey, whose "Irony and Structure in Catullus 64," *Latomus* 24 (1965), 911–31, was not available to me until my paper was in the process of final revision, argues that Catullus' attitude to the Heroic Age is ironic, but in a different sense from that in which I would apply the word to the poem. His approach is summarized on p. 930: "...the poem is at no high level of seriousness. Catullus does not take the grief of the mother or [Polyxena's] sacrifice seriously because neither he nor his audience take the stories of the Heroic Age seriously. His attitude is...that...of the realist ironically retelling a story found in some romantic novel which no one regards as anything except light entertainment." The irony Kinsey finds in the poem is much too good-natured and light-hearted.

In developing his thesis of the poem's fundamental lack of seriousness, Kinsey anticipates certain observations made in this paper, although the conclusions he draws from them, of course, reflect his own view of the nature of the irony. He rejects the autobiographical interpretation on grounds similar to mine (p. 912). "The gods are not presented in an entirely favourable light nor are they shown, even in the Heroic Age, as working for the happiness of mankind" (p. 912). "...the poet's attitude to the Heroic Age is not the apparently naive enthusiasm of Section I; there is much irony in the poem and the irony reaches a climax in the marriage song" (p. 914). Of the less pleasant details of the Peleus and Thetis story, among which Kinsey is concerned primarily with the role of Jupiter, he says, "If these discordant details are alluded to later on, it is permissible to infer that the reader is meant to notice the suppressions here and to detect a certain irony in Catullus' enthusiasm..." (p. 915). "Lines 1–15, reminiscent as they are of the *Medea* of Ennius, lead us to expect the tragedy of Jason and Medea..." (pp. 915 f.). He recognizes the unfavorable light the description of Prometheus casts upon the relationship between the gods (p. 923). He does not gloss over the Achilles passage: "Catullus' picture appears *intended* to alienate sympathy from Achilles. Secondly, the Fates are supposed to be recounting the future happiness of Peleus and Thetis, but here they dwell on the death of their son" (p. 926). "Catullus...here [405–8]... takes and appears to accept the statement that the sins of men alienated the gods, but his acceptance is ironical, since he refers to sins of which there were examples in his own poem and well-known examples in the Heroic Age" (p. 929).

# Bacchus and the Horatian *Recusatio*

EDMUND T. SILK

# Bacchus and the Horatian *Recusatio*[1]

HORACE is like the other Augustan writers in contriving to combine extravagant compliment to the emperor with protests of inability to cope with the magnitude of such a theme. But Horace's handling of the rhetorical *recusatio* is unusual if not unique in extent and complexity. Most writers pay the compliment and make the disclaimer in a single poem, or, if the need arises to repeat the process, it is undertaken afresh in a new idiom and different metaphor. This is usually the end of the matter. The poet has met his obligation and can now proceed with his work in his chosen genre with a clear conscience and unpreoccupied. It is otherwise with Horace.[2] While there are

1. The significance of Bacchus in the *Odes* of Horace has been touched upon several times by Professor Steele Commager in his *Odes of Horace* (New Haven 1962). While Professor Commager discovers more mysticism in the poet's approach to Bacchus than I do, his treatment of this subject is most suggestive and helpful. Certain specific points on which I hold a view superficially similar to, but actually different from, Professor Commager's will be mentioned in the notes to this paper. The striking difference between Professor Commager's interpretation and mine is that his comments on the poet's attitude toward Bacchus are, while often extensive, sporadic and isolated, whereas I believe that the poet's several treatments of his relation to the god are arranged in a meaningful sequence. The present paper is a by-product of a study of the prologues and epilogues of Horace's books of lyrics, the first results of which I endeavored to give in "A Fresh Approach to Horace, 2.20," *American Journal of Philology* LXXVII (1956), 255–63.

Walter Wimmel, "Kallimachos in Rom," *Hermes*, Einzelschriften 6 (1960), is the most recent as well as the only thorough study of the poetic apology as it was developed by Callimachus and passed on to Roman writers. Wimmel does not take up the subject of this paper and does not discuss the poems addressed to Bacchus by Horace.

2. I should not wish to be misunderstood here. Of course, Horace composes individual poetic apologies that have no relation to each other and that are written from various points of view and according to various traditional conventions. What I am trying to say is that these isolated

few poems in which he explicitly couples the *laudes Augusti* with protests of inability to undertake political epic, Horace continually reminds the reader that he is nagged by a feeling of obligation unfulfilled. Very early in the *Odes*, however, it becomes clear that the poet's dilemma is not merely the conventional literary frustration of the feeble genius confronted by the colossal theme. All three books of the *Odes* are solidly provided with encomia of Augustus. Side by side with these, however, and nearly engulfing them is the series of poems that directly or indirectly attack the growing depravity of the Roman people. These invectives vary in intensity but are ranged with a crescendo effect. The poet is plainly representing himself as torn between admiration for the great leader and anxiety over the decline of the *vulgus* that, it seems, not even Augustus can arrest. It is Bacchus who, at the close of Book III, resolves this conflict in the poet's mind and persuades him to forget his misgivings and become the herald and trumpet of the Augustan regime. *Recusatio* has been expanded into something like a drama in which the hesitant or recalcitrant poet and an overpowering god are the actors.

The preceding sketch is not fantasy. The poems in which the poet and the god confront each other, if placed side by side, present the unmistakable pattern of conversion in three stages: (1) scepticism and intolerance; (2) sudden revelation; (3) progressive ecstasy. If these poems are examined in the context of their respective books, it will be found that the Bacchic poems not only are in harmony with their near neighbors, but highlight and symbolize successive stages in the poet's thought and feeling. Regardless of one's view of Horace's principles of arrangement of his three books of lyrics, the fiction of the poet's struggle with the god imparts an element of forward movement to the collection and attracts other poems into this stream that, but for the Bacchic influence, might have had a quite neutral

poems are drawn into a larger complex and make their individual contributions to the "continued story" of the poet's pretended retreat that is fully developed in the series of poems addressed to Bacchus.

relationship to the collection as a whole.[3] The order of the detailed discussion below will be as follows: first a classified list of the poems that, in one way or another, are connected with the subject of this paper (table, below); secondly the conversion pattern in the poems to Bacchus; and thirdly the relation of the Bacchic poems to their context.

| Bacchus | Recusatio | Laudes Augusti | Vs. Vulgus |
|---|---|---|---|
| I.18 | I.6 | I.2 | I.2 |
|  |  | 6 | 3 |
|  |  | 12 | 14 |
|  |  | 37 | 15 |
| II.19 | II.1 | II.7 | (II passim) |
|  | 12 | 9 | II.1 |
|  |  | 12 | 15 |
|  |  |  | 18 |
| III.3 | III.3 fin. | III.3 | III.1–6 |
| 25 | (6 fin.?) | 4 | 24 |
|  |  | 5 |  |
|  |  | 14 |  |
|  |  | 25 |  |

3. Presumably most modern critics of Horace will look askance on an enterprise such as that which is the starting point of this paper. Professor Fraenkel (*Horace* [Oxford 1957]) has declared the absolute independence of the individual Horatian Ode and N. E. Collinge in his sometimes abstruse and difficult but always profound study *The Structure of the Horatian Ode* (Oxford University Press 1961) has warned of the folly of searching for any pattern of arrangement that can account for the order of the collection as a whole. Mr Collinge's own work, however, in revealing as it does so many effects of harmony and contrast in Horace's placement of poems, cannot help encouraging less cautious investigators than himself to pursue the problem further. The present paper is not part of an investigation of the *intentio auctoris Horatii* but is meant to be a description of what one reader has seen. In this kind of study, the genesis of the poem is of less significance than the comparisons it provokes with other poems that may be its near or more distant neighbors in the collection. Once totally unrelated objects of art have been assembled in a museum, whether we like it or not, they themselves become something in addition to what they were before. If the collection is a random one, observers are struck by felicitous or unfortunate juxtapositions. If the collection was made according to some principle, the principle should in time reveal itself. On the assumption that Horace

A number of poems to be cited in the course of the discussion
are not included in the lists, because they do not explicitly belong
to any of the categories. The lists by themselves bring out a few
interesting points. The explicit *recusatio*s are few in number.
Whereas the criticisms of the Roman people are more numerous
than the *laudes Augusti*, the latter are more or less evenly distributed throughout the three books. Every book has one poem to
Bacchus and Book III has two. It should be added that there are
some nineteen poems addressed to various divinities in the first
three books of the *Odes*, and that Bacchus is the only god to
whom as many as four poems are addressed, the only god
addressed in all three books, and the only god addressed in
Book II.[4]

It requires neither intensive nor prolonged study of the four
poems addressed to Bacchus to ascertain things about them
that have a bearing on my argument. In brief summary,
1.18, ostensibly a piece of advice to Varus as he plants his
estate, grows into a praise of wine as the dispeller of care, but
gradually becomes a defiance of the wine-god, or at least a
warning to him not to disturb the even tenor of the poet's life

arranged his own museum, the present writer has been in search of objective
indications and reasonable inferences and has endeavored to reduce subjective considerations to the minimum.

4. The following table shows the relationship of the Bacchus-poems to the
total list of pieces addressed to divinities; the poems to Bacchus are set off
by asterisks:

     1.2 *Iam satis terris*, which appeals to most of the Roman pantheon
         but is technically addressed to Mercury (disguised as Caesar)

    10 *Mercuri, facunde nepos Atlantis*

    12 *Quem virum aut heroa* (to Juppiter)

  *18 *Nullam Vare sacra* (addressed at the opening to Varus but
         becomes an address to Bacchus)

(*)19 *Mater saeva cupidinum* (to Venus, with whom Bacchus is associ-
         ated)

    24 *Quis desiderio sit pudor aut modus* (begins as an address to Mel-
         pomene)

    30 *Venus regina*

or invade his privacy beyond the limits prescribed by the poet himself:

> non ego te, candide Bassareu
> invitum quatiam nec variis obsita frondibus
> sub divum rapiam.   saeva tene cum Berecyntio
> cornu tympana, quae subsequitur caecus amor sui
> et tollens vacuum plus nimio gloria verticem
> arcanique fides prodiga, perlucidior vitro.   (1.18.11-16)

II.19 reports a vision of the god that the poet has had in the wilderness.[5] It is a step-by-step account as the poet feels him-

31 *Quid dedicatum poscit Apollinem vates*

35 *O diva gratum quae regis Antium* (this hymn is addressed to Fortune; 1.34 *Parcus deorum cultor* is the preface to it)

\*II.19 *Bacchum in remotis carmina rupibus*

\*III.3 *Iustum et tenacem propositi virum* (*hac te merentem* in line 12 directly addresses this poem to Bacchus)

4 *Descende caelo* (in part, at least, a hymn to the Muses)

11 *Mercuri—nam te docilis magistro*

18 *Faune, Nympharum fugientum amator*

22 *Montium custos nemorumque Virgo* (Diana)

\*25 *Quo me Bacche rapis tui*

27 *Impios parrae recinentis omen* (to Galatea)

28 *Festo quid potius die* (Neptune)

30 *Exegi monumentum* (Melpomene)

5. Professor Fraenkel's comment on *Ode* II.19 is interesting. He interprets the poem as a poetic record of a real experience, that is to say (or so I assume) the record of a dream or waking reverie. Horace had read and knew the traditional lore so well that, given the right circumstances, the vision or the dream was the result. In any case Horace's memory has been selective and even a little arbitrary. The reminiscences of Euripides should have involved some reference to the Bacchants; but Bacchus' followers here are not human but Nymphs and Satyrs. In other words, the poet is alone with Nature rather than a member of a *thiasos* of fellow worshipers. The intense emotion leads the poet to no violent activity of any kind but to a deeper contemplation and a constantly widening view of the universe until he sees everything from heaven to hell. In certain ways the poem resembles I.10, II.13, and, of course, III.4.

self overwhelmed and made to join the god's followers and
become the authorized divulger of the lore of the cult:

> fas pervicacis est mihi Thyiadas
> vinique fontem lactis et uberes
>     cantare rivos atque truncis
>         lapsa cavis iterare mella,
> fas et beatae coniugis additum
> stellis honorem tectaque Penthei
>     disiecta non leni ruina
>         Thracis et exitium Lycurgi.   (II.19.9–16)

*Iustum et tenacem propositi virum* (III.3) is addressed to Bacchus, the
poet's favorite among the demigods, whose possession of justice
and bravery carried them to a place in heaven:

> hac arte Pollux et vagus Hercules
> enisus arcis attigit igneas,
>     quos inter Augustus recumbens
>         purpureo bibit ore nectar,
> hac te merentem, Bacche pater, tuae
> vexere tigres indocili iugum
>     collo trahentes, hac Quirinus
>         Martis equis Acheronta fugit.   (III.3.9–16)

III.25 reports another visitation of the god, during which the poet
is being hurried through groves and caves where he receives
prophetic statements of the coming glory of the Augustan order.
The poet is to be the poetic voice of the regime and he is the
one to place Augustus among the immortals:

> quibus
> antris egregii Caesaris audiar
> aeternum meditans decus
>     stellis inserere et consilio Iovis?
>             *        *        *
> nil parvum aut humili modo,
>     nil mortale loquar. dulce periculum est
> o Lenaee, sequi deum
>     cingentem viridi tempora pampino.
>                         (III.25.3–6 and 17–20)

As they stand, the poems present the outline of a progressive religious experience. Stage one is that of *a priori* prejudice and intolerance. Stage two is that of sudden revelation, conversion and initiation. Stage three (III.3 and III.25) is that of belief, then doubt, then new ecstasy.

It may quite naturally be objected that, if one is prepared to wrench poems from their proper context, it is not difficult to make them present any pattern that one desires to discover. I think, however, it is quite clear that, while the poems have been lifted out of their context, they have been set side by side in the order of the books from which they have been taken. Conceivably it could be an accident that four poems concerned with Bacchus should, when brought together in this way, exhibit a pattern of conversion, but the possibility seems to me to be remote. The possibility of the conversion-pattern's being a matter of accident would be greater if the Bacchic series were simply a group of poetic exercises on a theme. But, as the last poem in the series makes unmistakably clear, the poet's resistance and his capitulation to Bacchus are part of a literary and political allegory. Each of the first three books of the *Odes*, as we have noted, contains one of these Bacchic poems. The inference seems to be reasonable enough that Horace has intended to represent himself as being in the first stage of his relationship to Bacchus in Book I, to have progressed to the second stage by the end of Book II, and the third in Book III. It is this inference that the following paragraphs are intended to support.

*Nullam Vare sacra* stands nearly in the center of Book I and at the close of a half-book that contains some extravagant panegyric, Horace's most explicit complimentary refusal to treat the praise of Augustus in heroic epic, four poems (2, 3, 14 and 15) that express great and increasing anxiety over the moral crisis of Rome, and two poems (16 and 17) that indicate a strong desire to run away from the whole business and take refuge in Arcadia.

The extreme of panegyric would seem to have been reached in I.12 (*Quem virum aut heroa lyra*), in which it is stated that the Augustan story is not only the greatest literary theme that

Horace could treat but that its hero should take over the supervision of the known world, excepting possibly Olympus where
Jove may remain to practise with thunderbolts. Horace's most
explicit *recusatio* (1.6 *Scriberis Vario*) more subtly suggests an
Achillean role for the emperor; unfortunately the poet lacks the
genius of a Homer or that of the great dramatists, both which
would really be needed for the adequate treatment of the theme.
*Iam satis terris* (1.2) concludes its recital of woe and frustrated
appeals to deaf deities with a panegyrical postscript, that
possibly the god Mercury has already responded and is hiding
under the mask of the youth Octavian. The happy idea is
clouded, however, by the haunting fear that Mercury too may
be alienated by Rome's depravity. Some hope there may be,
but it is the quickening pace of Rome's decadence that worries
the poet. In the prayer for Vergil's safety (1.3) the Romans
have become latter-day Titans on the point of a fresh assault
upon Heaven itself.[6] Surely the ship of 1.14 is the State and its
moribund people. Similarly the Trojan metaphor of Nereus'
prophecy (1.15) is another expression of horror and apprehension lest the Roman course lead to a disaster too terrible to
contemplate. Nereus has no real hope of making Paris and Helen
turn back by painting his contrasting pictures of war and the
cowardly dalliance of the lovers. Horace suddenly cuts short
his metaphorical treatment of Roman distress and writes a
Stesichorean palinode. The somewhat scholastic discourse on
the horrors of violence slams the door on thoughts of war.
*O matre pulchra filia pulchrior* (1.16) and *Velox amoenum saepe
Lucretilem* (1.17) are addressed to Helen—not, of course, the
heroine of Homer, but Helen with the allegorical overtones of
the moralists. Turning his back on war—as well as on thoughts
of writing heroic poetry—the poet makes his apology to love

6. The Romans actually continue the assault where the Titans left off:

> nil mortalibus arduum est:
> caelum ipsum petimus stultitia neque
>     per nostrum patimur scelus
> iracunda Iovem ponere fulmina.                              (1.3.37–40)

and invites "Helen" to come to his private Arcadia and sing beside him in the wilderness. The faint echo of the Trojan war can still be heard, but it is not heroic: it concerns a contest of women for the love of one man Odysseus.[7]

This is the collection at the close of which *Nullam Vare sacra* stands. The assertion in this poem (that the poet is a willing follower of the genial Bacchus who loves gaiety and is the companion of Venus but that he will have nothing to do with the Bacchus whose worship leads to strife) reads like a restatement in a new idiom of the poet's declaration in 1.6 and the apology to Helen of 1.16 and 1.17. As if to leave no doubt of his attitude at this point in his work, the poet follows *Nullam Vare sacra* with *Mater saeva cupidinum* (1.19), which begins with a reproof of the poet for having strayed from his proper field of activity:

> Mater saeva Cupidinum
> Thebanaeque iubet me Semelae puer
> et lasciva Licentia
> finitis animum reddere amoribus.

Retreat from war and aloofness from public concerns are, generally speaking, Epicurean attitudes. The present paper is not the place for exploring the matter further, but it may be remarked that Book 1 is the book in which Horace has concentrated most of his poems that contain what are popularly considered to be Epicurean views of life under the shadow of fleeting Time, uncertain Fortune and inevitable death. This is the book of *carpe diem*, an admonition never repeated in earnest by Horace after Book 1.[8]

7. To judge from Horace's treatment of Homer in *Epist.* 1.2, he would have expected readers to recognize in *matre pulchra filia pulchrior* an allegorical Helen just as he would have expected them to see an allegory of Roman moral decline in 1.15.

8. In this paper the labels "Epicurean" and "Stoic" are used for convenience' sake as terms that are not philosophically accurate but come as close as anything to being serviceable in describing two different attitudes towards life and the eternal verities, as they emerge in Horace. No attempt is made in this paper to take part in the debate over Horace's philosophy.

*Bacchum in remotis* (II.19) contains nothing within itself that would warrant its being interpreted as a poem of political significance (on the surface at least), and nothing about it that makes it the appropriate sequel to or endpiece for a book largely filled with poetic treatments of Stoic philosophy. Nevertheless, because II.19's *mise en scène* is strikingly similar to that of the obviously political III.25 and because its wording in part recalls 1.18, it seems justifiable to inquire whether II.19 may not in some way be intended to have a meaningful relationship to the poems that precede and follow it.

In an earlier paper I suggested but did not develop the idea that a poem of supposed Bacchic ecstasy was precisely the right thing for Horace to have set down immediately before the fantasy of II.20.[9] If anything could provide the dramatic motivation for a bizarre hallucination such as metamorphosis into a bird, *Bacchum in remotis* was the poem to do it. That idea still seems sound to me and I shall not weary the reader with further discussion of it here.

The appropriateness of II.19 as the sequel to Book II as a whole is more difficult to establish, but I believe the arguments for this are reasonable. Bacchus must have long had status among Stoic teachers as a symbol of spiritual and moral independence and security. The encounter between Dionysus and Pentheus in Euripides' *Bacchae* had, it seems, been taken over by the moralists as the classical example of the serenity of true wisdom and virtue when confronted by intolerance and tyranny. Horace paraphrases the scene as the conclusion of his discourse on the *vir bonus et sapiens* in the sixteenth epistle of Book 1.[10] On the pretext of anticipating Quinctius' inquiry regarding the character of Horace's farm, the poet in this letter propounds a whole philosophy. First there is an almost photographically exact description of the site, environs, and climatic conditions

9. "A fresh Approach to Horace II.20," *American Journal of Philology*, LXXVII (1956), 255–63.

10. *Epist.* 1.16.73–7. Cf. Eur. *Bac.* 492–8. On the Stoic use of this passage of the *Bacchae* see Heinze's note on *Epist.* 1.16.73 ff.

of the farm. Then an inventory of essential features that is adequate and terse enough for Cato and thoughtful enough for Thoreau. This is nature. Compare the picture of these fields, oak-groves and the living water with the pretty villas that the Tiber washes in Book II of the *Odes* and it is easy to see what Horace is doing. Before the reader realizes it, he has been shown that these trees are living in accordance with Nature. They provide food for beasts and shade for man. Therefore it is that such a grove is *amoenus*. This is truly philosophy in a nutshell. From here it is not difficult to go on to the definition of the *vir bonus et sapiens*. Whether it is the lilies of the field or the oaks of Tivoli, behold them and the rest is not difficult. One can face up to Pentheus without fear, because Nature's order and procedure are obvious.

It would be over-simplification to say that in *Nullam Vare sacra* (1.18) the poet poses in a smug suburban role like that of the benighted gentry addressed so often in Book II and that in *Bacchum in remotis* (II.19) he has reversed himself, shaking off the stuffy intolerance and ignorance of Pentheus (as the moralists interpreted him) to emerge as the disciple of the god of wisdom, a disciple who has contemplated Nature's truth so long that he is vouchsafed a glimpse of heaven. A great many important poems stand between 1.18 and II.19 and they pose innumerable problems of interpretation in detail. But it is nevertheless fairly obvious that the poet has reversed his attitude towards Bacchus and that the explanation of the change is to be sought in the poems that lie between. To determine the exact point at which the poet pretends to have experienced conversion is not my present concern. I shall be satisfied if I can make out the rough outline in Book II of the course of thought so subtly and yet sharply indicated in Epistle 1.16.

Partisans of an Epicurean Horace can find superficial evidence to support their position in Book II. But, if one leafs through this Book thoughtfully, it is impossible not to be aware of the austerity of the poet's thought and expression, despite

moments of near gaiety in the first half of the book.[11] The
hesitant portrayal of military scenes in *Motum ex Metello* (II.1)
belongs to *recusatio*, of course, but the reflection on the contention of Roman leaders for material prizes (*plenum opus aleae*)
hints at the beginning of a critique of Roman Society. Stoic
motifs sometimes stand out in sharp relief as in the poetic
diatribe on the true king (II.1). Proculeius, in the paradoxical
view of the Stoics, is a greater king than Phrahates, whom, if she
were censor, Virtus would disqualify. The true king can look
upon a heap of treasure without a sidelong glance of desire.
One might say that most of Book II is one way or another
concerned with the paradox relating to true wealth. Horace is
writing poetry, not philosophical discourses, and oftener than
not blends or joins the paradoxes for satirical effect, as in II.4,
where Xanthias is playfully consoled for having been smitten
with a slave-girl by the suggestion that the physically charming
Phyllis may be a princess in disguise. The ironic fusion of *topoi*
here defies analysis in a line, but a Stoic with a sense of humor
might identify the paradoxes relating to true wealth, true
beauty, and true royalty; he should be equally delighted with
the portrait of the lovely Barine (II.8), a kind of female Dorian
Gray, whose loveliness and power grow apace with her black
soul. *Aequam memento rebus in arduis | servare mentem* is good Stoic
advice, and one could cite more.

Throughout Book II, however, and especially after the fall of
the tree (*Ille et nefasto te posuit die*: II.13) Horace's sharpest remarks
are leveled at the Roman gentry who, blind to the lessons Nature
is forever teaching all around them, not only cut for their own
palaces the marble Numa reserved for temples but restlessly and
without enjoyment and unaware of their folly under the shadow
of death strive to counterfeit Nature's groves and streams with
sterile shade-trees and artificial waterworks.[12] They try to buy
release from fear with the treasure which is the stuff of fear.[13]

---

11. Cf. the ironic consolation to Xanthias (II.4) and the welcome home to
Pompeius (II.7).

12. Cf. II.3 and II.15.                    13. Cf. II.16 and II.18.

On the other hand, as the shadows deepen for the wretched seekers of material wealth, they fade for the poet, whom even sudden death might carry to the company of Alcaeus and Sappho (ii.13). By the close of Book ii it is plain that poet and *vulgus* are worlds apart. As we read we seem to be already in the atmosphere of the Roman Odes. Horace is speaking to Rome rather than to individuals and his manner is suited more to the rostrum than to the dinner-table. Pentheus and Dionysus are nearing a decisive confrontation.

In ii.18 (*Non ebur neque aureum*) the poet flings his challenge into the face of the world and boasts his personal victory over the mighty of this world. He possesses what they can never have. He has genius, which the gods gave him; he enjoys men's trust; although he is poor in material things, he has power. The rich and mighty of this world are the poet's clients. Indeed, he is far richer than they, for he is beyond need and fear, and indifferent to time and death:

> at fides et ingeni
> benigna vena est, pauperemque dives
>    me petit: nihil supra
> deos lacesso nec potentem amicum
>    largiora flagito,
> satis beatus unicis Sabinis.
>    truditur dies die,
> novaeque pergunt interire lunae...[14]

Gratitude to Maecenas required the inclusion of the Sabine farm among the poet's blessings, but it is clear that he looks upon his material comforts as corollaries and dividends and not as essential. Happiness is the state in which there is nothing left to desire. Modesty even in this poem prevents the poet's declaring that it is basically *virtus* that has placed him in his present state, but he is unmistakably enjoying the rewards that *virtus* alone has the power to bring.

Still the question may be asked: well enough, but why should

14. ii.18.9–16.

a vision of Bacchus be the sequel to a candid confession of
felicity achieved? My answer is this. Philosophy has given its
definition of happiness: it is not what the *vulgus* prizes but what
the philosopher-poet has. Horace can go no further in definition
except by resorting to symbol and metaphor. In the first three
books of the *Odes* Bacchus—god of madness as he is supposed to
be—represents the opposite to the unheroic, to retreat from
reality, retreat to the tempting luxury of a decadent "Troy."
Bacchus can take arms against a sea of troubles and win. The
miracles he performs for his votaries (not unskillfully adapted
by Horace in II.19 from the messenger's speech in the *Bacchae*)[15]
are close poetic equivalents of those luxuries to which the poet-
sage falls heir as the result of his genius and his character in
II.18. And Bacchus seems to have taken his faithful quite
suddenly to the abode of the blest which had to be reached by a
long sea-journey in *Epode* 16. Or, turning the problem another
way, Bacchus' votaries in II.19 seem to have arrived in heaven
or somewhere from which there is a good view of heaven and
hell. And Bacchus' own first trip to heaven (to be recorded in
III.3) came as the result of his possession or acquisition of
qualities very similar to those to which the poet lays claim in
II.18.

By way of summarizing a tedious argument, it seems reasonable to conclude that *Bacchum in remotis* (II.19) stands at the
close of Book II as the poetically logical culmination of Book II.
As I have suggested, it provides also the dramatic motivation
for the poet's imagined metamorphosis into a bird of heroic
song.

The point is a familiar one but can bear repeating here:
Bacchus is the patron god of poets in both the genres in which
Horace has occasion to write in the *Odes*: *quamquam choreis aptior
et iocis*, Bacchus was nevertheless Jove's stand-by in the battle
with the Giants.[16] Naturally, in Book I, when the poet was
running away from heroic poetry, he lauded Bacchus the god of
gentle revelry and love but abused the god of the heroic

15. Lines 672 ff.                    16. II.19.25.

madness. At the close of Book II the poet is in a mood for a spell of heroic madness.

The *amabilis insania* however wears off. As much as the poet is fired with *virtus*, which the god inspires, he loses heart as he contemplates in his vision the seemingly certain decline and fall of Rome. The poet doffs his swan's plumage for the *penna tenuis usitata*[17] and resumes the composition of lyric poetry as usual. This does not mean, however, a return to the mood of Book I. Neither the pretended retreat from exalted lyric at the close of III.3 nor the heartbroken and bitter final stanza of III.6 means that. There is no retreat to a cave of Dione. The poet's political position is about what it was in Book II. Augustus, if he has not quite displaced Jove in the administration of things in general, is given credit as *finire quaerens labores* and on the point of receiving divine honors in his lifetime. As for the *profanum vulgus*, although the subject is avoided in the part of Book III that immediately follows the Roman Odes, the poet's *odium* mixed with anxiety has not changed. This essay is not the place in which to consider the character of the poems of Book III. In diversity it resembles Book I, although it contains poems of greater length; in philosophical outlook it is closer to II, but less satirical. At times, in Book III, it almost seems as if Horace had been collecting material for a "legend of good women." As this book nears its close, the question that the poet had raised in *Iam satis terris* (I.2) is still unanswered: Will the god, whether in the shape of Mercury or Jove himself, be able to conquer the hostile forces in Rome's own soul as he has conquered her enemies abroad? The Roman Odes have left the possibility in our minds that neither Augustus nor any other can now arrest the decline of the Roman people. *Intactis opulentior* (III.24) puts the question in no uncertain terms. The degraded, effeminate generation of the day is treated more severely here than ever before; the crowning insult is an unfavorable comparison with barbarian neighbors like the noble nomadic Scythians, whose nobility, it seems, grows through their blessed separation from

17. II.20.1 ff.

the enervating influences of a complex urban civilization. But the poem is not an appeal to the Roman people but a call for a savior; the call comes as close as anything in the *Odes* to a challenge to such a would-be savior, to show now, if ever, what he can really do. If he is to receive honors as the father of his country, it is time that he did something about his children. The gap between the encomium of Augustus and this apparently sharp admonitory line seems impossible to close.

It is Bacchus, of course, with that power that can arrest the course of rivers, who, even before the poet's readers can have unrolled their *libelli* to iii.25, has already changed the course of history—or, perhaps, who opens the poet's eyes once more to the fact that, even while he harangued the people and their leader, the beneficent forces of reformation were at work. The poet is in mid-ecstasy as *Quo me Bacche rapis tui plenum* begins. Like the Bacchants, the poet is being rushed over rocks and through forests, through caves and groves, receiving ineffable prophecy, and, like the Bacchant, he emerges from the dark wood upon the bank of a great river, from which he has a glorious prospect of the new Augustan order. Anxiety and doubt melt away and with them any resistance to the proposal that he, Horace, should be the trumpeter of the new regime. He will be the one to give Augustus his secure position among the gods.

Thus Bacchus performs his final function as a *deux ex machina* and brings down the curtain on a drama that has been kept alive in the reader's consciousness but largely played out off stage. The reader, it seems to me, is permitted to witness just enough to make him curious, to arouse his curiosity and make him search the context of the Bacchic poems for clues to their meaning.

The expansion of a *recusatio* from an isolated poem of combined flattery and refusal into an intermittent narrative sequence with plot and suspense may have been Horace's invention, but my inadequate knowledge of Hellenistic models that can have influenced him prevents me from stating this with conviction.

It is possible that Horace had already experimented with literary devices for making the *recusatio* an organic feature of a collection of poems before he undertook the Bacchic sequence. It is my impression that in the *Epodes* Horace made use of Canidia in very much the same way as he used Bacchus in the *Odes*. The *Epodes*, as Horace later characterized them in *Epistle* I.19, were a series of studies in wrath after the fashion of Archilochus but without the element of personal animosity against real people. Horace created Canidia to be the straw target of his imitation of the *rabies Archilochi*. Canidia appears or is mentioned in only three poems: the playful invective to Maecenas (3), the melodramatic preliminaries to ritual murder (5), and the dialogue between her and the poet at the end of the book (17); but these three appearances on the stage of the *Epodes* are sufficient to establish her as the dominant and evil genius of the *Epodes*. She is the classical witch of the *fabula Milesia*, whose presence is felt even when she is invisible. She is the *pharmaceutria* who will conquer with her spells and potions the objects of her desire or destroy them. She is the appropriate adversary for the curious yet cynical Bohemian intellectual who, having felt her power, is not filled with passion for Canidia but is maddened by her spells and potions into a ferocious hostility towards the ugliness and evil of the whole world of which she is the hateful symbol.

The parallel between Canidia's role and that of Bacchus is not precise. The poet began by fearing and suspecting Bacchus but eventually capitulated to him as the power that represented forces that would conquer evil in the world. With Canidia the relationship entered into by the poet from curiosity or through accident mushrooms into a bitter and permanent hostility. In both cases, however, there is a contest, the uncertainty of whose outcome provides an element of suspense and continuity to the collection as a whole. The status of the poet's adversaries provides convenient dramatic motivation for the poet's behavior in each case. Bacchus' power enables the poet to soar suddenly into heroic verse. The spells of the witch help to explain and condone the extravagant tone and unrestrained expression of the *iambi*.

There has been considerable debate over the significance of Canidia in the *Epodes* and, in particular, over the meaning of her prophecy which she gives in her dialogue with the poet in *Epode* 17.[18] I am not prepared to make a full-dress entry into the controversy here. But is it unreasonable to conjecture that Canidia somehow symbolizes not just evil but the age-old forces that oppose progress, especially if progress means the rejection of ugly, selfish and shortsighted materialism? May Canidia not be a kind of representative in the *Epodes* of the *profanum vulgus*?

If Canidia may be thought to be the personal representative of the *vulgus* and its ideals, it is a little easier to make sense out of her grandiloquently worded prophecy. First of all, her prediction that, despite present reverses at the hands of the poet (the punishment she has received in the *Epodes*), she will one day be in the drivers' seat again, can be taken to mean that the cause of the *vulgus* is never lost against the forces of reform. In the end, the *vulgus* always wins.

The slightly wearying catalogue of the punishments that the poet is to undergo for his sacrilegious meddling and divulging of Canidia's rites I take to mean that the poet is to be condemned to the perpetual—albeit futile—practice of literary composition. He is to receive punishment that befits his crime.

Canidia is used, it seems to me, very much in the way Vergil used the Harpy Celaeno: to make an externally disagreeable messenger the unwitting bearer of uncomprehended good tidings. Some of the dilemmas and crises that Canidia sees ahead for the poet hint at similar emergencies common to lovers and love-poets. Why may not Horace be using Canidia to speak his epilogue? It is time for *plaudite* but the epode-poet will meet the *vulgus* again in another literary genre, namely that of the *Odes*.

18. Cf. V. Pöschl, "Horaz," in *Fondation Hardt, Entretiens sur l'antiquité classique*, II (1953), 91–127.

# Two Horatian Proems:
## *Carm.* 1.26 and 1.32

ROSS S. KILPATRICK

# Two Horatian Proems:
## *Carm.* 1.26 and 1.32 [1]

HORACE'S LYRIC PRAYERS for poetic inspiration from his Muses seem to fall into two categories. First, there are those odes which contain both the prayer and the poem requested, as do *Carm.* 1.24 and 3.4. Secondly, there are two odes in particular that consist wholly of the prayers themselves, and do not include the poem that is the object of the prayer. In *Carm.* 1.26 Horace addresses a formal prayer to his Muse (*Pipleis*) to inspire in him a poem of diversion and solace for Lamia. Similarly, in *Carm.* 1.32 he appeals to his *barbitos* to remember the old days, and speak forth at his request with a *carmen Latinum*. A question that has yet to be answered is this: if Horace did write the poems referred to in 1.26 and 1.32, did he include them in the collection of odes?

The hypothesis offered here is an obvious one, but one not (to my knowledge) explored before: namely that the poems asked for in *Carm.* 1.26 and *Carm.* 1.32 are the odes which immediately follow them. In other words, *Carm.* 1.26 is the proem to 1.27; and *Carm.* 1.32, to 1.33. What I hope to prove, then, is that in each of these two pairs of odes Horace has skillfully contrived to integrate with the dedicated poem an introductory ode that shares with it important features of theme, allusion, and meter, and to fashion of each pair an organic whole.

1. This study represents the substance of Chapter II of the writer's doctoral thesis, *MUSIS AMICUS UNICE SECURUS: A Study of Consolation in the ODES of Horace* (Yale, 1967). He wishes to express his gratitude to the editors of *Yale Classical Studies* and his director, Prof. E. T. Silk, for all their assistance and encouragement.

Carm. *1.26*/*1.27*

Writing in 1912, E. H. Sturtevant had this to say about these two odes: "No connection between them can be detected. Perhaps the tantalizing phrase *Opuntiae frater Megillae* in 1.27 hides some allusion to Lamia."[2] This remark was made incidentally to a discussion of *Carm.* 1.16 and 1.17, one of five pairs of odes that present consecutive odes in like meters.[3] (The general rarity of such pairs had already been noted by Wickham.)[4]

In 1939 Adelaide Hahn took up the problem of *Carm.* 16 and 17 where Sturtevant had left it (she called them "pendants"), and observed in a note[5] that *Carm.* 26 and 27 were a pair similar (in reverse order) to 16 and 17; that is, 1.26 is an invitation to a feast, while 1.27 is the feast itself, replete with "mock heroics, playful paternal raillery, yet with a serious undercurrent."

So far this pair of odes has been discussed in terms of matter and meter only by way of *obiter dicta*;[6] their difficulties, apparently, have seemed insoluble. But if Horace places a pair of Alcaic poems back-to-back (something he rarely does) he may have a reason for considering them connected in some way. *Carm.* 16 and 17, for example, appear to be addressed somehow to Helen. 34 and 35 are bonded together by the theme of *Fortuna*. The Alcaic meter is the poet's real *forte*, and he does not often employ it for trivial poems.[7] In Book 1 it is a kind of rhythmic thread that ties together some important themes: the

2. E. H. Sturtevant, "O Matre Pulchra Filia Pulchrior," *CR*, xxvi (1912), 122.

3. *Carm.* 1.16–17; 1.26–7; 1.34–5; 3.24–5; 4.14–15.

4. *The Works of Horace* (3rd ed. Oxford, 1896), vol. i, p. 29. *Carm.* 3.1–6 are, as Wickham points out, the one notable exception.

5. A. Hahn, "Epodes 5 and 17, *Carmina* 1.16 and 1.17," *TAPA*, lxx (1939), 226, n. 61.

6. E.g. Collinge, *The Structure of Horace's Odes* (London 1961), p. 46; J. Perret, *Horace* (New York 1964), p. 85.

7. Even 3.26 is significant as a *recusatio*.

delicate 1.9, the agonized 1.35, the resounding 1.37. *Carm.* 3.1–6 speak for themselves.

*Carm.* 1.26 shows evidence of careful composition and location. In form it is a prayer to the Muses,[8] delivered in the role he assumed with greater pomp in 3.1, that of the *Musarum sacerdos*. As *Musis amicus* (1), Horace acknowledges their gift to him: "nil sine te mei | prosunt honores" (9–10), echoing *Carm.* 1.1 and anticipating 3.30. And he points with pride to his proudest achievement: the Alcaic meter in Latin. This call for recognition is steeped in a Lucretian joy and fervor:[9] "O quae fontibus integris | gaudes, apricos necte flores, | necte meo Lamiae coronam, | Piplei dulcis!" (5–9). Wilkinson, who goes so far as to say that Horace's lyrics are "rarely lyrical, being the product of meditation rather than immediate emotion...," admits that 1.26 is one of the few exceptions. He sees this ode, however, simply as a "celebration of Horace's success in mastering the Lesbian metres and adapting them to suit his ears."[10]

While Wilkinson, along with Pasquali[11] and Heinze, is content with this simple interpretation, this conviction has not seemed so uncomplicated to others. Wickham, for instance, had this reservation to make: "It is difficult to see the point of connection between the first and the last parts of the ode, unless, indeed, as has been suggested, Horace has been holding up his own cheerfulness and its source to Lamia's imitation."[12] Compare too A. Y. Campbell's assessment of 1.26: "xxvi is one of those poems that somewhat mystify the modern reader; it is probably best explained as purporting to inspirit Aelius Lamia, who is anxious about the political situation."[13]

8. Cf. *Carm.* 1.12, where Clio, the "Proclaimer," is invoked for *encomium*.
9. Cf. Lucr. 5.192–7.
10. L. P. Wilkinson, *Horace and his Lyric Poetry* (Cambridge 1945), pp. 12, 123.
11. G. Pasquali, *Orazio Lirico* (Florence 1920), p. 30.
12. *Op. cit.* (above, p. 216, n. 4), p. 98.
13. A. Y. Campbell, *Horace. A New Interpretation* (London 1924), p. 223.

My sympathy is with those who have been bothered by a *nescioquid* in *Carm.* 1.26. If it were a little three-strophe poem used in isolation somewhere else or as a demonstration of some odd meter that Horace uses only once, it would never have caught much attention. But, as we have seen, it is one of a pair of Alcaic odes, a significant fact in itself. Surprisingly enough, no one seems to have suggested that it is a "fragment"; unless Lehrs' peremptory comment, "offenbar nur Einleitung-strophen,"[14] is moving in that direction. As a matter of fact, Lehrs' remark is (as far as it does go) correct in my opinion: the triad of strophes that comprises *Carm.* 1.26 constitutes an intro-ductory poem, to which the accompanying ode itself has been lost—or perhaps "lost-sight of" is more accurate, for it may not be beyond recovery.

To digress briefly, how much better it might have been if rather than "a light poem of only three stanzas"[15] whose unity and coherence have appeared less than satisfactory, a more impressive ode in Alcaics had been placed after *Carm.* 1.25 (in Sapphics). *Carm.* 1.27, for example, is a rollicking drinking song, Alcaean in both meter and manner,[16] into which Horace has woven a subtle web of literary allusion and reminiscence (Anacreon,[17] Plato, Theocritus) against a background of a Hellenistic banquet, with its teasing, drama, suspense, and *amour*. To all of this the "Alcaean form" lends a high stylistic level.[18] It ends with a finale that "seems to revel in grandeur," with "rolling sounds...awe-inspiring images...delightful mockery of thought."[19] The whole poem is Greek with the exception of one detail, *Falerni* (10). In short, it is an impressive

14. K. Lehrs, *Q. Horatius Flaccus* (Leipzig 1869), p. lv.

15. Wilkinson, p. 143.

16. "Alcaeus' drinking songs have an air of being spontaneous and almost contemporary. He looks to the immediate occasion and not to some ideal drinking party, and speaks of it as it is or as he wishes it to be" (C. M. Bowra, *Greek Lyric Poetry* [2nd ed. Oxford 1961], p. 157).

17. Anacreon, Frag. 11 (P); Plato, *Laws* 637–42, 722; *Symp.* 177D, 213A; Theoc. 14.18–20.

18. E. Fraenkel, *Horace* (Oxford 1957), p. 183.          19. *Ibid.*

piece of virtuoso composition. Then why did Horace not use *this* in isolation as a real "production number" in Alcaics? Perhaps (to return to the point of digression) he did.

There is one explanation that may reconcile this hypothesis with the hard facts that the MSS, without exception, present. *Carm.* 1.26 and 27 are in essence two components of one metrical recapitulation. The former's function in the collection is to introduce the spectacular 1.27, and dedicate it with grace and taste to Aelius Lamia, who, if the historical allusions are contemporary, was a very young man.[20] In other words, Horace is here following in the tradition of Catullus (65, 68 *a*) in dedicating a previously completed poem to a specific individual; but he has surpassed anything Catullus had attempted in integrating his dedication with the *munus* itself.

At this point one might well anticipate two substantial objections. (1) Where else does Horace use this type of dedication? (2) What are the verbal clues and internal links between the two that effect this integration?

With respect to (1), I would adduce, in addition to the pertinent analogues from Catullus just cited, Eduard Fraenkel's vigorous condemnation of *Systemzwang*, the insistence that

> no form or setting of a poem can be tolerated if there exists only one instance of it. If in such a case a scholar is afraid of resorting to the most radical cure, the obelizing of the obnoxious poem, he should at least extort from it such a meaning as to make it conform to a common type.[21]

If this *Systemzwang* dictates that there has never been found in the works of Horace a poem that dedicates the next (in the same meter and presenting a metrical pair in deliberate isolation), and that therefore there can be no such phenomenon, then I too reject it.

Objection (2) demands a less subjective defence. Since 1.26 is so short, a fairly complete analysis of it can be attempted here.

20. See Heinze, p. 113.　　　21. *Op. cit.* p. 188.

My text is exactly that of Wickham (1912) and Klingner (1950), who differ only by one exclamation mark after *dulcis* (9).

> Musis amicus tristitiam et metus
> tradam protervis in mare Creticum
>     portare ventis, quis sub Arcto
>         rex gelidae metuatur orae,
>
> quid Tiridaten terreat, unice
> securus. o quae fontibus integris
> gaudes, apricos necte flores,
>     necte meo Lamiae coronam,
>
> Piplei dulcis. nil sine te mei
> prosunt honores: hunc fidibus novis,
>     hunc Lesbio sacrare plectro
>         teque tuasque decet sorores.

> Beloved of the Muses, I shall give over gloom and appre-
> hension to the wanton winds to carry out into the Cretan
> sea. As for what prince causes alarm on the frozen strand
> by the northpole, (or) what is scaring Tiridates—with
> those things I am supremely unconcerned (1–6*a*).

In these six lines, Horace makes the first major declaration in the *Odes* of his role as *vates* and votary of the Muses. (The future tense may be intended to suggest a realization just reached, or attitude just formed.) It is in the *Alcaic* strophe too, that his definitive declarations of this role are to be made in Books III and IV. In *Carm.* 3.1 his full role as *Musarum sacerdos* (3) is revealed, along with the claim to an entirely new utterance arising from their personal inspiration:

> Odi profanum vulgus et arceo;
> favete linguis: carmina non prius
>     audita Musarum sacerdos
>         virginibus puerisque canto (1–4).

This later role is implicit in his prayer to the Muses (1.26.6*b*– 12). As their votary, he is under their protective *aegis*, as he elaborates in *Carm.* 3.4 (5–36) and (perhaps) 1.22. It is with the supreme confidence born of his awareness of this relationship that he can lay fears aside. But the poet is not merely the recipient of favor, or client of the Muses; he is their interpreter as well. The implications of this are clear: the *vates* has the power to impart comfort and solace, just as he receives it himself from the Muses, as both precept and *divertissement*. This is what Horace is telling us in *vv.* 1–6*a*. The question is, why?

Having declared his role as *Musis amicus*, Horace proceeds with his petition to one of them:

> O thou who delightest in unquaffed springs, plait thou the sunny flowers: plait for my friend Lamia a garland, sweet maid of Pipleia (6*b*–9*a*).

It is important to see the real meaning of *apricos* (7).[22] Coupled as it is with *gaudes*, the word provides a deliberate antithesis to *tristitiam et metus* (1): the sunny blooms are an antidote for "gloom and apprehension." Horace is immune; so it should be Lamia who is afflicted. The garland of flowers can only be, as commentators have realized right along, a poem dedicated in Pindaric fashion to Lamia,[23] to which the epithets *apricos* (7) and *dulcis* (9) can, by inference, apply. And the stress upon the *vates'* role as bringer of consolation, joy, and *divertissement* can be justified by what should be obvious, but has never seemed so: the poem dedicated to Lamia should be capable of this function. The anxiety to which Horace the *Musis amicus* is immune, but which Lamia has been suffering, is one to which we in the 1960's are no strangers: "wars and rumors of wars."

Now *Carm.* 1.26, in spite of its lyrical qualities, is surely not

22. H. Peerlkamp (*Q. Horati Flacci Carmina* [Amsterdam 1862]) conjectured *pudicos* (= *recentes, intactos*). But it was not the text that was lacking, only the proper emphasis that Horace intended.

23. For flowers as the symbols of poetry, cf. Sappho, Frag. 55 (L–P); *Carm.* 3.27.29–32 (see Chapter v of my dissertation); *Ep.* 2.2.96; Lucr. 1.197 ff.

the poem to provide the diversion to boost Lamia's morale; but
*Carm.* 1.27 *is.* And, if Horace has included the poem to which he
refers in 1.26 in his collection of odes, where else would one
expect to find it than immediately following? Merely to
speculate on the possibility that 1.27 was the poem that Horace
presented to Lamia would prove nothing. There is, however,
internal evidence, including correspondences of theme and
motif between the two, that might lead one to suppose that
Horace wrote 1.27 first, and then having decided (for one
reason or another) to dedicate it to Lamia, composed 1.26 as
an integrated *prooemium* to it.

The form of *Carm.* 1.26 is a prayer with a four-part structure:
I (1–6*a*) declaration by the poet of his freedom from worldly
care as a *Musis amicus*: II (6*b*–9*a*) invocation and prayer to the
Muses to "plait a garland of sunny flowers" to cheer Lamia;
III (9*b*–10*a*) acknowledgement of the poet's debt to the Muses
(i.e. the sanction) for his power to confer *honores*; IV (10*b*–12)
recapitulation of prayer to Muses to present Lamia with a
poem—and in the great new meter they have taught him.
Using a prayer to the Muses for a dedication seems the obvious
and natural thing for the *vates lyricus* to do.

There is one more aspect of *Carm.* 1.26 that may have a slight
bearing upon its function as *prooemium* to 1.27. This is the interpretation of the word *sacrare* (11). It is translated universally as
"immortalize": "consecrate" (Shorey), "heiligen" (Heinze),
"canonize" (Wickham). But *sacrare* is sometimes capable of a
slightly different meaning. At *Aen.* 12.141, for example, Juno
addresses the nymph Juturna in an appeal for Turnus' rescue.
She speaks of the origin of her powers as follows: "hunc illi rex
aetheris altus honorem | Iuppiter erepta pro virginitate
sacravit." In that context *sacrare* can only mean "confer upon,
award, bestow" ("...appropriate of an inalienable gift con-
ferred by a god"—Conington). If *hunc...sacrare* is construed as
*hunc* (sc. *honorem*) *sacrare*, rather than our assuming that *hunc*
refers to Lamia, perhaps *vv.* 9*b*–10 might be translated as
follows:

To naught without thee come the honors I have to give;
this one with lyre new, this one with Lesbian pick it doth
behoove thee and thy sisters to bestow.[24]

*Hunc* (...*sacrare*) with its repetition would parallel *necte flores,
necte...coronam* (7–8), and would pick up the dative *meo Lamiae*
from the same line. At the same time, it would look ahead to the
following poem which is to be dedicated. One might compare
the use of this demonstrative pronoun in Catullus' dedication
poems: "quare habe tibi quidquid *hoc* libelli" (1.8); "mitto |
*haec* expressa tibi carmen Battiadae" (65.16); "*haec* tibi non
tribuo munera, cum nequeo" (68.32).

Is the emphasis of this ode upon Lamia or the power of
poetry and the poet? This too might relate to the question of
the meaning of *hunc sacrare*. I believe that Wilkinson is right in
this regard: "It is not necessary to suppose that Lamia had done
anything; he was simply the first person upon whom the
excited poet could exercise his power of conferring honour..."[25]

24. For a parallel use of the phrase *honorem sacrare* in a prayer to the
Muses for a poem-in-honor see Silius Italicus, 12.309 ff., where such an
*honor* is to be bestowed upon Ennius:

> sed vos, Calliope, nostro donate labori
> nota parum magni longo tradantur ut aevo
> facta viri, et meritum vati sacremus honorem.

I see no difficulty with the ellipse of the dative in 1.26, since *hunc (honorem)
sacrare* would be parallel to *necte meo Lamiae coronam* (8) and have virtually
the same significance.

*Sacrare* in the sense of "immortalize" is rare in any event (L.–S.), and
usually takes a *thing* as object; e.g. poetry (*Ep.* 2.1.49), *eloquentia* (Liv. 39.40).
Of a *person* it seems to mean nothing less than "deify", as Ovid apparently
uses it of Julius Caesar (*Pont.* 4.8.64). In view of the rather modest reference
to Lamia, any significance as strong as this might here seem peculiar. These
considerations, plus the context of the *prooemium*, commend the *hunc* (sc.
*honorem Lamiae*) interpretation to me.

25. *Op. cit.* p. 13. Is there any harm in supposing that a conversation
with Lamia about his anxieties had led Horace to dedicate a poem to him to
cheer him up, with a declaration in conventional terms of his own position
as *Musis amicus...unice securus*? Or perhaps Lamia was being repaid for a
generous compliment to Horace. I feel that the context of *Carm.* 1.26 and its

If so, the emphatically repeated *hunc* is perhaps better taken as referring to the poem than to the addressee.

This interpretation of *hunc sacrare* would make the link between 1.26 and 1.27 explicit. But, even if the interpretation is not accepted, the proem-like character of the first poem is clear.

Adelaide Hahn, in the article already cited, also recognized some links between these two odes which may support our hypothesis.[26] She saw *Carm.* 1.26 as Horace's invitation to a feast to Lamia, with a mood that is the reverse of 1.27: the former is restrained and dignified, while the latter is "a scene of revelry that is fast degenerating into a barbarian brawl."

Each poem does offer a mirror-image of the other though the mood of each is progressive, not static. In 1.26 one proceeds from the extreme of *tristitia* to the mean of *securus*. In 1.27 the opposite is true:

> Natis in usum laetitiae scyphis
> pugnare Thracum est: tollite barbarum
>   morem, verecundumque Bacchum
>     sanguineis prohibete rixis.
>
> vino et lucernis Medus acinaces                         5
> immane quantum discrepat: impium
>   lenite clamorem, sodales,
>     et cubito remanete presso.
>
> vultis severi me quoque sumere
> partem Falerni? dicat Opuntiae                          10
>   frater Megillae, quo beatus
>     vulnere, qua pereat sagitta.
>
> cessat voluntas? non alia bibam
> mercede. quae te cumque domat Venus,
>   non erubescendis adurit                               15
>     ignibus, ingenuoque semper

probable connection with the following ode, as well as the appropriate emphasis upon the *poem*, not the man, lends support to this interpretation of *hunc sacrare*. But, either way, the language is suitable for a *prooemium*.

26. Above, p. 216, n. 5.

amore peccas. quidquid habes, age
depone tutus auribus. a! miser,
  quanta laborabas Charybdi,
    digne puer meliore flamma.                    20

quae saga, quis te solvere Thessalis
magus venenis, quis poterit deus?
  vix illigatum te triformi
    Pegasus expediet Chimaera.

From the extreme (*barbarus mos*) of the *laetitia* which the *arbiter*
decries, the mood shifts to the mean of *verecundus Bacchus* (3).
Just as *immane quantum discrepat* (6) applies to the incompati-
bility of conviviality and violence, it could apply also to that of
gloom and the power of song (26.1–2). And it is in language
very much that of the *Musarum sacerdos* addressing the rioting
Centaurs at the wedding of Pirithoos that the *arbiter* exclaims,
"impium | lenite clamorem sodales. . ." (6). It is surely the
same voice of sweet reason here appealing for moderation in
conviviality that appeals for moderation in anxiety in *Carm.* 1.26.
Finally, the rhetorical question at the end of *v.* 27, "quae saga,
quis te solvere Thessalis | magus venenis, quis poterit deus?"
suggests a glance back to the beginning of the pair of odes for a
kind of answer: "Musis amicus tristitiam et metus | tradam"
(1–2).

M. Treu[27] has presented some evidence to support the view
that 1.26 had, to some extent, an Alcaean original, which for
Horace's contemporaries would have provided an additional
link between the two. But there is at least one further nexus
of literary allusion that serves to bind and unify the two odes.
The name *Opuntiae frater Megillae* may allude (with an added
erotic temper) to the Lacedaemonian who features in Plato's
*Laws.* This has been noted frequently in the commentaries,
but never, to my knowledge, have its implications been ex-

27. See M. Treu, "Zu Alkaios 82 D (32 L) und Horaz C. 1.26," *Würz-*
*burger Jahrbücher für die Altertumswissenschaft* IV (1949–50), 219–25.

amined.[28] In Book 1 (637–42), the dialogue on Crete between the Athenian, Lacedaemonian (Megillus), and Cretan centers on the virtues of restraint at *symposia*. The observation is made (637E): Σκύθαι δὲ καὶ Θρᾷκες ἀκράτῳ παντάπασι χρώμενοι... Πέρσαι δὲ σφόδρα μὲν χρῶνται καὶ ταῖς ἄλλαις τροφαῖς. Heinze identifies the *rex* of *Carm.* 1.26 (4) as the Scythian king,[29] and the reader of 1.27 might recall the Scythian motive in the poem of Anacreon, which according to Ps.-Acro suggested the *sensus* of Horace's own ode:

> ἄγε δηῦτε μηκέθ' οὕτω
> πατάγῳ τε κἀλαλητῷ
> Σκυθικὴν πόσιν παρ' οἴνῳ
> μελετῶμεν, ἀλλὰ καλοῖς
> ὑποπίνοντες ἐν ὕμνοις.[30]

Scythians and Thracians are thus linked in 1.26 (4) – 27 (2) just as they are in the *Laws*.

At 640 Plato has his Athenian propound the requirements of a perfect *arbiter bibendi* (a phenomenon, to be sure, he has never beheld): a quiet person who understands psychology and can preserve and increase good feelings, as well as being sober and wise.[31] Maintenance of good order and discipline at *symposia* promotes convivial association—hence education in its own right:

> Drinking may indeed appear to be a slight matter, and yet is one which cannot be ordered rightly according to nature without correct principles of music; these are necessary to any satisfactory treatment of the subject.[32]

28. As far as I know, these detailed echoes from the *Laws* have not been put forward before: only the simple identification of Megillus. A. T. Cole has made the suggestion that the *topos* of non-Greek excess at banquets may be from Critias (rather than Plato), who wrote a *Lakedaimonion Politeia* in elegiacs: Frag. 4 (D). Indeed, if Horace was particularly interested in this particular *topos*, he might well have studied both works carefully. There certainly do seem to be echoes of the *Laws* in *Carm.* 3.4 (see my dissertation, p. 151, n. 45). See also Xenophanes, Frag. 1 (D).

29. Heinze, *ad loc.*                30. Frag. 43 (D) = 11 (P).
31. *Laws* 640D.                     32. *Ibid.* 642A (tr. Jowett).

Moderation is a theme in the Anacreon fragment too; for it ends: ἀλλὰ καλοῖς ὑποπίνοντες ἐν ὕμνοις: "but drink with moderation between beautiful hymns."[33] Both Plato and Anacreon set up a contrast between barbaric carousing and the decorous sort in conjunction with music, and we find an allusion to this conjunction in Horace too. Both poems refer to the notion that alien influences are responsible for man's misery and vices. In the former the Muses' civilizing role is explicit; in the latter it is present by allusion, and (by the diction of vv. 6–8) implicit. *Impium lenite clamorem* (echoing 3.1.1–4) suggests also the famous riot at the marriage of Pirithoos and Hippodamia, in which the feat of Apollo in quelling the "ungodly row" stood recorded on the pediment at Olympia. The traditional role of Apollo as patron of musicians is common in Horace's odes,[34] as is the mad exploit of the uncivilized Centaurs. The conflict of the Lapiths and Centaurs is a common theme in Greek sculpture, surely representing the age-old struggle between the forces of civilization and barbarians.

No matter which of Horace's literary models appear to have been uppermost in his mind when he composed 1.26 and 27, the nexus of motif, repetition, and complement is discernible. Moreover, if we read on into the *Laws* we shall discover what may have been a further motivation or inspiration for Horace to use a dedicatory prelude here. The Athenian interlocutor refers to what has been said up to that point (i.e. noon) as the *prooemia* to the actual laws in the technical sense:

> ...what has preceded was only the prelude of them...All discourses and vocal exercises have preludes and overtures, which are a sort of artistic beginnings, intended to help the strain which is to be performed; lyric measures and every sort of music have preludes framed with wonderful care.[35]

33. Tr. Bowra (*G.L.P.* p. 276).

34. For centaurs in Horace, see *Carm.* 1.18.8; 4.2.15. Although the settings of 1.27 and 3.1 are quite different, the roles of the *vates* as *arbiter* (*impium lenite clamorem*) and *sacerdos* (*odi profanum vulgus...favete linguis*) are complementary.     35. *Laws* 722 D (tr. Jowett).

It is not impossible that Horace's interest was drawn to the discussion of temperance and music in the *Laws* as a direct result of its similarity with the passage of Anacreon which he recalled. From this the thought of this pair of odes might have emerged, infused with the poet's self-conscious delight in his mastery of the Alcaic meter. The setting of the dialogue in the *Laws* (Crete) may lend meaning to 1.26.2 (*in mare Creticum*), a further hint from the poet, to couple with *frater Megillae* (27.11).[36]

Finally, as for the speaker in 1.27: is he not the wise, perfect, sober (*verecundus*) *arbiter* the Athenian has been longing to find? If he is, Horace has put his requisite psychological insight to the acid test with shrewd humor—to quell the riotous throng. He diverts their intoxicated attention from himself (he must perforce get drunk if he fails to outwit them) to the hapless Megillus who (here as in Lacedaemon) is to be the butt of abuse.[37] But instead of an elderly man with a Spartan bearing we meet a love-sick youth: *miser...puer!* The one Roman element in this very Greek poem appears at *v.* 9: "vultis severi me quoque sumere partem *Falerni*?" If the *arbiter* is intended as a Roman, who would be more likely than the poet Horace himself?

Many of the literary allusions in *Carm.* 1.26 and 27 have been discussed by Fraenkel, Brinkmann,[38] Heinze, Treu and others. To these, the *Laws* of Plato seem to add a further dimension of sophistication, increasing the delightful quality of sheer entertainment that submerges and transcends them all.

In short, the probable relationship between the two odes is this. Horace's description of himself (in conventional terms) as *Musis amicus...unice securus* (1.26.1–6) has no particular relevance either to its own poem or to the pair unless the converse is true: Lamia *is* troubled with anxiety. And, just as for Caesar (*Carm.* 3.4), the Muses can provide for Lamia comfort and solace, in the form of diversion and pleasure. It is "sunny flowers" that

36. *Ibid.* 642 c.                              37. *Ibid.*
38. O. Brinkmann, "Horaz der Künstler," *Humanistisches Gymnasium* VI (1936), 189–204.

Horace wishes for a garland for Lamia, to counteract the gloom produced by the international situation. The *corona* or *honor* for which he prays should be *Carm.* 1.27, so full of *doctrina* and sheer fun. It is perhaps intentionally ironic that the discomfiture of the hapless Megillus, who is beyond consolation, is actually intended to divert and amuse the poet's friend.

## Carm. *1.32/1.33*

In establishing a connection between the previous pair of odes, the fact that they were in the same meter was a clue, and an important one; for there was an *apparent* lack of connection between the two subjects. In dealing with 1.32 and 1.33 we find that the opposite situation prevails; the meters are different (although Alcaeus used them both), but there is a recognizable nexus of theme to provide a preliminary guide. This theme is once again *consolation*. In 1.26 the poet, as the Muse's beneficiary and spokesman, finds and gives comfort for life's anxieties. The same role is assumed explicitly in the final strophe of 1.32 when Horace resumes the solemn invocation of the ode, hailing the *barbitos* (13–16):

> o decus Phoebi et dapibus supremi
> grata testudo Iovis, o laborum
> dulce lenimen, mihi †cumque salve
> rite vocanti.[39]

Here *dulce lenimen*, as the last of three attributes, seems to bear some deliberate emphasis. Moreover, while the first two seem largely conventional, the last is particularly relevant to the sort of Alcaean lyric that Horace is alluding to—that which can console the poet (as we shall see) for the *labores vitae*.

In *Carm.* 1.33 the first three words are enough to restate the theme that runs through both poems: *Albi, ne doleas.* That these

39. On the crux that *cumque* presents, see E. Fraenkel, p. 169; also R. Reitzenstein, "Horaz Ode 1 32," *RhM* LXVIII (1913), 251–6. My conjecture for the *cumque* of *v.* 15 is *numque* (i.e. = καὶ νῦν). See Appendix B of my dissertation for my discussion of this crux.

two odes have a definite and wider relationship to one another
will be shown later on.

The hymnic aspects of *Carm.* 1.32 have been discussed very
fully by E. Fraenkel. In form, the ode is a prayer to a deity (or
*genius*), Horace's *barbitos*. One suspects that the *barbitos* has much
less basis in fact than the jar in *Carm.* 3.21, an ode which since
the appearance of Norden's *Agnostos Theos*[40] has been seen to be
a parody of a *kletikos hymnos*. The hymn to the lyre has pre-
cedents of course, and has been recognized for what it is, since
ancient times.[41]

> Poscimur. Si quid vacui sub umbra
> lusimus tecum, quod et hunc in annum
> vivat et pluris, age dic Latinum
>     barbite, carmen,
>
> Lesbio primum modulate civi,                                    5
> qui ferox bello, tamen inter arma
> sive iactatam religarat udo
>     litore navim,
>
> Liberum et Musas Veneremque et illi
> semper haerentem puerum canebat                                10
> et Lycum nigris oculis nigroque
>     crine decorum.

We are asked for a song. If ever while free from care
beneath the shade thou hast joined with me in improvising
a trifle to last out the year—and longer—come, *barbitos*,
utter thou a Latin lyric: thou who first wast tuned by the
man of Lesbos; him who though stout-hearted in battle
would, whether under arms or having lashed his battered
ship on the sodden strand, sing of Liber and the Muses,
and Venus, and the lad that clings ever to her, and Lycus
with black eyes and black hair—fair he was (1–12)!

40. E. Norden, *Agnostos Theos* (Leipzig/Berlin 1913), pp. 143–63.
41. Sappho, Frag. 118 (L–P); Theognis, 761; Bacch. Frag. 20B (Snell);
Pind. *Pyth.* 1.

Horace opens, I believe, by declaring that he and his lyre have been asked for a lyric in Latin.[42] Some scholars would draw a sharp contrast between this lyric and the poetic trifles mentioned in *vv.* 1–2. Bentley and Heinze, for example, propose the very doubtful syntax[43] of construing the *quod pluris* clause with *carmen Latinum,* and argue that it is only this *carmen* which Horace hopes will survive, not the trifles he is recalling. Others suggest that the trifles, unlike the *carmen,* were in Greek rather than Latin.[44] A more plausible interpretation of the passage, however, is provided by a comparison between our poem and the lines in which Catullus dedicates his *libellus* to Cornelius Nepos:

> namque tu solebas
> meas esse aliquid putare *nugas...*
> quare habe tibi quidquid hoc libelli,
> qualecumque; *quod* o patrona virgo,
> *plus uno maneat perenne saeclo.*[45]

In other words, Horace's use of the word *lusimus,* like Catullus' use of *nugae,* is simply conventional modesty: both poets hope

42. See Peerlkamp *ad loc.*; and Reitzenstein *op. cit.,* p. 251 on *poscimur.* For a survey of recent opinion see A. Magariños, "Horacio, I 32," *Emerita,* xx (1952), 423–6. In reading *poscimur* (passive) in *v.* 1 it is necessary to oppose the views of Bentley, Heinze, Klingner and Fraenkel, who all read *poscimus. Carm.* 1.31 begins with *poscere* in the sense of "pray" = *quid dedicatum poscit Apollinem....?* In fact 1.32 is the third in a triad of prayer odes: 1.30 (direct to Venus); 1.31 (indirect to Apollo); and 1.32 (direct to *barbitos*), in which two Sapphics frame an Alcaic. This concentration of prayer odes would seem to weigh heavily in favor of the active. (Certainly there are parallels for this type of prayer opening (cf. Sappho, Frag. 1.2 (L–P); Ar. *Thesm.* 1156; Pind. *Ol.*12.1); see Heinze *ad loc.*) Nevertheless, for reasons that will later appear, I prefer *poscimur.*

43. Fraenkel, p. 172; also Reitzenstein, *op. cit.* p. 252, against Bentley and Heinze.

44. Horace did experiment in Greek before deciding that his future lay in writing Latin. Cf. *Sat.* 1.10.31–5. N.B. the neoteric flavor of *Graecos versiculos* (cf. Catull. 16.3–6). See Reitzenstein, *ibid.* p. 252, on the meaning of *lusus* here.

45. Catullus 1.3–10; 68.15–17: "Tempore quo primum vestis mihi tradita pura est, | iucundum cum aetas florida ver ageret, | multa satis lusi."

that the poems referred to will survive.[46] And when Horace asks for a *carmen* on the basis of past *lusus* with the lyre he is merely being specific, not designating one portion of his work in contradistinction to another.

The real emphasis of *Latinum* lies in its antithesis to *Lesbio*, not to the *nugae* alluded to in *vv.* 1–2.[47] This distinction is made in the address to the *barbitos* for a good reason. Horace intends to devote the list of exploits or *aretai* conventionally found in a prayer to the lyric poetry the lyre performed long ago in the hands of Alcaeus. But he wishes an *Aeolium carmen* not in Greek (as Alcaeus would sing), but in *Itali modi*. Horace asks the lyre to make the genre of Alcaeus his own (for this poem at any rate), and with his own stamp.

Fraenkel saw that what Horace does *not* say here about Alcaeus' poetry is important. We have seen other sides of Alcaeus earlier in the *Odes*: the *carpe diem* (1.9), the *politicon* (1.14) and the convivial (1.27).[48] But it is not until *Carm.* 1.32 that a theme touched upon earlier (1.26) is developed by allusion to him. Recall that in *Carm.* 1.26 Horace declared himself *musis amicus* and thus *securus* from the worries and troubles that dismay lesser men: but he can also impart this state to others. And it is with *Lesbio plectro* and *fidibus novis* that he there proceeded to fulfill that function for Lamia. In *Carm.* 1.32, the power of the poet is developed further by generic examples from the career of Alcaeus, a man whose *labores* were greater than the average, to be sure. In the very thick of war

46. The Catullan echoes in 1.32 are strong and deliberate. Cf. also 50.1–2: "Hesterno Licini, die otiosi | multum lusimus in meis tabellis"; and 49.3: "aliis erunt in annis." See Reitzenstein, *op. cit.* p. 253, n. 1. The close of 1.32.2 (*hunc in annum*) has a Catullan ring, too. There is a difference between the contexts of the two poems though: Catullus is probably alluding to a specific symposium with Calvus, while Horace may be referring to experience of this kind in a general sense, even just using the poetic convention for his own purposes.

47. Fraenkel, p. 175.

48. These three odes are cited because they have certain or probable Alcaean characteristics. See Heinze, Fraenkel *et al.*

(*inter arma*) and the lonely isolation (*udo litore*) of exile he could find consolation in song; that is, in singing the praises of wine (*Liber*), women (*Venus*), and song (*Musae*).[49] Horace's account of Alcaeus' poetry is deliberately incomplete, because he wishes to emphasize its consolatory function.

If we re-examine the ode up to this point in the light of its obvious hymnic and formal character, we see that what Horace has given so far comprises the sanction (1–3*a*), the wish (3*b*–4), and the "god's" exploits (5–12). This is concluded by a final invocation to the lyre as consoler. As N. E. Collinge observes, this would seem to give *Carm.* 1.32 a kind of symmetry, even on a verbal level.[50] The words *o laborum | dulce lenimen* in turn recall faintly the *vacui lusimus* of *vv.* 1–2, consolidating the unity of the poem and stating clearly its central theme: poetry and the poet have the power to give consolation and release from cares—especially the quintessential form of music, Aeolian lyric, and the Muses' new interpreter, the *vates Romanus*:

> O thou, Phoebus' glory, Shell beloved at the feasts of Jove most high. O thou sweet solace for tribulation,...[51] receive my salutation as I duly invoke thee (13–16).

Horace has asked his lyre for a poem. In view of the epithet *lenimen*, and his references to Alcaeus, it is implicitly to be consolatory. But that is not all we can safely infer. Horace is clear on the sanction he claims for his petition: "si quid vacui sub umbra | lusimus tecum, quod et hunc in annum | vivat et pluris" (1–3). And we have seen (above, p. 231, with n. 46) how strongly Catullan this passage is in tone, diction, and rhythm. The previous poems Horace mentions are the products (at least conventionally) of leisure and light-hearted improvisa-

---

49. Theocritus' Cyclops (*Id.* 11) also finds consolation from loneliness in song.

50. Collinge (*op. cit.* pp. 112 f.) analyzes the poem as follows: (1–4) appeal to lute, (5–12) citation, (13–16) invocation. (C. reads *poscimus*.)

51. Omitting translation here of the MSS' *cumque*. See n. 39 above.

tion. The only specific instruction he has for the lyre is that the poem he asks for be in Latin; but in view of Horace's skill this is no handicap: as we see, the lyre is at liberty (by implication) to choose any of Alcaeus' lighter themes—wine, dalliance or song (9).[52] The distinctive Catullan echoes seem to help suggest a not-so-serious coloring for the whole poem, as do the themes of Alcaeus he suggests. The fact that the ode, like *Carm.* 3.21 (*o nata mecum*), is modeled after a lyric hymn, should reinforce this. The deification of an inanimate object requires great sensitivity on the reader's part to the poet's intent, and Horace's precise choice of the object of veneration bears close attention here.

In *Carm.* 3.21, for example, the jar is the symbol of Liber and the servant of Venus and her train:

> te Liber et, si laeta aderit, Venus
> segnesque nodum solvere Gratiae
> vivaeque producent lucernae,
> dum rediens fugat astra Phoebus.

What of the *barbitos*? In *Carm.* 1.1.34 this instrument is used generically, in contrast to the *tibiae*:

> si neque tibias
> Euterpe cohibet nec Polyhymnia
> Lesboum refugit tendere barbiton.

Horace there defines the two main functions or modes of lyric by referring to two Muses: their specific areas of competence are suggested by the etymology of their names. Euterpe with the *tibiae* and Polyhymnia with the *Lesboum barbiton* may represent (in *Carm.* 1.1 at least) the variety of the modes of lyric, perhaps here the joyous and the serious. After all, the full range of the human comedy is the preserve of lyric! Horace uses the word *barbitos* in only one other poem: *Carm.* 3.26.4. There the context makes its meaning clear: Horace is abandoning attempts at erotic poetry (1–6):

52. Cf. Reitzenstein, *op. cit.* pp. 252 f.

Vixi puellis nuper idoneus
et militavi non sine gloria;
    nunc arma defunctumque bello
      barbiton hic paries habebit,

laevum marinae qui Veneris latus
custodit.

    There the *barbitos* is part of the poet-lover's panoply; and he dedicates it to Venus after his glorious return from "campaigning." Why can it not have the same connotation in 1.32? True, the epithet *decus Phoebi*, which might suggest poetry of a higher plane than the erotic, is prominently placed in the final invocation; but this is really just part of the list of escape-clause formulae dear to the hearts of lyric poets, and is neutralized surely by the convivial attributes that follow: *et dapibus supremi | grata testudo Iovis* (13–14). The external evidence of *Carm.* 3.26 and the neoteric echoes of *vv.* 1–3 are corroborated by *vv.* 9–12, devoted exclusively to the symbols of the erotic side of Alcaean lyric: "Liberum et Musas Veneremque et illi | semper haerentem puerum canebat | et Lycum nigris oculis nigroque crine decorum" (9–12).

    If we analyze what Horace's words to the lyre really imply, it becomes clear that what he is asking for is a lyric that is (*a*) erotic and convivial, (*b*) in an Alcaean meter, and (*c*) in a consolatory vein. And judging by the neoteric echoes (1–4) we might expect (*d*) *doctrina* to be a requirement. We do not need to go far to find an ode that fits this description perfectly: *Carm.* 1.33.

Albi, ne doleas plus nimio memor
immitis Glycerae neu miserabilis
decantes elegos, cur tibi iunior
    laesa praeniteat fide,

insignem tenui fronte Lycorida                 5
Cyri torret amor, Cyrus in asperam
declinat Pholoen; sed prius Apulis
    iungentur capreae lupis,

> quam turpi Pholoe peccet adultero.
> sic visum Veneri, cui placet imparis                    10
> formas atque animos sub iuga aenea
>     saevo mittere cum ioco.
>
> ipsum me melior cum peteret Venus,
> grata detinuit compede Myrtale
> libertina, fretis acrior Hadriae                        15
>     curvantis Calabros sinus.

The ode to Albius (Tibullus?) is a consolation offered to him for the "pangs of dispriz'd love." And it is in an Alcaean meter: a four-line strophe consisting of three lesser asclepiads plus one glyconic, a form used eight times in Horace, and appearing at least twice in the remains of Alcaeus: A5 and D9 (L–P). Its *doctrina* (as we now should call it) has been well demonstrated by W. C. Helmbold.[53] He has shown an ingenious parataxis (A–B:B–C) in the deployment of the lovers' names; e.g. *Lycoris–Cyrus: Cyrus–Pholoe, Albius–Glycera: Glycera–X,* and *melior Venus–Horace: Horace–Myrtale.* Helmbold also sees possible subtle literary puns: *laesa fide* (4) "your lute is off key," *immitis Glycerae* (2) "that bitter-sweet grape of yours," and *elegos miserabilis* (2) "pitiable or dreadful elegies." In addition, *miserabilis elegos* could also mean, in the erotic sense of *miser,* "love-sick elegies." In short, Helmbold goes as far as to class 1.33 as a piece of advice to Tibullus to abandon a cycle of elegies devoted to a Glycera, saying in effect: "My poor man, you're losing your style with that one." The evidence for this is doubtful.

J. de Decker, writing in 1937,[54] had also tried to find the meaning behind the ode, but placed undue emphasis on a reconstruction of actual events, in which *Carm.* 1.33 resulted from a specific visit to Tibullus' villa. But all we can really consider probable about the two poets (assuming that Albius *is* the poet Tibullus) is that they shared a deep and abiding love

53. W. C. Helmbold, "Horace, *C.* i, 32," *AJP* LXXVII (1956), 291 f.
54. J. de Decker, "Horace et Tibulle," *RPh* XI (1937), 30–44.

for the Italian countryside.[55] It seems likely, as well, that Horace respected his literary judgements. If we recall the latter in the light of the conventional allusion to a leisurely scene of improvisation among congenial fellow-poets implied in 1.32.1 f., 1.33 begins to take on the form of a programmatic manifesto made in conventional and playful terms by poet to poet.

But what is the exact relationship of 1.33 to 1.32? The consolation of 1.33 is of a somewhat rhetorical nature. Horace begins immediately with an admonition to Albius to forget his anguish over Glycera, and cease droning love-sick elegies. The implication of excess (*plus nimio* [1]) makes the rebuke even more telling. This is a typical introduction to a rhetorical *consolatio*, as seen, for example, in the letters of Seneca. He begins a letter to Lucilius: *Plus tamen aequo dolere te nolo.*[56] In another he begins with a rebuke for Lucilius' womanish behavior.[57]

Horace's introduction sets the stage for the lovers' triangle, *Albius → Glycera → iunior.* The second triangle, *Lycoris → Cyrus → Pholoe,* offers an *exemplum* for the consolatory *topos*: "you are not the only one to suffer so." The *exemplum* proves to be an even more complicated and frustrating lovers' triangle: the girl whom Cyrus does love will have nothing to do with him. This leads to another *topos* of formal consolation: "we all must suffer the same fate": *sic visum Veneri* (10). In fact, the *iuga aenea* (11) and the *saevus iocus* (12) seem just as appropriate to the god of

55. E.g. *Carm.* 1.17.44 ff.; *Sat.* 2.6; Tibull. 1.5.21 ff. A. Brouwers, "Horace et Albius," *Etudes Horatiennes* (Brussels 1937), pp. 53–64, presents the evidence pro and con the identifying of Albius with Tibullus the elegist. He concludes that, whoever Albius is, Horace attempts to encourage (*Ep.* 1.4) him to write tragedy and avoid elegy (*Carm.* 1.33). Brouwers' insistence upon identifying Horace's Melpomene with the Muse of tragedy is most unfortunate.

56. Sen. *Ep. Moral.* 63.1: "Moleste fero decessisse Flaccum, amicum tuum, plus tamen aequo dolere te nolo. Illud, ut non doleas, vix audebo exigere."

57. *Ibid.* 99.2: "Solacia exspectas? convicia accipe. Tam molliter tu fers mortem filii?" The *topos* of womanish behavior on the part of the mourner goes back to Archilochus, 7 (D). As used technically of mournful elegies, cf. *Carm.* 2.9.9 f.; and (perhaps) *Epod.* 16.37–9.

death as to his fair but fickle niece. But Horace is not content to leave the poem with a simple situation–example–precept structure. He adds one final *exemplum* (his favorite): himself—and in just such a triangle: *ipsum me* (13).[58] With a twist of ironic hyperbole he portrays himself madly in love with Disaster personified, while a better love longs for him—unrequited.

Basically simple in its design, *Carm.* 1.33 shows some typical features of the rhetorical *consolatio*. It is really a kind of parody of the genre, embellished with much *doctrina* in its subtle plays and word-arrangement, and cast into a lyric—in fact Alcaean—form.

If there is an "occasional" side to 1.33 it properly belongs within the realm of speculation.[59] There is, however, one explanation of the poem's presence in Horace's collection that could free it from the encumbrance of actual events and rely solely upon internal evidence and the context of convention and genre. *Carm.* 1.33 is intended to represent the product of the very sort of *lusus in tabellis* that Catullus describes (and to which Horace deliberately alludes in 1.32.1–2): "scribens versiculos uterque nostrum | reddens mutua per iocum atque vinum" (51.4–6). Its very stuff is that of the Horatian love lyric: the *Glycera* of *Carm.* 1.30.3; the *iunior* of *Carm.* 1.5.1; the frustrated and inept lover of 1.23 and 1.5.[60]

In other words, this lyric consolation is a set piece, whether on terms conceived by Horace or suggested by Albius, who is probably Tibullus the elegist. Its goal is to challenge playfully, with a lyric, the supremacy of elegy in the conventional matters of the broken heart and its consolation. These requirements are presented in the prayer to the *barbitos* for the inspiration to succeed. Does it not seem reasonable, therefore, that the

58. See esp. H. Jaffee, *Horace. An Essay on Poetic Therapy* (Diss. Chicago 1944).

59. In spite of the arguments of de Decker and Helmbold, the "occasional" aspects of 1.33 are very doubtful.

60. *Carm.* 1.5 is especially revealing. There too are the *iunior* (*gracilis puer*) who steals the mistress' affections, and the *laesa fides* (*fidem...flebit*).

challenge should be specifically referred to in the very first word of the earlier poem? If this is so, then the obvious choice between the two variants is *poscimur*: "We are challenged." In this way the textual difficulty would be neatly solved by the context.

These two poems seem to have been composed together, as *prooemium* and *opus*.[61] *Carm.* 1.32 in a mood of ironic professional seriousness asks the lyre for the poem to which *they* have been challenged. Then *Carm.* 1.33 delivers it, a lyric consolation to an elegiac lover, worked out with neoteric *cura* and *doctrina*, plus the *dissimulatio* and *felicitas* which are the trademarks of Horatian art.

61. That *Carm.* 1.32 was a proem of *some* kind had been observed frequently by Horatian scholars; e.g. Orelli, Shorey, Heinze, Pasquali and Reitzenstein. Orelli did take the trouble to ask (reading *-mur*) who had done the asking. Since there is a definite case for classifying 1.32 as a proem, and since the addressee of the poem it introduces is known, the case for *poscimur* (sc. *ab Albio*) seems very strong.

Reitzenstein despaired of finding the poem that 1.32 introduced: "Es handelt sich ja nicht um einen bestimmten Stoff, sondern um die Aufforderung zum Liede, und nichts deutet selbst dem feinhörigsten Leser an, welches Lied diesem Präludium einst gefolgt ist, ja, ob das Lied überhaupt in unserer Sammlung steht" (*op. cit.* p. 251).

# Ovid and the Law

E. J. KENNEY

# Ovid and the Law[1]

## I

OVID'S KNOWLEDGE OF THE LAW was first discussed in 1811 by J. van Iddekinge.[2] This was pioneer work; unfortunately it was antiquated almost at once by the discovery of the Verona codex of Gaius in 1816, and in any case Van Iddekinge exaggerated, as pioneers will, certain aspects of his subject. That Ovid was deeply learned in the law—"juris scientia consultissimus"— can hardly be demonstrated and will not be maintained in this paper. If legal words and ideas crop up not infrequently in his poetry, the same is true of, for instance, Propertius. One fact, however, distinguishes Ovid from the other Roman love-poets who drew on the sphere of law for metaphor and illustration, his attested practical experience of legal matters. It was part of the elegist's *credo* to despise official, established values and occupations, all the activity summed up in that most Roman word, *negotium*. But Ovid's father, as he tells us, was ambitious for his son, and pointed out that poetry was all very well but that there was no money in it; and in spite of his dislike of business the

1. The appearance of legal and historical learning worn by this paper will not deceive the instructed. I have relied heavily on obvious secondary sources, in particular A. Berger's invaluable *Encyclopedic Dictionary of Roman Law* (*Trans. Am. Philos. Soc.* N.S. vol. 43, part 2, 1953). An early draft was read to the Cambridge Roman Law Group, whose members contributed helpful suggestions. Mr M. H. Crawford and Dr T. P. Wiseman have kindly supplied additional references, and Professor D. Daube corrected certain rash inferences in a most friendly letter. My chief debt is to Mr J. A. Crook, who has read and criticized two successive versions and caused me to modify the argument (apart from correcting my legal howlers) in a number of places. For what I have allowed to survive his amiable but penetrating scrutiny he must not be held in any measure responsible.

2. *Dissertatio Philologico-juridica de insigni in poeta Ovidio Romani juris peritia*, Amsterdam 1811.

future poet of the *Metamorphoses* was embarked on the initial stages of an official career. It was not long before the *tuta otia* of literature reclaimed him, but in the interval he had figured in several capacities connected with the administration of the law. It is the thesis of this paper that these experiences can be shown to have left their mark on his poetry.

Ovid refers explicitly to this part of his life four times. In his autobiography, after mentioning the death of his brother, older by one year than himself, he speaks of his first official post:

> cepimus et tenerae primos aetatis honores,
> eque uiris quondam pars tribus una fui.[3]

What kind of triumvir was he? In choosing between the two possibilities of *tresuiri monetales* and *capitales* we have little but general probability to guide us. Mr Wilkinson leaves the matter open;[4] in the absence of a specific indication it is perhaps marginally more likely that the more conspicuous *capitales* should be intended. If Ovid was one of this body, no more unpropitious initiation into public life could have been devised for the sensitive poet: their responsibilities included the superintendence of executions. How much law he would have learned one cannot tell; it has recently been held that the *capitales* were more than mere policemen.[5] For Ovid's career the importance of this first office was that it was one of those which belonged to the vigintivirate (before the reforms of Augustus the vigintisexvirate) and which qualified their holders for the quaestorship and the Senate.

The next office held by Ovid was of an indubitably judicial character. In the *Fasti* he describes a conversation which is

----

3. *Tristia* IV.10.33–4.

4. L. P. Wilkinson, *Ovid Recalled* (1955), p. 15. Schaefer, *R.-E.* 2. R. VIII A 2, 2580.56, thinks that Ovid was *iiiuir monetalis*.

5. See W. Kunkel, *Untersuchungen zur Entwicklung des römischen Kriminalverfahrens in vorsullanischer Zeit* (*Abh. bay. Akad. d. Wissensch.* Phil.-Hist. Kl. N.F. 56, 1962), pp. 71–9, arguing against the older view represented by e.g. Mommsen, *Röm. Staatsrecht*[3], II 1.597, that they had no judicial responsibilities. On their possible civil functions Mommsen, *ibid.* 599–600; M. Kaser, *Das römische Zivilprozessrecht* (1966), p. 27 n. 19.

supposed to have taken place at the games held on 6 April, the
anniversary of Thapsus, between himself and a retired military
man in the next seat, who comments on the achievements which
had qualified them for their privileged position:

> hanc ego militia sedem, tu pace parasti,
>     inter bis quinos usus honore uiros.[6]

The reference can only be to the *decemuiri stlitibus iudicandis*.[7] The

6. *Fasti* iv.383–4.

7. On the ground that no individual could hold more than one office
belonging to the vigintivirate Nipperdey, with the qualified approval of
Mommsen, conjectured *denos* for *quinos*, thus making the passage refer to
Ovid's membership of the vigintivirate as triumvir. This interference with
the transmitted text is unwarranted, and editors of the *Fasti* ought to feel
under no obligation to mention the conjecture. (*a*) There seems to be no
real evidence for the view that it was illegal to hold posts in the xx(vi)virate
more than once. The often cited case of P. Paquius Scaeva (*CIL* ix
2845 = Dessau 915; cf. C. Cichorius, *Röm. Studien* [1922], p. 289), as
Mr Crook points out to me, must have been a special one in that he held his
vigintiviral posts *post quaesturam*, i.e. after entering the Senate. Radford
(*Ph. Q.* vii [1928], 48, n. 7) was right to style Nipperdey's objection
"trivial." (*b*) There is a chronological uncertainty which I have not seen
mentioned and which as a matter of principle ought to prevent any attempt
to emend the text: for if one is to emend the tradition to give a required
sense one must be certain what that sense is. At some time not later than
13 B.C. (Dio 54.26.5) Augustus abolished the offices of *ivuiri uiis in urbe
purgandis* and *iiuiri uiis extra urbem purgandis*, thus reducing the vigintisexvirate to a vigintivirate. If Ovid's appointment as triumvir occurred, as is
reasonable to suppose, when he was about twenty, i.e. in 23 B.C., and *if*
Mommsen's dating (*Staatsrecht*, ii 1.604; "ohne zwingenden Grund,"
Cichorius, *op. cit.* 291) of Augustus' reforms to 20 B.C. is correct, Ovid had
been a vigintisexvir, not a vigintivir. Of course, writing the *Fasti* about
A.D. 5, he might have thought it unnecessary—always supposing that he did
think about it at all—to be pedantically accurate in referring to his past
membership of a body now of twenty years' standing in its revised form.

This note would perhaps not have been worth writing if its sole purpose
were to remove one superfluous conjecture from the critical apparatus of
future editions of the *Fasti*—though every little helps—but there is one
curious fact connected with the problem which I think ought to be
mentioned. This is that Ovid refers to his membership of the decemvirate
neither in his autobiography nor in his *apologia pro uita sua*, and this silence

precise function of this body at the time of Ovid's membership is unfortunately obscure. At some time during the principate of Augustus it underwent a change of status, losing its independent judicial responsibilities, whatever they were,[8] to assume some sort of presidential role in the centumviral court.[9] In view of Ovid's evident familiarity with the proceedings *in iure* of this court, of which more will be said presently, it seems reasonable to hazard the guess—it can be no more—that he was one of the reformed decemviri.

In the curious poem (*Tristia* II) that forms his apologia to Augustus for his life and work Ovid dwells with some emphasis on his membership of the centumviral court:

> nec male commissa est nobis fortuna reorum
>     lisque decem deciens inspicienda uiris.
> res quoque priuatas statui sine crimine iudex,
>     deque mea fassa est pars quoque uicta fide.[10]

In this poem, it should be remembered, Ovid is less concerned to recount his career than to remind Augustus that before his fatal indiscretion he had been a respected and trusted member of society. Thus the emphasis in these lines is on the confidence that was reposed in him as centumvir and *iudex* and on the fact that this confidence was allowed by disinterested witnesses to be deserved.[11] The cases that concerned this court are listed,

is surely a little odd. On the other hand there need be no mystery about why he should have held two vigintiviral posts: I recur to this below (p. 249).

8. Cic. *pro Caec.* 97, *de domo* 78.

9. Suet. *Aug.* 36. Very little can be established about the activities of these decemviri at any stage of their existence: Kaser (above, n. 5), 40–1.

10. *Tristia* II.93–6; the fourth reference to Ovid's judicial career, at *ex P.* III.5.23–4, adds nothing.

11. The interpretation of *v.* 93 has been discussed. The couplet 93–4 is best taken as a single utterance; *reorum* might, I suppose, be used here in its primitive sense of a party to legal proceedings, *omnis quorum de re disceptatur* (Cic. *de Or.* II.183; cf. Festus, p. 336 L.); but it is more probable that Ovid is referring to the functions of the court in terms appropriate to criminal proceedings, in which the defendant was traditionally a figure of sympathy (*reos tueri* as an *officium*, etc.).

not without a hint of irony, by Cicero in the *de Oratore*.[12] In case this formidable catalogue gives an inflated idea of the technical qualifications required in a centumvir, it should be remembered that the court formed a *consilium*, something more akin to a jury or a panel of assessors than a bench of judges.[13] This raises a difficulty rightly accentuated by Mr Crook. The preliminary proceedings *in iure*, that is before the praetor, when a case was to come to the centumviri, were always in the form of the old *legis actio*, even after this had been generally superseded by the more flexible and convenient formulary procedure;[14] and it will be shown below that Ovid possessed an evident if not always accurately exemplified familiarity with the technical language of the *legis actiones*. Is there, however, an inferable connexion between these facts? The proceedings *in iure* did not concern the centumviri as such; need Ovid's show of legal technicalities have been acquired as a result of his membership of the court? May it not be rather that these were odd and un-digested scraps of jargon that he picked up because they were, so to speak, in the air among Romans of his class and milieu? I concede that no certain connexion can be demonstrated which would satisfy the demands of historical proof on the evidence available; but a connexion seems to me more probable than not, for two reasons. (1) These particular technicalities are peculiar to Ovid; and Ovid, as has been remarked, is peculiar in having been a member of the very court where they figured in the preliminary proceedings. The most economical of com-peting hypotheses is not necessarily the true one, but other things being equal one may reasonably prefer it. (2) If Ovid "picked up" these technicalities he must have picked them up

12. "causis centumuiralibus, in quibus usucapionum, tutelarum, gentili-tatum, agnationum, adluuionum, circumluuionum, nexorum, mancipiorum, parietum, luminum, stillicidiorum, testamentorum ruptorum aut ratorum, ceterarumque rerum innumerabilium iura uersentur" (1.173); cf. Kaser (above, n. 5), 38–40 nn.

13. W. Kunkel, *An Introduction to Roman Legal and Constitutional History*, tr. J. M. Kelly (1966), pp. 64–5.

14. Gaius, *Inst.* IV.31.

somewhere. Where? It is true that in the *Ars Amatoria* he recommends the courts as possible places of resort for the man about town on the lookout for a mistress:

> et fora conueniunt (quis credere possit?) amori,
> flammaque in arguto saepe reperta foro.[15]

Yet if Ovid himself, as he no doubt did, frequented the courts purely as a stroller, it was not primarily to hobnob with lawyers and litigants. It seems more probable that, if he witnessed the proceedings *in iure* (which there was nothing to stop him from doing), it was because he had in any case to be in the vicinity— as centumvir. (That he had seen the proceedings and not simply heard about them I argue below.) More than this one can hardly say, and it does not add up to proof, but in terms of a balance of probabilities I believe that it is reasonable to suggest a connexion.

Ovid seems to mention his activities as a *iudex* in *res priuatae* almost in the same breath as his membership of the centum-viral court, but in fact the two things were not directly con-nected.[16] As a knight *equo publico* he would have been on the list of *iudices selecti*[17] and was therefore liable for service as *iudex unus*, the single *iudex* before whom many (perhaps most) private suits were tried, a service which might entail considerable responsibility. The functions of the *iudex priuatus* cannot, it would seem, be disentangled from those of the *arbiter*;[18] and in this connexion it is worth drawing attention to the fact that, whereas in the rest of Augustan poetry the words *arbiter* and

15. *A.A.* 1.79–80.

16. The *iudices priuati* are distinguished from the centumviri by Cic. *de Or.* 1.173, 177–8; Quint. *Inst. Or.* v.10.115; Pliny, *Epp.* vi.33.9. Cf. Kaser (above, n. 5), 34, n. 23. At *Tr.* ii.95 *quoque* qualifies *iudex* rather than *res priuatas*.

17. This technical term occurs at *Am.* 1.10.38. For the lists from which *iudices* and *arbitri* were drawn cf. Kaser (above, n. 5), 36.

18. "There was no fundamental distinction; an *arbiter* was a *iudex*" (W. W. Buckland, *A text-book of Roman Law...*[3] (rev. P. Stein 1963), p. 636); cf. Kunkel (above, n. 13), p. 83; Kaser (above, n. 5), 41–3; J. A. Crook, *Law and Life of Rome* (1967), p. 78.

*arbitrium* are rare, in Ovid they are relatively frequent.[19] To this extent there is some ground for thinking that his experience of arbitration, whether as single *iudex* or one of a panel, left an impression on his mind and on his poetic vocabulary. However that may be, that the duties of an *arbiter* were taken seriously emerges from an interesting passage of Gellius;[20] and the parties to a case, if they chose their *iudex*, were in effect expressing confidence in him even before the verdict.[21] Some element of publicity was also entailed, in that an oral judgement was required to be given in the presence of the parties.[22] Thus, in spite of the fact that in Book II of the *Tristia* Ovid is making out a case for himself, there is no reason for not taking his words at their face value and recognizing that in this part of his legal career he may well have demonstrated more than average ability or at any rate conscientiousness.

One point should perhaps be made in conclusion about Ovid's legal experiences. It has been observed above that, though no legal bar probably existed to the holding of two vigintiviral offices, it was distinctly unusual to do so. That Ovid was both triumvir and decemvir does not mean that he was especially favoured; probably the reverse. In the current shortage of suitable candidates for these *magistratus minores* anybody who could be persuaded to step into the breach by holding them more than once was doing a service, not so much to the State as to his more ambitious contemporaries, for whom they formed a necessary but no doubt tiresome stepping-stone to higher things. It may be that Ovid's good nature led him to do a friend a good turn; it may be that he was manœuvred or pressured into the second office; certainly if the double tenure had been evidence of distinction we should have heard about it in the *Tristia*. Thus it is at any rate a tenable hypothesis that his strongly expressed dislike of public life may have had something to do with this episode.

19. See the table below, and cf. Radford, *Ph. Q.* VII (1928), 48, n. 8.
20. *N.A.* XIV.2.
21. Cf. Pliny, *N.H. Praef.* 8.   22. *Dig.* 42.1.47.

17

## II

Of any formal legal training in Ovid's case we hear nothing, but he studied declamation under the most distinguished teachers that Rome could boast.[23] From their very inception the schools were criticized as remote from the realities of the courts, and Quintilian is hard put to it to defend them against this charge. Bonner in his useful *Roman Declamation* has argued that these criticisms were exaggerated: "...the majority [*sc.* of the declamatory laws] are, if often not demonstrably Roman as they stand, far closer to Roman Law than has been generally supposed."[24] However that may be, it is unlikely that Ovid can have absorbed very much law from this source, whatever was on offer, since we have it on Seneca's authority[25] that he tended to shirk that type of exercise in which the argument turned on points of law, preferring *suasoriae* and the so-called *ethicae controuersiae*, in which the emphasis lay on psychological motivation. We shall notice below a passage where the law involved seems to show signs of declamatory influence, but in general the legal terms which figure in his poetry derive from the courts and not the schools; indeed, as will be seen, the language is on occasion almost aggressively technical. In support of the suggestion that these legal words and ideas stem from his own experience it may be noted that the majority of the obviously technical terms employed occur in his early work. Generic differences alone will not account for this: it seems to me to imply that he used this material while it was fresh in his memory and experience.

As has been said, the use of legal terms and concepts in Roman poetry by way of illustration and metaphor is not confined to Ovid. Comedy and Elegy had exploited ideas, such as the *seruitium amoris* or the bond of love as a *foedus*, that lent themselves to the play of quasi-juridical fantasy. Moreover the

23. *insignes Vrbis ab arte uiros* (*Tr.* IV.10.16).
24. S. F. Bonner, *Roman Declamation* (1949), p. 131.
25. *Contr.* II.2.12.

elegiac poets had enriched and deepened their exploration of love by conducting it in part in terms derived from characteristically Roman ideas of friendship and obligation: *amicitia, officium, beneficium*, and all that these words implied. The subject has been discussed by Reitzenstein in an authoritative article which has left subsequent contributors to the debate little to add but slight changes of emphasis.[26] One important conclusion that emerges is that this is a peculiarly Roman phenomenon, hardly paralleled in Greek poetry. Ovid could accordingly count on a receptive public with ears attuned to this type of metaphor; and, if he exploited the fact by laying under contribution hitherto untapped areas of terminology, that is no more than, knowing Ovid, we should expect. In fact he makes little use of the idea of *amor* as *amicitia*; indeed (as Reitzenstein remarked) he explicitly dissociates the two:

> nec semper Veneris spes est profitenda roganti:
>> intret amicitiae nomine tectus amor.
> hoc aditu uidi tetricae data uerba puellae:
>> qui fuerat cultor, factus amator erat.[27]

But another idea which he does use belongs as much, one would say, to the sphere of *officium* as to that of law, the special kind of contract based on trust which the Romans called *mandatum*. In an interesting passage transmitted in the first book of the *Ars Amatoria* (though its precise position in the text is disputable) he writes:

> tuta frequensque uia est, per amici fallere nomen;
>> tuta frequensque licet sit uia, crimen habet.
> inde procurator nimium quoque multa procurat
>> et sibi mandatis plura uidenda putat.[28]

26. "Zur Sprache der lateinischen Erotik," *Sitzb. d. Heidelb. Akad. d. Wissensch. Phil.-Hist. Kl.* 3 (1912), 12. See also Alfonsi, *Aevum* xix (1945), 372–8; La Penna, *Maia* iv (1951), 187–209; S. Lilja, *The Roman Elegists' Attitude to Women* (*Ann. Acad. Sc. Fenn.*, Ser. B, vol. 135, 1, 1965), pp. 69–73.
27. *A.A.* 1.719–22.
28. *A.A.* 1.585–8.

The same idea is exploited in the *Heroides*: Paris is made to justify his overtures to Helen by the argument that Menelaus' action in confiding his guest to her care during his absence is a *mandatum* which she ought not to neglect. The language, as in the *Ars*, is technical:

> †esset et† Idaei mando tibi" dixit iturus
> "curam pro nobis hospitis, uxor, agas."
> neglegis absentis, testor, mandata mariti:
> cura tibi non est hospitis ulla tui;[29]

and a few lines later:

> paene suis ad te manibus deducit amantem:
> utere mandantis simplicitate uiri.[30]

The passage from the *Ars* bears on a technical question that need be no more than mentioned here, the relationship of *mandatum* to *procuratio*. Watson may well be right in discounting Ovid's evidence on the point and in ascribing the link between the two things which the passage, when taken at its face value, suggests to "poetic licence."[31] As will be emphasized presently, Ovid is often imprecise in his use of technical terms, and from a poet using language and ideas for rhetorical and emotive effect one can hardly expect pedantic accuracy. Nevertheless he may on this occasion have meant exactly what he seems to imply, and his evidence should not be ruled out because it happens to be inconvenient. What concerns the present enquiry is that he is seen here exploiting in legalistic, if not legal, language an idea of obligation that in its origins as "a social concept"[32] belongs to the sphere of relationships mentioned above as a source of erotic metaphor.[33] Moreover (to reiterate a point already made)

29. *Her.* xvi.303–6. In *v.* 303 Madvig's "*res, et ut...*" for *esset et* receives support from xvii.159–60, but is not free from objection.
30. *Her.* xvi.315–16. *Deducere* is a technical word, common in this special sense in both legal and non-legal contexts.
31. A. Watson, *Contract of Mandate in Roman Law* (1961), p. 50.
32. Watson (above, n. 31), 17.
33. Cf. Cic. *Sex. Rosc.* 111–12, *de nat. deor.* iii.74.

the idea of *mandatum* is not exploited by the other elegists, though they have a good deal to say about *fides* in general, and it does not, as far as I can see, figure in the school declamations. It is therefore economical, if not inevitable, to infer that in using this idea as a source of imagery Ovid drew on some personal experience of *mandatum* cases. It is in any case an amusing and original stroke of invention.

Numerical comparisons in the matter of vocabulary must be used with caution, since the bulk of Ovid's surviving writing is so much greater than that of any other classical Latin poet and ranges so widely over different genres. It is difficult, for instance, to say what weight we should attach to the fact that the word *legitimus* occurs sixteen times in Ovid but is otherwise unknown to the "high" genres of Latin poetry before Lucan. The table below offers some figures which no doubt need further analysis; but even presented in this rather crude way they may give some sort of quantitative notion of the extent to which legal words and ideas occur in Ovid's poetry, and in-

|  | Ovid | Lucret. | Catull. | Virg. | Hor. (*Od.*) | Prop. | Tib. (I, II) |
|---|---|---|---|---|---|---|---|
| *ius* | 134 | 9 | 5 | 18 | 5 | 21 | 1 |
| *lex* | 74 | 10 | 1 | 19 | 9 | 18 | 3 |
| *legitimus* | 16 | — | — | — | — | — | — |
| *iudex* | 47 | — | 1 | 4 | 3 | 4 | — |
| *iudicium* | 39 | 2 | — | 2 | — | 3 | — |
| *index* | 26 | — | — | — | — | 1 | — |
| *indicium* | 36 | 4 | — | 4 | — | — | — |
| *arbiter* | 7 | — | — | — | 3 | 1 | — |
| *arbitrium* | 23 | 1 | 1 | — | 3 | 1 | — |
| *lis* | 23 | — | 1 | 3 | 3 | 3 | — |
| *reus* | 23 | — | 1 | 1 | 2 | 1 | — |
| *uindex* | 26 | — | 1 | — | 2 | 2 | — |
| *uindico* | 16 | — | — | 1 | — | 5 | — |
| *uindicta* | 11 | — | — | — | — | — | — |
| *assero* | 3 | — | — | — | — | — | — |
| *assertor* | 1 | — | — | — | — | — | — |

deed it may be occasionally dominate his modes of thought and expression. I have not aimed at completeness or minute accuracy.[34]

No doubt a number of interesting points arise from this table,[35] but I wish here to dwell only on the last group of words in it, those connected with the process of making a legal claim called *uindicatio*: *uindex*,[36] *uindico, uindicta, assero, assertor*. The last three words, it will be seen, occur among our group of poets only in Ovid. In classical prose and post-Augustan verse these five words are by no means limited to their technical legal significations; and it seems highly probable that the credit for removing them from the legal and prose sphere and introducing them to the metaphorical resources of high poetry belongs to Ovid. Unobtrusive linguistic innovation of this kind is one of the hallmarks of the Ovidian style. In this connexion it may for once be permitted to press an argument from silence. Nowhere in Lucretius do the words *uindex, uindico* or *uindicta* occur. Considering that his purpose in writing the *De Rerum Natura* was, as he tells us, to release mankind from the bondage of superstition,[37] it is remarkable that he does not avail himself, in his most Roman poem, of this characteristically Roman image. This it was left for Ovid to do in a didactic poem of quite another stamp:

> publicus assertor dominis suppressa leuabo
> pectora: uindictae quisque fauete suae.[38]

34. The figures are based on concordances and indexes; I have ignored spurious or dubious works (*App. Verg., Nux, Halieutica*), but I have not scrutinized the individual instances closely. Nor have I differentiated between the legal and non-legal uses of a word like *iudicium*; indeed I think that for the present purpose it would be wrong to do so.

35. For instance, that Propertius, when the modest bulk of his work is taken into account, yields a surprisingly high proportion of the non-Ovidian instances of *ius* and *lex*.

36. In fact the *uindex* does not belong to the *uindicatio*-process, but to the *legis actio per manus iniectionem*: see below, p. 255, n. 40.

37. VI.62–3 *rursus in antiquas referuntur religiones | et* dominos *acris adsciscunt.*

38. *Remedia Amoris* 73–4.

The concentration of legal terms appropriate, or partially so,[39] to the process called *uindicatio in libertatem* is most remarkable, and offers imagery quite unparalleled in other Augustan poetry. Similarly Hermione protests to Pyrrhus in language reminiscent of, if again not wholly appropriate to, the *actio in rem*:

> "quid facis, Aeacide? non sum sine uindice" dixi:
> "haec tibi sub domino est, Pyrrhe, puella suo."[40]

Again Acontius (of whom more will be heard) expostulates with his beloved's official fiancé in legalistic phraseology of a similar type:

> elige de uacuis quam non sibi uindicet alter;
> si nescis, dominum res habet ista suum.
> nec mihi credideris: recitetur formula pacti...[41]

Here the technically correct use of *res* = "chattel" applied to a human being deserves attention: compare Gaius: "[res] corporales hae sunt, quae tangi possunt, uelut fundus, *homo* [= slave], uestis, aurum, argentum."[42] These passages and others[43] show that Ovid was particularly fond of parodying and

---

39. It is no part of my purpose to vindicate Iddekinge's claim that Ovid was an accomplished lawyer; and the point must be made firmly that in this and in most of the other passages cited there is a rather casual mixture of terminology. The point is, however, that, even where the terminology is mixed and inexact, it is real legal terminology exploited for poetic and rhetorical purposes, and that in a way peculiar to Ovid: this is the literary interest of the subject. What effect it had on a contemporary ear, how far these imprecisions were appreciated or even noticed by Ovid's readers, and whether there is a real gain in poetic terms when imagery drawn from a technical source is exactly applied, are questions which are either unanswerable or lie outside the scope of this paper.

40. *Her.* viii.7–8. *Actiones in rem* were *uindicationes* (see below), but the *uindex*, as already remarked (p. 254, n. 36, above) had nothing to do with *uindicatio*. For Ovid's purpose, however, *uindex* = *is qui uindicat*: he needed the short syllables. Cf. Margaret W. Herr, *The additional short syllables in Ovid*, Language Dissertations pub. by the Linguistic Society of America, no. 25, 1937.

41. *Her.* xx.149–51.     42. *Inst.* ii.13.     43. *Am.* iii.11.3, *Her.* viii.16.

playing with the language of the *uindicatio*-process.[44] The fact that this type of legal allusion also appears to be peculiar, or almost so,[45] to him suggests again that he was likely to have been drawing on personal experience rather than on a common stock of legal concepts and phraseology already belonging to Latin love-poetry.

It has already been mentioned that the old *legis actiones* continued in use in cases that were to come to the centumviral court after they had been superseded elsewhere. Gaius refers to all *actiones in rem* as *uindicationes*,[46] and his description of the procedure followed before the praetor evokes a picture of a stately legal minuet: "si in rem agebatur, mobilia quidem et mouentia, quae modo in ius adferri adduciue possent, in iure uindicabantur ad hunc modum: qui uindicabat, festucam tenebat; deinde ipsam rem adprehendebat, uelut hominem, et ita dicebat: HVNC EGO HOMINEM EX IVRE QVIRITIVM MEVM ESSE AIO SECVNDVM SVAM CAVSAM; SICVT DIXI, ECCE TIBI, VINDICTAM INPOSVI, et simul homini festucam[47] inponebat. aduersarius eadem similiter dicebat et faciebat"[48] (note also *iusti dominii* a little later). As has been previously remarked, there was no need for Ovid to have witnessed any of these proceedings *qua* centumvir, but equally there is no reason why he should not have witnessed them. They were just the sort of thing to appeal to the future poet of the *Fasti*, and both the passages that we have already examined and those that will be quoted in a moment suggest to me at any rate that he was more than once present and that the dramatic possibilities of the ritual impressed themselves strongly upon him. In the poetic exploitation of this material, as has also been remarked, scholarly accuracy came a poor second to rhetorical effect, and the

44. Cf. Pokrowskij, *Philol.* Suppl. XI (1909), 395.

45. Cf. Prop. II.34.15–16 *te socium uitae, te corporis esse licebit,* | *te dominum admitto, rebus, amice, meis.*

46. *Inst.* IV.5; cf. Kaser (above, n. 5), 66; Crook (above, n. 18), 144.

47. This rod should probably be distinguished from the *uindicta* that is so frequent in Ovid: cf. Kaser (above, n. 5), 70, n. 25.

48. *Inst.* IV.16.

passage from Gaius just quoted allows us to amplify this point. In the amusing poem (*Amores* 1.4) in which the poet lectures his mistress on her deportment when she is in company with himself and with her current official protector (so *uir* must be glossed in this context) he threatens that, if the other man's attentions should be suffered to go too far, he will declare his own prior rights in due form:

> ...dicam "mea sunt" iniciamque manum;[49]

and the same combination of phrases is put into the mouth of Medea:

> uix me continui quin sic laniata capillos
> clamarem "meus est" iniceremque manus.[50]

Elsewhere in the *Amores* (II.5) a claim is asserted in similarly technical language:

> "quid facis?" exclamo, "quo nunc mea gaudia defers?[51]
> iniciam dominas in mea iura manus.
> haec tibi sunt mecum, mihi sunt communia tecum:
> in bona cur quisquam tertius ista uenit?"[52]

These two passages from the *Amores* have recently been discussed with a characteristic blend of wit and learning by Professor David Daube.[53] His remark that "we should be...careful not

---

49. *Amores* 1.4.40.    50. *Her.* XII.157–8.

51. *defers*, not *differs*, is the correct reading: cf. H. Fränkel, *Ovid* (1945), p. 187, n. 60. "*Differre* is not technical," as Daube remarks (art. cit. n. 53 below, p. 230), whereas *deferre*, though not exactly a term of art, has something of a legal flavour: cf. Berger (above, n. 1), s.v. *Deferre hereditatem*.

52. *Am.* II.5.29–32.

53. "No Kissing, Or Else...", in *The Classical Tradition: Literary and Historical Studies in Honor of Harry Caplan*, ed. L. Wallach (1966), pp. 222–31. I am grateful to Professor P. W. Duff for calling my attention to this article. On the legal formula in *Am.* 1.4.38 *oscula praecipue nulla dedisse uelis*, also discussed by Daube, see now A. Ollfors, *Textkritische und interpretatorische Beiträge zu Lucan* (Acta Reg. Soc. Sc. et Litt. Gothoburgensis, Humaniora, 2.1967), pp. 36–43.

to place too much reliance on the exactitude of the legal details involved"[54] is amply borne out by a confrontation of the first of the *Amores* passages and Medea's outburst with Gaius. The procedure of *manus iniectio* formed part of, though it was not confined to, a *legis actio* which in Gaius[55] is quite distinct from the *legis actio* from which the extract quoted above (p. 256) is taken and to which the phrase "meus est" belonged. It is true that neither element is necessarily or exclusively legal: we are not bound to see legal terminology in Virgil's "haec mea sunt, ueteres migrate coloni," and the phrase *inicere manus* occurs in a variety of non-legal contexts.[56] Nevertheless, when they are thus found in company it is difficult to deny each its legal flavour. This does not mean that Ovid was indulging in a small pleasantry for the benefit of learned readers, merely that in the interests of making his point and investing his speech with a high legal tone he was careless about the accuracy of the technical details. Here too I am inclined to think that personal experience was the source of the idea. Daube concludes that Ovid "made use of bits of lore which formed part of the... traditional knowledge of the educated" and observes that the procedure of *manus iniectio* was already in Ovid's day "something of an archaism."[57] Possibly it was this archaic character that caught Ovid's fancy: the *legis actiones* and their associated ritual were very old, going back to and beyond the Twelve

---

54. (Above, n. 53), 231.

55. *Inst.* IV.21.

56. Cf. Ovid, *Fasti* IV.89–90 *Aprilem...* | *quem Venus iniecta uindicat alma manu* (see Bömer *ad loc.*); Catull. 35.10 (an embrace); Hor. *C.* 1.17.26·(an attack). In the legal texts the singular *manum* is normal (*T.L.L.* VII 1.1613. 67–9); Ovid's usage seems to be determined only in part by metrical convenience.

57. (Above, n. 53), 231. For the connexion of the *iiiuiri capitales* with *manus iniectio* see Kaser (above, n. 5), 27, n. 23. It seems to have been abolished by the *leges Iuliae* somewhat after Ovid's time in the courts. For a parallel to the mixed terminology of the Ovidian passages cf. Quint. *Decl. min.* 359 (p. 391.16 Ritter): "translatis [*sc.* unionibus] manum inicit et suos dicit."

Tables.[58] The introduction of this time-honoured, by now "quaint," phraseology into Ovid's very modern[59] poetry was a piquant stroke of invention; and it seems to me more likely that his imagination was stimulated by actually seeing the rituals enacted before the praetor than that he picked up his knowledge in some unspecified way at second hand.

### III

So far I have been suggesting that Ovid's use of legal phrases and ideas is likely to have derived from actual legal experience, and that the dubious or manufactured law that figured in the schools of declamation played relatively little part. This indeed is what we should expect of a poet using law for metaphorical illustration, for illustration that did not stem from realities familiar to the poet's readers would have no poetic value. However, there is one piece of legal or pseudo-legal fantasy in Ovid's love-poetry that seems, as it were, to have a foot in both camps. It occurs in a particularly interesting pair of poems which have received scant measure from commentators, the epistles of Acontius and Cydippe. I have elsewhere[60] discussed the problems which confronted Ovid when he came to adapt the story as he found it in Callimachus (where it is strictly subservient to genealogical and aetiological matters) to his epistolary form. What interests us for our present purpose is the way in which he brings out and exploits a legal—really a pseudo-legal—situation which could be made, as in Callimachus' treatment it was not made, crucial in the motivation of the characters and the argumentation given to them in this *controuersia ethica*. Acontius in his letter explains that the stratagem of the message on the apple was inspired by love.

58. Kaser (above, n. 5), 37.

59. Cf. *A.A.* III.121–2 *prisca iuuent alios; ego me nunc denique natum | gratulor: haec aetas moribus apta meis.*

60. *Philol.* CXI (1967), 215 ff.

His language is technical, describing a consultation with
Cupid in terms appropriate to the briefing of a client by a
barrister:

> te mihi compositis, siquid tamen egimus, a me
>   adstrinxit uerbis ingeniosus Amor:
> dictatis ab eo feci sponsalia uerbis,
>   consultoque fui iuris Amore uafer.[61]

Later comes the passage already quoted (above, p. 255), with
its heavy concentration of *uindicatio*-terms. It is consistent that
Cydippe is made to take up the argument on the same pseudo-
legal plane in her reply. Acontius had harped on one theme, the
binding nature of her oath. As legal argument what he says is
worthless, for, as he admits, the oath had been extracted from
Cydippe by deceit, *dolo*, and no claim purporting to be based
on such an oath could have any legal validity in the contemporary Roman legal system.[62] Moreover the conflict is not
in fact between two legally based claims, the oath and Cydippe's
prior betrothal, but between human ordinance and divine
caprice.[63] However, the unreality of his premises naturally did
not worry Ovid, whose interest lay in extracting the maximum
of psychological tension from this typical declaimer's situation.
Thus Cydippe's reply, or the part of it with which we are
concerned here (for the psychological subtleties of these epistles

61. *Her.* xx.27–30. *Sponsalia* is a highly technical word otherwise unknown to "high" poetry.

62. See Berger (above, n. 1), s.v. *dolus*. Mr Crook points out that the
remedies against *dolus malus* were only invented in Cicero's day (Cic. *de
Off.* iii.60). However, I doubt whether Ovid worried about this fact, even
if he knew it, or envisaged Cydippe's plight as that of a victim of a code of
"objective" law. In this I differ from Mr Crook, who doubts the propriety
of seeing in Cydippe's pleas a reflection of the *scriptum* )( *uoluntas status*. It is
true that, strictly speaking, there is a difference between this *status* and what
one might call the ἡ γλῶσσ' ὀμώμοχ' situation, but the terms in which
Cydippe is made to argue suggest strongly, to me at any rate, the influence
of the *status*: 139 *uolui*, 142 *uerba*. Here, as elsewhere, technical accuracy and
relevance were a minor preoccupation with our fluent and inventive poet.

63. *Her.* xx.160 *ille homines, haec est testificata deam.*

belong to another enquiry) is also conceived and delivered in declamatory terms. She is made to extend herself at great length on the argument that the words she uttered were not a true oath and were not binding because there was no intention behind the utterance:

> quid tibi nunc prodest iurandi formula iuris
> > linguaque praesentem testificata deam?
> quae iurat, mens est: nil †coniurauimus illa;        135
> > illa fidem dictis addere sola potest.
> consilium prudensque animi sententia iurat,
> > et nisi iudicii uincula nulla ualent.
> si tibi coniugium uolui promittere nostrum,
> > exige polliciti debita iura tori.        140
> sed si nil dedimus praeter sine pectore uocem,
> > uerba suis frustra uiribus orba tenes.
> non ego iuraui, legi iurantia uerba:
> > uir mihi non isto more legendus eras.
> decipe sic alios: succedat epistula pomo:        145
> > †si ualet hic magnas diuitis aufer opes.
> fac iurent reges sua se tibi regna daturos,
> > sitque tuum, toto quidquid in orbe placet.[64]

The commonplace on which Ovid is here making his heroine embroider, though commentators on the *Heroides* do not tell one so, is instantly clear: this is the conflict between the letter and the spirit of the law, technically known in the rhetorical sources as the *status ex scripto et ex sententia*. The doctrine of the στάσις or *status*, the basic point of a case on which the argument turned, was prominent in Greco-Roman rhetorical theory, and this particular *status* was one of the commonest, affording as it did an opportunity to manœuvre the argument off the arid plane of *strictum ius* into the lusher pastures of *aequitas*. That it figured prominently in the schools of declama-

---

64. *Her.* XXI.133–48. *v.* 135 *nil tum iurauimus* Itali: *nil nos iurauimus* Bentley: *sed nil iurauimus* Palmer. *v.* 145 *alios* ed. Parm. 1477: *alias* edd. temere. *v.* 146 *hoc . . . ditibus* uulg.

tion we are told by Quintilian, and the declamations attributed
to him offer several instances of its application. Clearly the
rhetorical possibilities of this *status* were rich in a type of exercise
in which more stress was usually laid on imparting a superficially plausible twist (*color*) to the argument than on rigorous
logic; but unlike many of the doctrines of the handbooks and
the schools this one seems to have had some importance for
actual courtroom practice. Quintilian indeed, in the passage
just mentioned, states that its prominence in the schools was due
precisely to its practical importance: "scripti et uoluntatis
frequentissima inter consultos quaestio est, et pars magna
controuersi iuris hinc pendet. quo minus id accidere in scholis
mirum est: ibi enim ex industria fingitur."[65] The *status* was
handled by the author of *ad Herennium*[66] and by Cicero in the
*de Inventione*;[67] and Cicero several times in his oratorical works
refers to the celebrated *causa Curiana* as an important document
in this connexion.[68] Whether or no Büchner is right to query the
relevance of that particular case to this *status*,[69] there seems to
be no doubt that the antithesis *scriptum* )( *uoluntas* or *uerba* )(
*uoluntas* might play a considerable part in the argument in
certain types of case.[70] This is surely the bearing of such a passage as "in conuentionibus contrahentium uoluntatem potius
quam uerba spectari placuit."[71] But, though the idea behind
Cydippe's plea is genuinely legal, the situation to which it is
applied and the manner of its application are purely Gilbertian.
However, it is worth noting in conclusion that the *reductio ad
absurdum* with which the passage quoted above ends is not all
that far from the sort of thing that might be heard in a Roman
courtroom. Cicero in the *de Inventione* suggests this sort of

65. *Inst. Or.* VII.6.1.          66. 1.19.          67. II.121 ff.

68. *Brut.* 144–5, 194–8; *de Or.* 1.180, 243–4, II.140–1; *de Inu.* II.122.
Cf. Bonner (above, n. 24), 46–8.

69. K. Büchner, "Summum ius summa iniuria," *Humanitas Romana*
(1957), pp. 80–105 (= *Hist. Jahrb.* LXXIII [1954], 11–35).

70. Cf. A. E. Douglas, *M. Tulli Ciceronis Brutus* (1966), on *Brut.* 143.12.

71. *Dig.* 50.16.219.

argument as one of those that might be used by a speaker pleading for *aequitas* and against the strict construction of the law: "...deinde nullam rem neque legibus neque scriptura ulla, denique ne in sermone quidem cotidiano atque imperiis domesticis recte posse administrari, si unus quisque uelit uerba spectare et non ad uoluntatem eius, qui ea uerba habuerit, accedere."[72] The whole passage is a remarkable mixture of the real and the declamatory such as only Ovid could have given us.

## IV

Ovid found public life most uncongenial to him, and he wasted no more time in it than he had to. In the words of his autobiography:

> nec patiens corpus, nec mens fuit apta labori,
> sollicitaeque fugax ambitionis eram,
> et petere Aoniae suadebant tuta sorores
> otia, iudicio semper amata meo.[73]

Yet these experiences, uncongenial as they were, left a mark on him that cannot be wholly deplored, since they were such that they could be transmuted unexpectedly but on the whole successfully into poetry. There is no telling what elements of a varied experience a poet cannot turn to account. Ovid's brushes with the law seem to have lacked the traumatic quality that later clamours imperiously for release in artistic shape: it was not a case of Dickens in the blacking factory or Kipling at Westward Ho! But the law left its mark on him, and may claim some small part in the formation of the most versatile poet of classical antiquity.

72. *De Inu.* ii. 140.        73. *Tristia* iv.10.37–40.